W9-AVX-261

When Our Words Return

1996

To: Bill & Mary Bergen
It has been
wonderful knowing you
even for a short time.
Our best to both of you.
Jim & Elsie Mather

When Our Words Return

Writing, Hearing, and Remembering Oral Traditions of Alaska and the Yukon

Edited by

Phyllis Morrow and William Schneider

UTAH STATE UNIVERSITY PRESS
Logan, Utah
1995

Copyright © 1995 Utah State University Press
"The Weight of Tradition and the Writer's Work" copyright © 1995 Mary
Odden. Photographs on front cover and pp. 12, 19, 78, and 88 copyright ©
1995 James H. Barker. All rights reserved.

Utah State University Press
Logan, Utah 84322-7800

All royalties after expenses from the sale of this book will be donated to support
the Alaska Native Elders in Residence Program
Alaska Native Studies
University of Alaska Fairbanks

Cover photo: Martina Phillip of Alakanuk skins a seal caught in 1982 by her
husband, Joe, who is in the background talking. Photo by James H. Barker.
Cover design by Michelle Sellers.
The book was typeset in TEX from WordPerfect files by The Bartlett Press, Inc.

Library of Congress Cataloging-in-Publication Data

When our words return: writing, hearing, and remembering oral traditions
of alaska and the yukon/Edited by Phyllis Morrow and William Schneider.
    p. cm.
    Includes bibliographical references.
    ISBN0-87421-199-9.–ISBN0-87421-195-6(pbk.)
    1. Indians of North America–Alaska–Folklore. 2. Indians of North
America–Yukon Territory–Folklore. 3. Indians of North America–Alaska–
Writing. 4. Indians of North America–Yukon Territory–Writing. 5. Oral
tradition–Alaska–History and criticism. 6. Oral tradition–Yukon Territory–
History and criticism. 7. Tales–Alaska–Structural analysis. 8. Tales–Yukon
Territory–Structural analysis. I. Morrow, Phyllis. II. Schneider, William,
1946- .
E78.A3W44   1995
398.2'089970798–dc20   95-32445
                                                                CIP

Contents

Illustrations

Map by Robert Drozda.

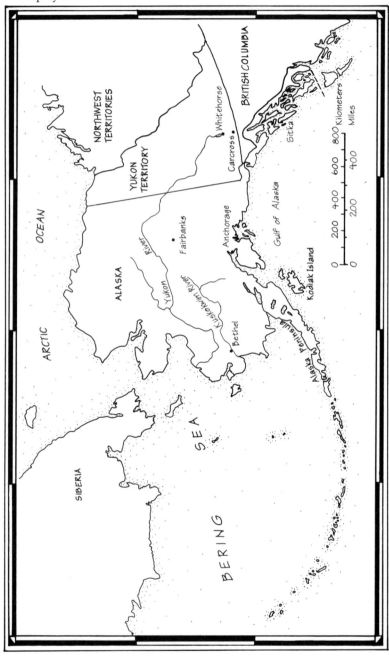

Acknowledgments

We offer our deep and heartfelt thanks to the following:
Robert Drozda for translating his love of place into maps, and
James H. Barker for translating his love of people into photographs;
Our proofreader, Sue Mitchell, for her microscopic attention to
misplaced commas despite impeding (or was that impending?) child-
birth; Linda Schandelmeier for a last proofreading;
Barre Toelken for his solid and encouraging affirmation that we
had something to say, for his incisive commentaries, and for shep-
herding us through the publication process; Pete Sinclair and Catherine McClellan, who along with Toelken acted as observant and
stimulating reviewers of the original manuscript;
Kitty Broderson for patiently sorting out conflicting masters (while
pursuing her own master's degree) as she typed the manuscript, and
Clarice Dickess for careful proofreading;
The Alaska Humanities Forum for that essential ingredient without which no humanistic work of this type can proceed: money; the
College of Liberal Arts at the University of Alaska Fairbanks, for a
bit more of that incentive; and the Elmer E. Rasmuson Library for the
many necessities that add up fast: telephone, fax, photocopying, et al;
Supportive spouses (and secretaries, students, and colleagues),
who suspended their needs, left messages, warded off callers, and
picked up loose ends while we sequestered ourselves to work on the
book;
The authors and editors for accepting both criticism and encour-
agement across the miles separating Bethel, McGrath, and Anchorage, Alaska; Vancouver, Canada; and Cambridge, England; from
Fairbanks, Alaska, and Logan, Utah.
Finally, beyond enumeration are all of the oral (and written) tradition bearers—the wits, the raconteurs, the faithful conduits, and the
trenchant observers; the family, friends, and strangers named and
unnamed in this volume—who have led us to love words, images,
and ideas. Our words return to you above all.

respect? How can we negotiate the linguistic and cultural biases that separate us from each other and from our audiences? How can we appreciate and convey some of the intellectual sophistication inherent in these oral traditions?

The obstacles in our way have become increasingly apparent. As researchers, we have only recently begun to understand in what ways our notes, tapes, and transcripts are mere artifacts of the telling. While they are important clues to meaning, the settings, speakers, audience, and reasons for telling the stories need to be known and described. We must go beyond the themes ("this is a story about . . .") and learn how the stories speak to people ("this story, told at this time, demonstrates . . .").

We are beginning to realize the obvious: a story does not exist as something to be captured but as something to be passed on. As we come to understand this in the role of storytellers, it shifts our sense of ourselves as writers. We, too, are prompted to take responsibility for our retelling of stories, not simply to analyze texts in a scholarly vacuum.

Then, if the stories are really going to be recognized as cross-culturally important, we must contemplate them in relation to our own lives and values. Without this perspective, they remain in the realm of the exotic and esoteric, important to a relatively small number of participants and students of culture.

The authors of this volume share these recognitions because they are either writing from a Native cultural tradition or from longtime associations with Native cultures. Fortunately, in Alaska and the Yukon, as these essays point out, there are many settings where we can experience a rich oral tradition and explore the integration of themes with particular settings; where we can see tellers and listeners make meaning through story. This is a place where ancient stories are rekindled in new settings and retellings bring meaning to the present.

We work at the place where folklore studies intersect with sociolinguistics and contemporary interpretive anthropology. In this interdisciplinary area, we can integrate previously disparate approaches to oral narrative in action. The contributors to this volume view oral narratives as a reflection of complex processes of communication which are continually renegotiated between tellers and listeners.

Julie Cruikshank's essay illustrates this point. She tells us how Mrs. Angela Sidney chose to tell the Kaax̱'achgóok story over the years to mark important events such as the return of her son from war and the dedication of the new Yukon College. We learn from Mrs. Sidney that this time-honored story was a powerful guidepost in her life, a gift that she knew she could share with others and a way to bring meaning to very diverse events. The story's meanings are inseparable from the reasons Mrs. Sidney chose to tell it.

All the essays in this volume focus on these questions of interpretation and representation: how oral narrative is produced and understood in a given time, place, and cultural context;[1] who it is addressed to; and how its meaning is intricately linked to both speakers and listeners. These processes, in essence, involve a series of dialogues between tradition bearers and their audiences, between writers and those they write about, and between interpreters of the oral tradition. The dialogues are interlinked in complex ways, and it is the purpose of this volume to explore some of their complexities in the context of a very exciting and challenging setting: the contemporary North. Each essay is preceded by an editorial note.

In the first section of this book, "Writing," we begin with Elsie Mather's 1986 address to the Alaska Bilingual Multicultural Education Conference. Mather, a Yup'ik Eskimo culture and language specialist and author, introduces us to her work documenting her own culture and language. She explores the ways that writing about culture differs from traditional cultural ways of learning and experiencing. Where the oral tradition responds to variation in personal meaning, Mather finds that books create a distanced dependency. Literacy, she says, is a "necessary monster" with which people "have to come to terms." Mather writes from her lived experience, negotiating that oral/written continuum which Tannen (1982) has drawn to our attention elsewhere.

This theme is also pursued by Phyllis Morrow, who discusses collaboration with Mather. She highlights the tension inherent in collaboration. Using Foucault as one point of departure to consider the implications of written and oral forms, she suggests that the question of who is entitled to speak and about what is cross-culturally variable. This perspective is significant because it shifts our understanding of what is involved in writing about cultural tradition, brokering differences between writers from Native and non-Native backgrounds, and deciding what to present and how far to interpret for the public. For collaborators, this can indeed be "shaky ground."

Julie Cruikshank describes her collaboration with Mrs. Angela Sidney, a Tagish and Tlingit woman from the Yukon Territories. In their long relationship (seventeen years), Mrs. Sidney taught Cruikshank how oral tradition gave meaning to her life and provided a context and way for her to understand contemporary issues. At one level, Cruikshank's essay is about the story of Kaax̱'achgóok and its importance to Mrs. Angela Sidney. At another level, the essay describes Cruikshank's education into the oral tradition and how she came to understand and learn to write about it in ways that reflect sensitivity to the culture and people who tell the stories. Finally, in the largest sense, it documents how a story may become appropriate in different ways.

All three authors focus on the challenges of writing about knowledge that is meant to be learned over many years of listening and experiencing and meant to be learned personally, not shared with an anonymous public.

"Hearing," the second section, features articles which struggle with issues in cross-cultural interpretation. Whether we consider people who are members of the narrator's cultural group or those who come from a different one, listeners bring their own orientations and experiences to bear on their interpretations of stories. In cross-cultural contexts, this is exaggerated by major cultural differences. Robin Barker pursues the educational implications of these differences. She uses the story "How Crane Got His Blue Eyes," as told by Maggie Lind, to demonstrate that Yupiit often understand the story to be about vision and observation while the tendency of Euro-Americans is to see it as a lesson in the importance of telling the truth. Confusion in the classroom often results.

Barker's essay is followed by Robert Drozda's. He describes cross-cultural interpretation within the context of a major government project to document Native historical places and cemetery sites. He emphasizes the learning process that occurred as government workers progressively came to realize that the people's conception of the landscape was very different from their own. These cultural differences posed serious challenges to the researchers in the course of gathering histories and determining land boundaries.

James Ruppert's work with Athabaskan elder Belle Deacon explores the fact that storytelling can vary depending on who the audience is and what language is used to tell the story. Ruppert compares variations in stories that Deacon told in Deg Hit'an that were then translated into English with the same stories told strictly in English. He makes a strong case for accepting the English telling as a telling, valid and instructive in itself. Although he is unable, at this point, to determine why the stories differ when told strictly in English,

Ruppert makes the very important point that traditional stories are shaped by "ongoing cultural conversations." That is, tellings in different languages and with new audiences provide opportunities to emphasize disparate aspects of a story. Various themes may be chosen for emphasis without the teller feeling that he or she has changed or distorted the meaning.

The essays in the third section, "Remembering," address issues of the way stories are remembered and interpreted by listeners over time. Following Sandra Stahl (1989), we recognize that listeners are, in the end, the ones who interpret, find meaning, and retell the stories to the next generation. This means that, in most cases, the "natural" condition for stories is to change over time as they are influenced by tellers and listeners and the events that shape their lives.

This point is dramatically illustrated by Patricia Partnow, who observes that classification of oral tradition from the Alaska Peninsula has undergone a marked change since the major Katmai volcanic eruption of 1912, which forced the villagers to relocate. The event became the prominent time marker in Alaska Peninsula Aleut oral tradition. Partnow reports that after the eruption, the preexisting genres of stories merged into two categories, stories about events before and events after the disaster. The implication is that today's elders grew up with the eruption as a key event so powerful that it changed the way they remember and talk about their past. Her observation makes an exciting contribution to folklore studies, because she has captured a moment when a community is defining its history meaningfully through folklore.

William Schneider's essay illustrates how and why oral traditions are remembered. In contrast, oral recordings are often devoid of sufficient information to allow an adequate interpretation and represent an attempt to capture tradition at one point in time and preserve it in a sort of freeze-dried state. This is antithetical to all that we know about the way oral narratives are passed along, interpreted, understood, and ultimately changed over time. He concludes with some suggestions about preserving a fuller oral record, recognizing that this medium, with all its limitations, may in some cases be all that remains for future generations.

In the final essay, Mary Odden continues the theme of how oral tradition affects an individual's understanding. Her piece bears witness to the way personal experiences with recorded and unrecorded oral tradition are sifted and sorted in our minds and become the basis of what we understand, value, and choose to share with others. At the same time, she writes in a style true to her desire to encourage dialogue. The essay is written in the first person, inviting the reader to see how its author is personally shaped by the oral traditions that she hears and reads.

The maturation of our work owes much to our national colleagues, particularly Alan Dundes, Dennis Tedlock, Richard Bauman, Charles Briggs, Edward "Sandy" Ives, and Barre Toelken. The impact of their work is evident in all these essays. In our emphasis throughout this collection on collaboration and dialogue, we take our lead from Dennis Tedlock (1979) and Stephen Tyler (1986), who argue that anthropologists should see narrators and their audiences as partners in a dialogue, commentators whose critiques are an integral part of the record to be preserved and reported. In this volume, Mary Odden's essay lays out this argument with particular attention to collaborative reportage. She sums up "the creative ambiguity at the heart of our disciplines" that each contributor to *When Our Words Return* has explored in his or her own way—the difficult necessity to examine our frames of representation, to recognize and acknowledge our biases and the role our presence has on the tellings we hear, and to take responsibility for the power relations that develop in any process of re-creation. It is our hope that the essays in this volume illustrate not only the ambiguity but also the creativity inherent in writing, listening, and remembering oral traditions.

Notes

1.   Oral narrative refers to personal stories generated from the experiences of the teller as well as accounts that have been passed on from generation to generation, often referred to as myth, folktale, and legend.

References

Stahl, Sandra Dolby. 1989. *Literary Folkloristic and the Personal Narrative.* Bloomington: Indiana University Press.

Tannen, Deborah. 1982. "The Oral/Literate Continuum in Discourse." In *Spoken and Written Language: Exploring Orality and Literacy*, edited by Deborah Tannen, 1–16. Norwood, N.J.: Ablex Publishing Corp.

Tedlock, Dennis. 1979. "The Analogical Tradition and the Emergence of a Dialogical Anthropology." *Journal of Anthropological Research* 35(4): 387–400.

Tyler, Stephen. 1986. "Post-Modern Ethnography: From Document of the Occult to Occult Document." In *Writing Culture: The Poetics and Politics of Ethnography*, edited by James Clifford and George Marcus, 123–140. Berkeley: University of California Press.

A Note on Consistency

Readers will notice that different terminologies and forms of address are used by the authors of these essays. The authors follow the conventions for group and individual designation considered appropriate by the people of the area where they work. For example, indigenous Canadian groups are called "First Nations," whereas Alaskan groups prefer to be called "Alaska Natives." Similarly, the authors have chosen personal designators which best reflect their relationships with individuals or follow the local custom. For instance, Mary Odden refers to Wendy Arundale and Eliza Jones as Wendy and Eliza, Phyllis Morrow calls Elsie Mather by her full name, and Julie Cruikshank prefers to use a more formal title for Mrs. Angela Sidney to reflect the respect she holds for this elder. Preserving this variation makes the point that local conventions are important (e.g., "Mrs. Angela Sidney" because Mrs. is the common respect term in the Yukon, but not amongst Yup'ik people in Alaska, where first names are often used even in situations non-Yupiit may consider relatively formal).

There are also differences in group self-designations. The terms "Yup'ik" and "Iñupiaq" are used by peoples known collectively as Inuit (in Canada) and Eskimos (in Alaska). "Eskimo" carries no negative connotations in Alaska and is often considered preferable because the Yup'ik people do not share the term *inuit* as their word for people. When referencing specific groups, authors also use other locally preferred terms (e.g., Inuvialuit, Tagish, Cup'ig, etc.)

Even with self-designation, there is variety in usage due to historical convention and the transference of Native language forms into English phonology, spelling, and plurals. In English-language writings, for example, Yupik (plural, Yupiks) is widely acceptable, while in the Native language orthography, an apostrophe is used in the singular, Yup'ik, and the plural is Yupiit. This book employs the latter variations.

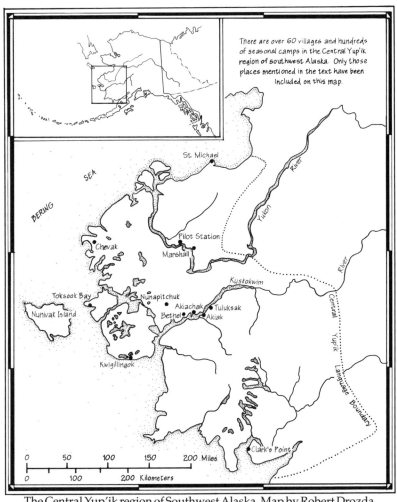

There are over 60 villages and hundreds of seasonal camps in the Central Yup'ik region of southwest Alaska. Only those places mentioned in the text have been included on this map.

BERING SEA

St. Michael

Yukon River

Pilot Station

Chevak

Marshall

Kuskokwim

Toksook Bay

Nunapitchuk

Akiachak Tuluksak

Nunivak Island

Bethel Akiak

Central Yup'ik Language Boundary

Kwigillingok

Clark's Point

| 0 | 50 | 100 | 150 | 200 Miles |

| 0 | 100 | 200 Kilometers |

The Central Yup'ik region of Southwest Alaska. Map by Robert Drozda.

PART I

WRITING

Mt. Edgecumbe, Anchorage, and Bethel, Alaska, as a nurse and interpreter for Yup'ik patients.

In the early 1970s when bilingual schools started in the Bethel area, I was hired by what was then the Alaska State-Operated Schools to teach a bilingual kindergarten class. In the late 1970s, I worked at the Kuskokwim Community College as a language specialist and also did some part-time teaching in Yup'ik orthography and grammar. At this time I started working on some Yup'ik traditional stories, which I continue to do today.

In 1984, I was hired by the Lower Kuskokwim School District (LKSD) to do research on Yup'ik traditional ceremonies. The resulting book, *Cauyarnariuq* (*It Is Time for Drumming*), was published in 1985 by LKSD and the Alaska Historical Society as a text to be used in Bethel-area high schools in their cultural heritage programs. It is a description of Yup'ik traditional religious ceremonies which are now no longer performed. It includes traditional stories as they were told by older people, in their seventies at the time of the research, who themselves had participated in some of these ceremonies.

The following essay was presented as a keynote speech at an annual bilingual-multicultural conference sponsored by the Alaska Department of Education in 1986 in Anchorage, Alaska.[1] By then, many villages in western Alaska had started various programs in bilingual education, which also included cultural heritage programs. In the Bethel area and its surrounding villages, the modern Yup'ik writing system was taking hold, particularly among high-school and college students.[2] The older writing systems, introduced by early missionaries, were being replaced by the modern one. With this modern writing system and the introduction of Yup'ik language classes, interest in Yup'ik stories was born. Efforts began to be made to record these stories.

There were still almost no original Yup'ik texts or other materials for use in classrooms by 1985. Translations from English into Yup'ik were the norm in materials production. We were made to feel that what we as Yupiit had to express about ourselves was not important, to the outside world or ourselves. Most of the "original" Yup'ik material appeared as transcribed and translated traditional stories, along with transcriptions of elders' reminiscences about the past.

Yupiit have long felt the failure of outsiders to understand their traditional ways. This includes our language and traditional stories, which are still very much a part of our everyday lives. In hunting and other subsistence pursuits and even in our everyday social activities, the ideals and values which underlie our ancient worldview are always near the surface, still operating to guide us in our behavior and way of life. Stories are often told spontaneously during daily activities when similar situations are recalled from the past. Admonishments and rules for living are part of the stories. Even when the older people tell about events in the modern day, they use references and allusions to old Yup'ik beliefs and their worldview.

So, even with the advent of a writing system that is now widely known in the Yup'ik area, reading and writing in Yup'ik are not the norm for transmission of information. Instead, literacy in the language is promoted separately, through the educational institution. This represents almost a foreign activity among traditional Yupiit, where lifeways and ideals are promoted through oral tellings. It is these everyday expressions that are not often in print, expressions that recall both the past and the present, interweaving them to voice our sense of who we are in this part of the world.

Yup'ik stories are not limited to bookshelf items, to be picked up for entertainment or reading. As I have tried to illustrate in the following essay, they were, and still are, part of our everyday lives. And they are still best appreciated by Yupiit when they are shared and experienced. Part of this appreciation comes from the way these stories take on variation, depending on the experiences of the storyteller. The storyteller becomes part of the experience. When stories are written down, they lose a kind of fluidity. Words and phrases become fixed, more like objects. They also become the subjects of more interpretation, acquiring definite meanings through analysis. And since most of the old stories refer to the mysterious, that part of our life that can not be interpreted, we who dare to pin meanings down do so precariously. For one thing, we can never really know exactly the message another person receives from hearing one of these stories.

Oral Traditions in an Age of Literacy

As I interviewed the elders for the book *Cauyarnariuq* (*It Is Time for Drumming*), they taught me many things. Many of these elders, with their knowledge especially of the past, are fast disappearing. Many of my teachers during my research were in their seventies. One of them, Thomas Moses of Chevak, recently passed away. He was a kind man who, always smiling and in his special, wise, and dignified manner, told me that I asked too many questions. He said this without resentment and with humor. We both knew that to ask many questions, especially of an elder by a younger person, was one of the no-no's in our way of learning. But we were also aware that our elders have a lot to teach us. And they don't often have the chance to impart their knowledge today, with young people away in schools and parents away at jobs. These once-important teachers are often left alone and forgotten in nursing homes. Even when they are among us—in meetings, for instance, where we conduct ourselves according to alien procedures that are confusing to them—they are lost and ignored. We need to involve them in the process of our education in our villages and elsewhere.

While trying to get information from the elders, I was especially apprehensive because of the nature of the subject, which had a lot to do with our religion. Our religious feelings and the traditions and customs related to them are usually not talked about openly. What compounded my apprehension was that I had previously ventured to ask some questions about our old beliefs and shamans. I knew many of our customs came from those old beliefs about our origins: what we thought about the dead or how we looked at our world in general. Maybe I had asked the wrong people, or maybe I had sounded stupid. Or maybe I felt apprehensive because some, especially the younger group, have learned to dismiss this kind of information as nonsense. Or did my reaction stem from the fact that our language and therefore our traditions have in the past, and even today, been regarded as something to be ashamed of?

Anyway, when I explained my purpose—that the information I was seeking would be used in high schools—the elders were more than willing to teach me and answer my questions patiently, even though one of them nicknamed me *apqanertuli*, or "one who asks too many questions." But it was important for them to see me demonstrate a little bit of knowledge about what I was asking. They know they teach us best by building upon our experiences.

When the elders teach, they have great expectations for us. They expect the learner not only to become knowledgeable but also to grow as a firm and upright human being—a responsible tradition bearer and eventually even a teacher of timeless, carefully thought-out ways of behavior.

I was impressed when I read Catherine Attla's keynote speech from a previous bilingual-multicultural conference.[3] She mentioned the elders a lot. I felt that her most important education had come from her elders and that she had a meaningful relationship with them. I notice many times that those who have been deeply influenced by their elders are often well adjusted, with a sense of direction in their lives. Usually they are very caring people because they have received that special knowledge about concern and responsibility from their elders.

Many of our Yup'ik traditional stories are about a grandmother and grandchild. Usually the grandchild is portrayed as someone with special abilities, someone extraordinary. Many times this young person is a beginning shaman, a profession that was respected and taken up by very intelligent people. These people were close to their elders. The gap that has developed between our elders and our young people may be why it is so hard to teach this next generation about our values. They are often not around their grandparents enough.

The elders I met were eager to pass on our traditions, and stories related to them, to us. They knew that in them we could learn about ourselves. A lot of things in my culture became much clearer to me through my teachers, especially from the stories they told. Another thing I learned is that they don't spell things out for you or theorize. Usually they will tell a story that illustrates what they are teaching you. It is not their story. It was passed on to them. They claim no authority about what they tell you. More importantly, they are telling you what a great responsibility it is to be able to learn from others, to cherish that knowledge, and then to pass it on carefully. They seem to feel the enormity of this situation, and often they have no way to pass on their sense of responsibility and their knowledge to the rest of the people.

We, as materials developers, writers about our cultures, researchers, or teachers, should feel that same respect for the information we receive from our elders. Like them, we ought to make it clear that some knowledge is not our own but that we are passing something on that we acquired from a respected source. Our traditions are very important to us. They carry something immortal, and to make them sound as if they are coming from us is an insult to our culture and our elders, who themselves make it very clear that they are only vehicles.

In the past few years, I have had the chance to work on some Yup'ik traditional stories which have been passed on carefully by our storytellers. Some are told, perhaps, in much the same way they have been told for thousands of years. When you think about something handed down by word of mouth for that length of time, you have to give a lot of credit to those who have the art of telling these stories. If the stories didn't have some value in people's lives, and if these storytellers did not think they were important, would they have survived this long?

Today we often hear elders lamenting that young people are not listening to what they have to say. They are frustrated with us, and they have a reason to be frustrated. For one thing, we have lost their art of learning, and we don't pay attention to their methods, which we often dismiss as nonsense or old folktales. Elders try to teach us indirectly, for instance through stories, but we regard these as mere fairy tales. We categorize them and say they don't apply to us. More often we want to be told something explicitly, directly. Or we want to get something in a nutshell and become instant experts. We forget that some of life's most important values are understood slowly over the course of a lifetime. We love to tear something apart and analyze it to death. We hardly leave anything to the imagination. Things always have to make sense. We forget that human beings are spiritual and there is a part of us that is not explainable in mere words. Elders don't spell things out for us. Like good teachers, they open doors for us to explore. They leave us to wonder, not merely to reason things out.

One important reason why we have bilingual/bicultural programs is to help students become familiar with their respective cultures. We want them to know something about ourselves. We have that human need to want the best for them. Many of them are turning to their roots. People want to identify themselves with something, or they want to stand for something. There is the feeling that teachers have something to offer and pass on to the students, something that will help them throughout their lives, so that life can be more meaningful for them.

We have a tremendous job to do, especially those of us who are involved in developing teaching materials. Many of us know our own cultures and languages well, but I think in many cases, we rely too much on our own interpretations or perceptions about our cultures, or we lose our sense of direction because we, too, have become lost and disoriented. We become more and more influenced in our thinking, and even in the use of our languages by the culture we are adopting. Many of us grew up in that era when our languages were repressed in schools.

I think the most important ingredient in our programs is promoting the use of our language. It still serves us in many of our villages. Just recently, I was attending some meetings held by our church leaders and village pastors of the Moravian Church. It was an all-Yup'ik group, and there were many older men talking about how best they can minister to the people in the villages. One man, Calvin Coolidge of Nunapitchuk, mentioned that they could best accomplish this task by using the Yup'ik language, which was, he said, the single most important gift to the Yup'ik people from God before Christ—it was given to them for their use. He said that we disobey God by not speaking our own language.

I was impressed with the idea of our language as an important gift. It got me thinking about how we regarded animals we hunted in the past. We also considered them as gifts and treated them with care and respect. We were careful not to offend the *yua*, or the "person" of the animal. The animals gave themselves to us to be used and shared. By sharing them with others, we paid them our greatest respect. And so our language, as a gift, ought to be used and shared. I thought about how we have become so disrespectful of our language by the way we use it. We do this partly when, for instance, we literally translate from English and produce awkward sentences that can be meaningless. We can talk about English concepts without adopting English sentence structure.

Back in 1970, some of us were thrust into the classroom and in effect were told, "Here, you can speak your language; teach!" We didn't have any materials besides the few that had been developed hastily during our summer workshops in Fairbanks. Many of us knew nothing about methods of teaching. The only requirement was that we speak our language. But what we lacked in materials and methods, we made up for in our enthusiasm and the feeling that we were on the right track. One of our more important enthusiasts was Irene Reed of the Alaska Native Language Center (ANLC) in Fairbanks. She put up with a lot from us because some of us, like myself, were completely carried away by the feeling that our way of pronouncing a certain word was better than the other person's. We were a motley crew—a bunch of ethnocentric people.

I would like to thank Irene, Michael Krauss, and others at ANLC who are doing a fine job of researching and recording the various languages of Alaska. Through their research, they're paving the way for those who might be interested in studying their own language. I know from experience that studying one's language can be very rewarding. We also need more Native scholars in this specialty, especially now, while we are still linked to the past and while our resources, our elders, are still alive.

Since teaching in that first bilingual classroom in Bethel, I have been involved one way or another in teaching materials. In order to get better acquainted with my language, I enrolled in Yup'ik grammar courses taught by people like Steven Jacobson, a linguist at the University of Alaska in Fairbanks, and Osahito Miyaoka, a linguist from Japan who has studied the Yup'ik language extensively. With their help and understanding, I was greatly encouraged and gained great appreciation for my language and therefore my culture for we know these go hand in hand—or should.

To do an effective job as transmitters of our language and culture, we need to reassess our situations and take a good look at our credentials and what we are doing. Let's not be fooled into thinking that just because we have multiplied and diversified in our programs, we are doing the job we set out to do. The gap between our students and the past is widening. We must see whether we are building a solid bridge. One way to help build that bridge is to work on meaningful materials or literature for our students. We should turn to our elders for a good part of our education about getting ourselves reoriented.

Today we are all aware that learning was different in the past. Our classrooms were our homes, our community houses, and all the land which was close around us. Our elders guided us from the time we were little and throughout the rest of our lives. Now, for many of us those tight, close-knit families are no more, and much of our education takes place in the world of books.

We are living in the age of literacy. We write everything down, and we expect everyone to be able to read. Our message is, "If you can't read, your chance of succeeding (however we interpret success) is zilch."

In a way, it's sad that we are becoming so dependent on reading for information. You and a book—you can closet yourself anywhere and learn (or not learn), depending on the quality of your reading material. You can be thousands of miles away from your source of information. When you have that book, it doesn't matter where your learning takes place. We now have village libraries, and we expect our students to use these facilities. So we have to come to terms with this monster that is upon us—this dependency on books. I call it a monster because of the distance it puts between us and our sources. Nevertheless, it is a necessary monster, and we have to deal with it.

In the past, we learned by word of mouth as we interacted with each other. Even our exercises (if I may call our dances exercises for now) were done while interacting with others, often in very delicate situations, for instance when we danced in front of other villagers. Young girls, mothers, prospective husbands, danced for all to see.

Theresa Charles, at the Cama-i Dance Festival in March 1991 in Bethel, Alaska, during the last dance of the last night, when the Bethel dancers, the host dancers, gave their final performance. Photo by James H. Barker.

Would some father or mother decide to choose a marriage partner for their son from these girls dancing?

Today we can turn on the TV in our living rooms and exercise all by ourselves, maybe with no real feelings involved—no apprehensions and no excitement. Exercise has become just that. Native people knew the importance of this fast-growing pastime of today, but the way they did it was different. Exercising while interacting with others in a meaningful way and learning in a real situation, a life situation, were our ways in the past.

When we start learning through books, there is a danger because we can be greatly affected by what we read. This was demonstrated to me clearly when I was in a certain class in college. The teacher had a preconceived idea about some aspect of Eskimo behavior. He was clearly influenced by literature written by an outsider who had concluded that a certain stereotype was actually our way of behaving. The teacher took it for granted that what he was saying was true in every Eskimo culture. I was uncomfortable, but I never spoke up. I even started to believe what he said.

Keeping in mind that what we read can influence our thinking and the way we use language, we need to take a good look at the content of the books in our programs. We know that language is the most important transmitter of our culture. Written words should reflect our language and culture. One area I'm concerned about is the way we use the Yup'ik language. As I read some of the literature and teaching materials in Yup'ik, I can't help but feel that we have fallen short of transmitting our cultural knowledge through them.

Since bilingual programs began in our area, we have had to make do with what materials for teaching we had. Many of our books were translations. *Goldilocks, Peter and the Wolf,* and other children's classics were translated or adapted. There were very few books written by Natives. And that was understandable then—in the beginning. Most of us working in the classroom didn't have time. But now, bilingual materials development centers have sprung up everywhere, although these are usually staffed by non-Native speakers. Native speakers at these centers have often not been encouraged to write original things. Most often, someone else writes something in English, and then it is the so-called language specialist's job to translate it. Too often, the result is books that have very little appeal as far as language expression is concerned—to say nothing of the content. We, as translators, are, in effect, cogs in a machine—a machine used in the business of transmitting English concepts to the Natives.

When we use translations from English to Yup'ik, for instance, we often end up teaching awkward expressions. We not only put these awkward expressions into books but we also adopt literal translations and use them in our speech. Take an expression like *cangacit*, which is now a common word of greeting between Yup'ik and non-Yup'ik people. It's a literal translation of the English "How are you?" and is not used as a greeting among Yupiit themselves. Even the response, *assirtua*, is a translation of "I am fine." This form of greeting is becoming common, but it's not used by older people. It exists only to accommodate English speakers. For them, it is just a greeting, but an older Yup'ik speaker might take it as a literal question. One non-Native person once asked me why older people in the villages started telling him a long personal story when he greeted them.

We do a lot of injustice to our language when we rely on literal translations. Sometimes we even structure our sentences after English, and a lot of times we ignore some of our everyday common expressions. In Yup'ik, for example, we avoid directness in our speech. We do not like to make statements such as, "I'm going fishing tomorrow." We use the equivalents in English of "perhaps," "maybe," and "it seems like." When I invite someone to go fishing with me, I might say, "Perhaps you wouldn't want to go fishing," or, "I'd like to go fishing this morning." We avoid abruptness. When we translate from English, we lose these forms.

In Yup'ik, we also use those little appendages at the end of our words called *enclitics*. Some express a hope or wish, but one that we use a lot is *-gguq*, to indicate that what we are saying has come from another source and that we are only passing on information. We even use it when we ask someone to do something, usually when we address a child who is not paying attention. In a way we are saying, "Look, what I'm telling you to do is not coming from me. This is something you should do." It is a way of not calling attention to ourselves, a way we let others know that this information is not our own, but we respect its source. When I talked about elders earlier, I mentioned that they treat information in a respectful manner and that is why some of our very old stories have lived on so long.

Our Native languages have long been treated like something inferior. It is time we recognize their worth and use them as they were meant to be used—as expressions of our cultures. Our cultural expressions, in every sense of that word, are worthy of being recorded.

We need not be tied to a replica of English usage and concepts. Our cultural expressions should not be confined to a few stories or fairy tales, as some are described. The rich vernacular of our everyday lives should be part of our language learning. We need to hear it and read it.

As we enter this age of literacy, we, as writers, should try to use our language creatively and provide interesting reading material that will enrich Native language and at the same time expand cultural knowledge. Let's not only teach our children the structure of our language but expose them to a variety of natural speech. After all, our lives are composed of many interesting aspects. Our ceremonies, for instance, are rich and so is our language—rich in abstract expressions that humor, cajole, or ridicule. Let's not just teach our children the skeleton of our language which is cold. Let's bring our language to life through imaginative use in all its flesh, warmth, and vitality.

As mentioned earlier, we can be influenced by what we read. A good part of our education now comes through reading. It scares me to think of the consequences of learning through reading because, for one thing, we can be misinformed. We can be misled about our own culture also. Or people outside our culture can receive the wrong information about us. We are well aware of literature that has been written by outsiders who portray us in very unflattering ways. We are right to be annoyed when we are stereotyped, misconceived, and misunderstood.

Let's be aware that we are writing down our history not only for our children but also for the world. We need to be concerned not only about what we write but also how we write. We can never really erase all that has been written about us, but we can do something about it now. Those of us producing materials for reading have this power in our hands. We need to speak up and not start believing an untruth about ourselves and then hand it down to our children, who are turning to their roots for direction.

Let me also quote one of the villagers whose testimony appears in Justice Berger's book, *Village Journey*. Edgar Ninguelook of Shishmaref, Alaska, says,

> We are the only ones who can save ourselves. We keep looking at the outside world for someone to come and do it, and it's not going to happen. We are expecting someone out there to save us and, in fact, there is nothing in the outside world that is really that important. . . . I think our people ought to understand that it is

possible to maintain their identity and their spirit, their language, their traditions, and history and their values and still function in the twenty-first century. We know what we need to know, how to make decisions, how to analyze situations, how to speak many languages and understand technology. (Ninguelook 1984: 50–51)

There is a lot of good stuff that could be in our literature. We need not always look elsewhere for subject matter. True, we could use information from books already published, written by people like Edward Nelson (1983), who gave pretty accurate descriptions as an outsider to our culture. I have used some of his descriptions of Yup'ik ceremonies. But if we are going to use sources like these, we should acquire the critical ability to sort out what we can include. We need to know how to weigh information, and we can do it best by knowing our own culture.

By not depending so much on outside sources, by doing things ourselves, we have the means to preserve a good part of our culture. Even though we are faced with modern technology, an important part of our culture—our language and our values—can endure. We can hunt with snowmobiles, but the ideas and customs that go along with hunting, for instance, can be kept alive. That is why I feel that knowing about our Yup'ik ceremonies, such as the Bladder Festival, is important. Describing these ceremonies tells us something about our relationship to others and our relationship and responsibility toward our land and all living things around us. They are our gifts, like our language, given to us not to be exploited and trampled but to be used responsibly with a vision beyond our immediate needs. We must also think of generations to come.

It is an awesome task, this recording of our way of life and our values. We must be preservers not only of the past but also of the here and now for the future—like our ancestors with the Bladder Festival. They preserved the culture, and by putting the bladders of hunted animals back into the water, they provided for the future. They did this not only to help themselves in the next hunting season but, I suspect, with a view that those animals would continue to come to them for all time to come. So we must also treat our oral literature in the same way as we write it down. As we preserve our values and customs, let's do it so that they will continue to serve future generations and, I hope, give them the same sense of responsibility and respect that our ancestors felt toward their environment, animals, the future, and most importantly, their language.

Notes

1.   The original speech appeared as "Preserving Our Culture Through Literacy" in the *Report of the 1986 Bilingual Multicultural Education Conference* (Juneau: Alaska Department of Education). It was revised and provided with a new introduction for this volume.
2.   This standardized writing system was developed by the staff of the Eskimo Language Workshop (the predecessor of the Yupik Language Center) and the Alaska Native Language Center in the 1960s. It was later described in the textbook, *Yupik Eskimo Orthography* (Bethel, Alaska: Yupik Language Center, Kuskokwim College, 1978; revised and reprinted, 1979), which I coauthored with linguist Osahito Miyaoka. (Editor's note: Mather has also conducted research on Yup'ik grammar with Miyaoka since the 1980s.)
3.   Catherine Attla is a Koyukon Athabaskan.

References

Berger, Thomas R. 1985. *Village Journey: The Report of the Alaska Native Review Commission.* New York, Hill and Wang.

Nelson, Edward W. [1899] 1983. *The Eskimo about Bering Strait.* Reprint, Washington, D.C.: Smithsonian Institution.

Ninguelook, Edgar. 1984. Hearings Transcribed February 1984–March 1985, box 9, folder 1. Series 1 of Alaska Native Review Commission Records, 1983–1985. Elmer E. Rasmuson Library Archives, University of Alaska Fairbanks.

On Shaky Ground
Folklore, Collaboration, and Problematic Outcomes

Phyllis Morrow

In Yup'ik society, hunters and fishers who are lucky enough to catch anything are individuals who pay attention to what they have learned. It is they to whom game returns. Storytellers, too, are people who are said to be "lucky enough to have caught a tale." Implicitly, people have this luck, too, when they pay attention to a store of ever-changing experiences, both individual ones and those shared as members of a common culture. Such experiences contextualize a story's meaning for any given person at a particular time and place. Removed from this cultural context, any of us may catch a Yup'ik story, but we may not know what to do with it once we have it.

As long-term friends and collaborators in the activity of passing Yup'ik stories on to be caught by readers, Phyllis Morrow and Elsie Mather have wrestled with the most effective and conscientious ways to convey tales. In the process, they have encountered some intractable problems in bridging the expectations and understanding of a culturally diverse, anonymous audience of readers. Should stories be presented with little or no commentary, so that any individual's right to make meaning is respected? Or should some of the context of the tales be explicated, at the risk of limiting personal interpretation? As writers, our voices become authoritative, implicitly contributing a more fixed sense of meaning than the one caught by a Yup'ik listener. Can we retell these stories without losing the subtleties of the storytellers' words? And who will be lucky enough to catch those subtleties?

In this essay, Morrow frames a discussion about meaning, authorship, ownership, and authenticity in terms of the ongoing dialogue between herself and Mather. The issues seem fundamentally unresolvable, yet they do not seem to warrant giving up the work.

The Yupiit know and feel that the world is experienced in different levels. There is much to wonder about. To learn to live comfortably in this is being Yup'ik. The world speaks to us, for one, in and by our feelings. It does not articulate clearly, but we make inferences and leave it at that. I feel strongly that interpretations should be very limited, leaving the information in the stories open. We are on shaky ground when we presume to know what the message is for the Native hearers.   —Elsie P. Mather

Much of our knowledge about other cultures must now be seen as contingent, the problematic outcome of intersubjective dialogue, translation and projection.   —James Clifford (1986: 109)

Since the early 1980s, Elsie Mather and I have collaborated on the transcription, translation, and representation of Central Alaskan Yup'ik stories. She was born and raised in the Kuskokwim delta, where her education started—and continues—with Yup'ik oral tradition. She spends much of her time in subsistence pursuits; she has also been a nurse, a teacher, a lecturer, and an author of high-school and college textbooks. Her grounding in the oral tradition puts her book learning in a certain perspective. I, on the other hand, was born on the East Coast of the United States, and my education was always pointed toward the written word. As a graduate student in cultural anthropology, I came to southwestern Alaska in the mid-1970s, expecting to stay for a year but remaining for over a decade. I was willingly snared by berry picking, fish cutting, friendships, and stories. This immersion put my book learning in a new perspective, and in retrospect I began to realize how important oral narrative had been in my life, too. Coming from different directions, then, Elsie and I found our interests converging on the problematics of shifting oral performance to paper and the question of whether such a move is wise, not to mention even possible.

Our conversations as friends and colleagues continue unabated, even though I now work at the University of Alaska Fairbanks, several hundred miles away. The most recent exchange is a coauthored paper that begins with a story told by Phillip Charlie (to which I will refer later),[1] offers a few explanatory notes, and then becomes a collaboratively written dialogue, reconstructed from our letters and telephone conversations, about the whole issue of collaboration and its implications for dialogue between cultural traditions.

This essay draws heavily from that conversation and represents some of my subsequent reflections on our personal struggle to decide what and what not to say about Yup'ik stories. The struggle relates, I think, to a theoretical and methodological discussion among anthropologists and folklorists that, like my relationship with Elsie, has developed since the 1970s. In this sense, I am offering a dialogue between and about dialogues.

On one level, the collaborative "dialogue," as we began to conceive of it, is not strictly between us—it is with you, in some sense the most problematic partners in this process. "You" include everyone who has made comments on our work in the past or whose comments on related topics we have heard or read. In our imaginations, you include perceptive critics with a deep level of understanding and a ready store of relevant personal experiences, as well as our own worst stereotypes of those who misconstrue, misappropriate, overromanticize, and/or overanalyze Native Americans and their folklore. You include Yup'ik people, to whom we feel responsible and about whom we remain constantly conscious, whether or not you eventually read this article. To complicate this process even more, what we imagine you to be is also what we sometimes project onto each other. We collaborate as both our most eager and appreciative audiences and as the alternately frustrated, misguided, and reluctant representatives of our respective cultures.

As reluctant cultural representatives, Elsie Mather and I have found that collaboration underscores certain basic contrasts between our traditions, contrasts which have a profound effect on "the work of interpretation" (see Tedlock 1983). A Yup'ik generally grows up encouraged to reflect on the personal meaning of stories but discouraged from detailed analysis and public explication. From this perspective, a preoccupation with hidden meanings and symbolism can lead to confusion, while the purpose of oral tradition is not to confuse or mislead the listener. Much of Western schooling and socialization, on the other hand, encourages probing, contending that addressing conflicting interpretations openly can illuminate subtle meanings and generally enrich an audience's understanding. Elsie and I acknowledge these as cultural differences that can be difficult to negotiate and that, to some extent, are reflected in our own intellectual styles.

As individuals, however, we also often delight in and partake of other traditions; it is no simple dichotomy. We both indulge in curious speculation; we both stop to wonder without trying to draw conclusions. Each drawing from diverse experiences, we try to construct a middle ground where we can collaborate, and we have found that it is shaky ground. The problematics of "intersubjective dialogue, translation and projection" are nowhere more complex and subtle than in the collaborative process of transferring a performance event to a static medium aimed at an hypothesized audience.

The first level of concern, then, is how to move beyond some naive concept of "bridging two cultures" to develop an awareness of ourselves and our audiences so that we may interact. The second level has to do with more general issues of representation. The interplay of these two levels is at the heart of this essay. When a storyteller speaks, he or she does so in a cultural context. It is a different task to write about that context from a position both/neither within it and/nor outside of it. In academic circles, postmodernist criticism has led to a theoretical, methodological, and political consideration of writing about "the other," as well as portraying in subtle ways "the self," that is, the author. In this academic movement, critics of anthropology have led us to see ethnographic writing as (having always been) a literary enterprise. One problem is that the authors of ethnographies have almost never been raised in the cultural tradition they are describing, and their objectively authoritative voice and selective presentation of their role in the "participant-observation" process often subsume and distance the voices of the people they depict. Although it is the basis of the work, little of the dialogue between anthropologist and informant, or folklorist and storyteller, ever appears in the resultant books and articles (Tedlock 1983). Since depiction and representation are filtering—and therefore distorting—processes, what we then read are artful constructions, produced under particular historical, political, and personal conditions. In short, the authorial tone offers a disguise of certainty that prevents readers from noticing the contingent nature of "our knowledge about other cultures."

The relatively newfound concern with a lack of Native voices in print has stimulated the production of alternative ethnographies that use a variety of devices in an attempt to rectify the omission. Dennis Tedlock, for example, has championed dialogic representations, arguing that they permit reinterpretation by readers. That is, it is better to read what the people say than only to read the author's conclusions about what they say. Clifford Geertz (1988: 144–47) aptly points out that no matter what devices are used to bring out Native viewpoints, an "un-get-roundable problem" persists: all ethnographic descriptions are those of the describer, not the described. The real authorship problem, as Geertz conceives it, remains: how can one get a description down on paper in a comprehensible and evocative fashion so that the reader may come to glimpse another life? The same question applies to conveying a moment of oral performance.[2]

Logically, one thinks of Native authorship and Native/non-Native collaboration as the next, better step toward balanced representation, but there are authorship problems here, too, and they are even more fundamental than the challenge of writing effectively. These problems stem from the fact that authoring itself is, and exists in, a peculiarly Western cultural milieu. Is it then possible for a Native author, or a collaborative team, to create—or represent—a discourse that departs from the conventions and cultural implications of authoring? This may be an unanswerable question, but even to approach it, we must not only consider our individual actions as authors (what and how we write) but also all that is entailed in Authoring, writ large, at least to uncover some of the implications of cultural difference in the process of cointerpretation.

Michel Foucault sees authoring ("the author function") as a particular epistemological stance of Western civilization. In "What Is an Author?" (1984), he points out that certain questions which have typically preoccupied "our civilization" since the seventeenth or eighteenth centuries center around the need to attribute works (and also theories, traditions, disciplines, and in the grandest sense "possibilities and . . . rules for the formation of other texts," (114) that is, entire potential discourses)[3] to "authors." The author function, then, is a cultural tradition, a way of conceiving of and ultimately regulating expression, and not at all a simple process of merely attributing ideas to individuals.[4] Although we think of authors as proliferating meaning, Foucault claims, we actually fear the idea of living in a state in which the fictive, by which he seems to mean a certain freedom of expression, "would be at the disposal of everyone" (119). The (ideological existence of the) author, then, is a way to "reduce the great peril, the great danger with which fiction threatens our world" (118). I paraphrase this to say that the author function limits or constrains the unbridled production of meaning by positing the author (by implication, over and above the rest of us, the readers) as meaning maker.

Stating that "the modes of circulation, valorization, attribution and appropriation of discourses vary with each culture and are modified within each," Foucault imagines a future culture in which there is less fear of fiction and all the dangers inherent in its "proliferation of meaning." In such a culture, the author function will disappear, and meaning will be less constrained, although necessarily still limited in some as yet unexperienced fashion:

We would no longer hear the questions [about authorship] that
have been rehashed for so long: Who really spoke? Is it really
he and not someone else? With what authenticity or originality?
And what part of his deepest self did he express in his discourse?
Instead there would be other questions, like these: What are the
modes of existence of this discourse? Where has it been used, how
can it circulate, and who can appropriate it for himself? What
are the places in it where there is room for possible subjects?
Who can assume these various subject functions? And behind all
these questions, we would hear hardly anything but the stirring
of an indifference: What difference does it make who is speaking?
(119–20)

If the author function is a culture-specific pattern, then to contemplate collaboration, we must consider two things. First, what
questions already shape discourse production and attribution of
meaning? Here we are considering the cultural contexts of folklore
transmission for the people whose lore we are representing. And
second, how do differences in the conception of discourse shape
its production between collaborators? In the case at hand, how
can we, coming from different discourse traditions, construct the
representation of one group's folklore for members of both traditions?

With respect to the first question, my understanding is that the
Yup'ik stance on meaning comes closer to that represented by Foucault's imaginary culture than to the ideological position occupied
by the author function. To begin with, the narrative function (to coin
a phrase) is preoccupied with things other than individual authority
or originality. Elsie Mather comments: "The most respected convey-
ors of Yup'ik knowledge are those who express things that listeners
already know in artful or different ways, offering new expressions of
the same." Whatever elements of individual expressiveness a teller
brings to the narration are thoroughly enjoyed, but they are not the
stuff of the story.

A common way for a storyteller to begin a Yup'ik narrative is to
set himself, the recorder, the story, and those from whom he heard
it in a web of relationships, a network of people, places, and events.
In this way, he makes it clear that this is a situated performance of
a repeated tale, authentic and faithful to the way he heard it. One
effect of this kind of opening is to invoke the collective authority of
many storytellers. Part of what makes a tale traditional is the way it reflects a timeless past and many retellings, rather than any individual's

experience or authority.[5] The teller may assert that he did not make it up: "it is truly a tale" and one of the "first of the tales." Responsiveness to listeners and dramatic effects like voice quality and pauses add variety and affect to every telling, but the stated goal is consistency with what one has heard.

For Yup'ik listeners, then, the search for authenticity does not involve looking for an author but an appreciation of the fact that discourse circulates from teller to teller. Ideally, changes in the telling result from differences in the hearing. When telling stories or describing traditions, it is common for narrators to invite variation: "This is the way I heard it. Perhaps others have heard it a little differently."

Second, in the Yup'ik oral tradition, meaning is not assumed to be fixed, to center in the storyteller, or to be deeply questioned. When we discussed the explication of stories, Elsie Mather wrote to me:

> Why do people want to reduce traditional stories to information, to some function? Isn't it enough that we hear and read them? They cause us to wonder about things, and sometimes they touch us briefly along the way, or we connect the information or idea into something we are doing at the moment. This is what the older people say a lot. They tell us to listen even when we don't understand, that later on we will make some meaning or that something that we had listened to before will touch us in some way. Understanding and knowing occur over one's lifetime. I am born into a culture which values certain things and ideas, but most of these I absorb during everyday experiences.
>
> Storytelling is part of the action of living. I do not question it much. The phrases, the themes or ideas expressed become a part of me, yet I do not understand half of what is said. But they are there. They are part of why I pick my berries or why I ask someone to have tea with me. Whenever my mother had the urge to pick on my head for lice or nits, she yanked me from whatever I was doing and proceeded. I rarely ever asked her to tell me stories. To quiet my protest at having my head picked on, my mother told me stories. The time was both pleasant and painful—a part of life.
>
> Why would I want to spoil the repetition and telling of stories with questions? Why would I want to know what they mean? Is not the hearing and the comforting repetition enough? They brought comfort and added to my well-being even when (in my case) they added to my discomfort and annoyance. I really don't suppose my

mother had grandiose ideas about instruction and knowledge as she told the stories. She just wanted me to be still so she could get rid of the little beasts while she had the pleasure of hunting for them.

In the view Elsie Mather expresses, meaning is not a question of the storyteller's intent ("I really don't suppose my mother had grandiose ideas about instruction and knowledge"), nor is it something to find out, once and for all ("Understanding and knowing occur over one's lifetime."). Neither the storyteller nor any other individual fills an author function. Instead, personal meanings proliferate through tellers and listeners. Furthermore, in a general sense, explication has the perverse effect of trying to erase mystery in the world; it contradicts the sense of awe that derives from "the Yup'ik belief that things just happen with no explanation," as Elsie Mather phrases it.

Implicit in this comfort with proliferation of meaning and non-explanation is a lack of concern with what Foucault assumes to be the "great dangers" of fiction, dangers that are held at bay, in the Western tradition, by the author function. To my concern with accuracy in explaining cultural contexts for our readers, Elsie Mather retorted: "What is accurate information? Accurate for who? Even if an explanation is not wrong, it is not complete."

In the past, the author function has prevented folklore collectors from seeing such contrasts and grappling with their deep implications. An author's explanations might be challenged, but no reader objected to the fact that explanations were offered. In the Yup'ik area, at least, this is no longer true. A brief review of the documentation of Yup'ik folklore shows that the dilemmas of collaboration are historically recent. As the review moves closer to the present, I will try to show when and how the author and narrative functions began to rub against each other.

Stories fascinated even the earliest non-Natives to travel through or settle in southwest Alaska. Like many other European world travelers, Russian and American explorers in Alaska wrote down indigenous tales, in addition to recording various customs they found intriguing. What they wrote and how they presented it depended largely upon their specific reasons for being there. For example, those with economic interests wanted information that would help them establish trade relations and guide them safely across regional boundaries. As a result, they were especially interested in stories detailing peoples' origins and their relations with neighboring groups. Most travelers also clearly enjoyed writing about exotica for the readers back home.

When Moravian and Catholic missionaries entered the region, they, too, began recording or mentioning tales in their diaries and letters, many of which subsequently appeared in mission publications, such as church magazines and missionary biographies.[6] Their concern was with the spiritual life of the people they encountered, so they noted stories that said something about indigenous religious beliefs. They often set down Raven creation stories and other tales, accompanied by their own Christian-influenced interpretations. In general, missionary writings, even through the mid-twentieth century, conveyed the impression that Yup'ik stories and other cultural expressions revealed a people at once primitive and full of potential: "There is a rich store of human culture for the educator to work on in the native," in the words of Paul O' Connor, S.J. (1947: 21). The sentiment had changed little since 1886, when Moravian missionary Edith Kilbuck wrote:

> In looking over our experience with the natives thus far, we have no reason to feel disheartened, altho [*sic*], as is to be expected in an unenlightened people, we have met with men who have to all appearance, no true manly principles, still we have met with those, in whose hearts are to be found those gems, which when polished by the grace of God will shine out brilliantly, and add new lustre to the crown of our Eternal King. There is something about these people that makes one long so for them, feel for them, to love them. We see a rich harvest, a great one, and one that requires earnest, hard, prayerful work. (Henkelman and Vitt 1985: 95)

Since one intent of these early collectors was to justify and facilitate their own work in the region and invite financial support from government agencies or wealthy parishioners back home, they wanted to show (and they believed) that there was a lot of work to be done but there was a good chance it could be accomplished. They were heartened when they could cast indigenous ideas in a Christian framework, since apparently parallel conceptions provided footholds for conversion, and they were determined to change any ideas that they identified with "idols" or "devil worship."

Missionaries obviously found Yup'ik stories both entertaining and useful in their efforts to learn the language as well. Catholic priest Francis Barnum, S.J., for example, recorded tales verbatim, with interlinear and free translations, in his grammar of the Yup'ik language (1901). Among the archived papers of missionaries, one can find other examples of stories that Jesuit priests apparently transcribed and used as the basis of religious lessons or to improve their language skills. The Moravian missionary John Kilbuck, himself a Delaware Indian, saw in the Yup'ik culture parallels to his own past and was "strangely stirred" by their customs. Among his papers is a short ethnography, written as if intended for eventual publication, including war and origin stories (see Fienup-Riordan 1988: 29–57).

A common strain in Moravian and Catholic missionary writings is the emphasis on the moral basis for Yup'ik teachings, and this parallelism continues to shape contemporary Yup'ik understandings of their own past; it is common for people to draw comparisons between Biblical precepts and the more traditional Yup'ik lessons for living embodied in lore. Naturally, the same emphasis on correspondences and contrasts between missionary and Yup'ik beliefs (intended in missionary writings for fellow Christians elsewhere) informed local mission efforts; thus, some aspects of Yup'ik lore and beliefs were syncretically reinforced more than others.

At the same time, the author function itself was apparently of little interest to Yupiit. We have a hint about Yup'ik conceptions about writing in the nineteenth century because some Moravian converts, known as Helpers, began to develop a writing system so that they could remember Biblical teachings (see Henkelman and Vitt 1985). They were particularly impressed that writing allowed the missionaries to repeat what they said in exactly the same words each time. Here the concern with faithfulness to what one heard was apparently paramount, along with the antiquity and divine source of the words themselves. Given the Yup'ik emphasis on other things than the attribution of original ideas to specific people, it is not surprising that their writing system was used almost exclusively for transcribing Biblical passages and parables and was never adapted to individual authorship.

There is also one nineteenth-century author, Edward Nelson, who attempted a more comprehensive description of Yup'ik life. *The Eskimo about Bering Strait* (1983) represents materials he collected between 1877 and 1881. Nelson gathered an excellent corpus of tales, noting provenances and including a sample text in the Yup'ik language. Trained as an observer of natural phenomena, he approached ethnography with an attention to detail and an objectively descriptive tone similar to those of other scientific reporters of his day. He was an effective practitioner of the author function: he "got it down" in a way that is still useful. Yet he unknowingly defined an authenticity both partial and potentially limiting. In my graduate folklore class, for example, I have on several occasions asked students to compare a variant of one Raven tale collected by Nelson with a telling that Elsie and I transcribed verbatim in 1981. Invariably, students prefer Nelson's version because "it is more detailed" and "explains more." I suspect that it was Nelson, as author, who skillfully wove the explanations into the text, for they refer to beliefs that would have been implicitly obvious to a Yup'ik audience. Students, however, assume that his version is verbatim, more complete because it was told a century earlier and therefore more original.

In the midtwentieth century, Yup'ik tales continued to be collected slowly, not only in missionary and travel publications but now also in academic writings. Margaret Lantis began anthropological research on Nunivak Island and along the Kuskokwim River, publishing results beginning in 1946. She (1946, 1953) and Hans Himmelheber (1951, 1953) were the first to offer scholarly analyses of Yup'ik folklore. Later Wendell Oswalt produced several ethnographic and ethnohistorical works, including a history of Moravian missionization that featured references to storytelling and summaries of some war stories (1963) and a short article about storyknifing, an activity in which girls simultaneously narrated tales and illustrated them with stylized symbols in the mud (1964).[7] Like missionaries and explorers, these academics wrote for restricted audiences whose characteristics seemed relatively predictable. Each knew what he or she wanted to write and could hazard a fair guess as to what the audience would want to have explicated.

This was also a time when Yup'ik tales began to make their way into American children's literature, targeting yet another restricted audience. Two collections of tales edited by Charles Gillham were in my own school library in Maryland in the 1950s. These books reflected a widespread European and American conception of folklore as unauthored public property, particularly suitable for the entertainment and moral instruction of children.[8] In a very un-Yup'ik fashion, Gillham was careful to separate what he saw as truth from fiction for his young readers. In *Medicine Men of Hooper Bay* (1955), for example, he undoes much of the effect of a story in which a hunter falls asleep, then wakes up and follows a crane to its humanlike village, by ending with a caution: "Sometimes you have dreams that are silly / And sometimes they seem to be true/ But it's usually something you've eaten/ When a dream ever comes to you" (94). He also appends morals throughout: e.g., "The beavers are busy people. Everyone has his own job and knows how to do it. It would be fine if everyone were as busy and as good as they" (103). The storytellers themselves, if mentioned at all, became subjects in Gillham's own tale: "an old Eskimo ... is the source of the following folk stories of these interesting people" (10). Only after publication did the stories become authored—by Gillham.

While these early folklore collectors varied tremendously, they had one thing in common: they wrote either for themselves, as in the case of missionaries learning the language, or for an audience that shared their cultural tradition. Yup'ik and non-Yup'ik discourse remained largely parallel traditions. That is, the writing activity of outsiders never stimulated the development of authorship in Yup'ik, nor did Euro-American authors see writing down stories as challenging in any deep philosophical sense. Tales were treated as translatable, reducible, and amenable to summary and editing. Thus, neither verbatim accuracy (except when taking linguistic samples) nor "intersubjective dialogue" with tradition bearers posed difficulties. In effect, the locus of activity, except for the initial telling of a tale, was elsewhere. Aesthetics were managed by the collector and publisher; interpretation took place at a distance.

In the 1970s, as civil rights, bilingual education, and ethnic pride movements blossomed, many people became actively interested in preserving their own folk traditions in writing and other nonoral media. Local language, authorship, and ownership were newly empowering. Many authors began to consider local audiences. In the Kuskokwim region, young students enthusiastically recorded narratives and photographed elders making sleds, kayaks, baskets, and other items of material culture. High-school cultural heritage magazines flourished and were proudly filled with the results of their work (see, for example, *Kaliikaq Yugnek* 1974–77).

This was a transitional period. The collectors were now the folk, the potential inheritors of their elders' lore. Their readers were also more diverse. This was a historical moment when roles began, for the first time, to overlap. Writers, readers, and listeners were no longer distinct and separate. Readers now included Yupiit as well as the wider public, diverse in age, cultural background, and interests. Under different historical circumstances, the cultural heritage projects might have faced the dilemma of collaborative representation, but their school-based nature preserved some sense of role separation. The young Yup'ik students were learning the non-Yup'ik author function because their teachers envisioned the cultural heritage magazines as ways of improving their students' English and shaping their essayist writing. Elders were seen as informants, students as writers and editors, and teachers as supervisors.

Further, because they conceived of this project simultaneously as *teaching* writing and *preserving* cultural heritage, teachers and students were unaware of the often-subtle cultural shifts that the *Foxfire* approach entailed.[9] An anecdote illustrates the type of shifts that occurred. I remember acting as a substitute teacher for the cultural heritage class at Bethel (then Regional) High School in 1977. The teacher explained that when the students asked elders to tell about their lives, they all started their recollections in the same way: "When I was young, we lived in mud houses." The teacher "solved" this by helping the students edit out repetitions, name the stories, and make them "more distinctive."

In retrospect, at this point we can see the author and narrative functions begin to rub against each other. It is no surprise that at the time nobody recognized a cultural significance in the uniformity of each elder's opening statement or the fact that Yup'ik stories do not have names,[10] given that there was little awareness of orality versus writing, and only one model existed for authoring. In fact, however, even naming stories as part of the author function is a way of limiting meaning. That is, it is because Euro-Americans are uncomfortable with indefinite proliferations of meaning that they name texts. Like Alice in *Through the Looking Glass* (1946),[11] one may feel moorless when one does not know what to call a thing:

"The name of the song is called '*Haddocks Eyes.*' "
"Oh, that's the name of the song, is it?" Alice said, trying to feel interested.
"No, you don't understand," the Knight said, looking a little vexed. "That's what the name is *called*. The name really *is* '*The Aged Aged Man.*' "
"Then I ought to have said 'That's what the *song* is called'?" Alice corrected herself.
"No, you oughtn't: that's quite another thing! The *song* is called '*Ways and Means*': but that's only what it's *called*, you know!"

"Well, what *is* the song, then?" said Alice, who was by this time completely bewildered.

"I was coming to that," the Knight said. "The song really *is* '*A-sitting on a Gate*': and the tune's my own invention." (131–32)

Each of these names highlights a different aspect of the song, giving that aspect primacy in a reader's consideration of its meaning. But Yup'ik stories have no names—no storyteller begins by explicitly stating, "The name of the story is X," and a storyteller is equally unlikely to say that the tale is "*about* X." What the tale is about is implicitly relational; meaning is created in any listener's connections between a telling, a teller, a life, a time, and a setting.[12]

Cultural heritage teachers, however, encouraged their students to supply an "appropriate" name for each tale. Furthermore, editors tended to sort the tales into named categories such as Yup'ik fables or short stories.[13] Since sorting and naming is a prized early educational skill, one which is routinely included in standardized multiple-choice tests ("Read the following paragraph and choose the *best* name for it"), the "need" to name and sort Yup'ik texts became, for high-school educators, a "teaching moment." But the apparently simple and justifiable step of naming narratives in the process of moving performance to paper is, on a subtle level, constitutive.

Not only does naming restrict interpretation by pointing the reader toward one aspect of meaning but it also ignores the care many Yupiit take not to state things too strongly because of a sense that, in stories and in the rest of life, words can make things happen. That is, words limit meaning because they potentially establish what is. A person, then, should ideally consider what he says carefully and be sparing with his words. In a meeting of a cooperative fish-management group, I remember that one speaker, Michael Chase, emphasized what he was about to say by twice reminding listeners: "I don't say much. But I *listen*" (Morrow and Hensel 1992: 48). If meaning is newly made in each moment of reflection on oral tales, then naming and sorting them—as well as expending verbiage in elucidating them—are antithetical processes.

Sorting narratives is also constitutive in that it predisposes a reader to see certain analogies to Western genres with all of their connotations. This, of course, simply accentuates a normal cultural tendency to understand the unfamiliar in terms of the familiar. Non-Yup'ik students, for instance, commonly expect Yup'ik stories to be like European fables and fairy tales. An example is the tale told by Phillip

Charlie in which a man's exhaustion after a long day's hunt leads him to ask his wife to bring his catch up from the shore, a task which is properly his to do. On the beach, she is abducted by a hunter from a distant village. The husband eventually finds her and laments his predicament as he cleans a walrus skull that he has found buried in the sand. He becomes the walrus and in this form drowns the abductor. He then swims away with his wife and leaves her in the form of a rock as a visible reminder of their story. Reading the tale (in English translation) to a college class, I found that, even after cultural referents that puzzled them were explained, students were disturbed because they could not figure out a moral to the story and because the separated couple, once rejoined, did not live happily ever after.

Elsie Mather, on the other hand, felt that once the events of the tale were set in motion, a transformation was required for the man to reach the state of "nothing to trouble his well-being," as Phillip Charlie put it. For her, the transformation of woman to rock and man to walrus left "a sense of permanence afterward, a feeling that they went to their rightful place, where they belong." To think of the tale as a fable or fairy tale is, clearly, more than a matter of convenience.

One collector during the 1980s did honor the Yup'ik practice of referring to stories simply as *quliraq* or *qanemciq* (which he translated as "tale" and "narrative," respectively) without descriptive titles. Anthony Woodbury's collection of stories from Chevak (1984) was informed by linguistic training and the performance school of folkloristics, and so he adopted Native genres.[14] Elsewhere, however, the misfit between author and narrative functions remains hidden. Writers continue to assign names for publication purposes, and contemporary audiences continue to expect them.

More overt problems surfaced as Yupiit read (or read about) the ethnographies, missionary reports, and other written sources describing their own culture. Often, when I was working with Yup'ik colleagues on writing projects, I heard serious concerns about misinformation that had been propagated by non-Native writers. The same people, however, were reluctant to author materials that corrected these impressions. Ten years later, when we talked about collaboration, Elsie Mather expressed what I think is the same dilemma they felt: "I have problems with interpretations of the Yupiit made by outsiders. I am also uncomfortable with making interpretations. I like the idea of people making meaning of life in their own terms."

The author and narrative functions, then, really came into conflict as people began to think about representing not just their lore or their language but themselves, *through* these cultural expressions. Yupiit who taught or cotaught Yup'ik language classes and conducted cultural awareness workshops with non-Native students, for example, were continually barraged with questions. Their students expected explication of customs and behaviors—they wanted "authors" to tell them how it was. Yup'ik teachers were often uncomfortable with this role; they expected others to extrapolate their own personal and private conclusions actively and variously as they accumulated experience interacting with Yupiit. This expectation did not succeed outside of a Yup'ik audience, for whom the terms by which people make their own meaning are largely shared. If they are not totally baffled, non-Natives are likely to become sidetracked by their cultural assumptions. They may, in effect, look in vain for the moral of the story, be disturbed because there is no "happily ever after" ending, or find some reference (innocuous, to Yupiit) shocking or offensive, as occurred with one story in which a fish, having been defecated on the outskirts of a village by the man who ate him, reflects gratefully on the man's careful action.[15]

It is obvious that values and daily experiences of life on the tundra and rivers are not likely to be absorbed during everyday living by readers or students from other traditions. It is less obvious that explaining such things is discouraged as a very part of the Yup'ik tradition that is being explained. And here we arrive squarely in the present, facing a catch-22 situation as collaborators. When I am concerned about inaccuracy, for example, I am reminded that one cannot be accurate, but one can be wrong. When I want to hear whether my ideas are wrong, Elsie Mather comments: "I find myself fluctuating between wanting to discourage some of your conclusions and at the same time I want to follow the Yup'ik way of respecting what others have to say. The Yup'ik expression for tolerating what is questionable is the saying, 'What is true will prevail.' "

So we return to the nagging question: can collaboration bring a dual perspective to bear on a narrative tradition? After all, even this notion of dualism is an oversimplification. The audience for a written tale not only will include non-Yupiit with a variety of backgrounds but also a diverse Yup'ik population: young Yupiit monolingual in English, living in larger urban communities, or less steeped in village subsistence activities; college-educated Yupiit; and so on. We begin to debate the very purpose of widening the audience for a narrative tradition beyond that of its original oral performance. Are we trying to increase cross-cultural understanding? ("Even if an explanation is not wrong, it is not complete.") In whose terms can we help people appreciate the tradition? ("I like the idea of people making meaning of life in their own terms.")

Clearly we are caught between the author and narrative functions, between saying too much and too little.[16] That cultural contexts require explication is no news to folklorists, nor is the dilemma of just how much contextual information is necessary; certainly there is no way to fully recreate the context of the original telling, not to mention the entire cultural background which informed it. Here, however, I raise a different issue: if, from a Yup'ik perspective, explication itself is counterproductive, does one shift the field of meaning of the tradition by approaching the question of its field of meaning at all? Is this a legitimate enterprise? It seems that collaboration creates a working space for the recognition of cultural difference, but it is merely a staging area for a more honest and self-aware interaction than that represented by the old researcher/informant dichotomy, not a solution.

What, then, have Elsie Mather and I done? We have agreed to limit explanatory notes and state openly that they are incomplete. We have also pointed out that these notes are addressed to non-Yupiit and those younger Yupiit who may be out of touch with narrative traditions. We have primarily restricted ourselves to explaining aspects of the motifs, themes, and general cultural setting which are clearly necessary for readers to understand the stories.

Beyond this, defining the limits and topics of discussion has not been easy. And, in addition to our common concerns about explication as culturally uneasy turf, each of us also finds the ground shaky in distinctly personal ways. As the academic member of the team, I have to grapple with the expectation that my contributions to the world of "the literature" will be valued only insofar as they are original, individually "owned" insights. This creates a certain pressure toward high-risk interpretations; that is, going out on an intellectual limb to say something new or at least express myself in a unique way. Because of its twin emphases on ownership and authenticity, the academy is suspicious of collaboration at the same time that it applauds the presence of Native voices. The author function asks, "Whose work is this really?" If Elsie Mather is assumed to be the "real" author, then I am undoubtedly guilty of appropriating her ideas. If I am the "real" author, then her byline must be mere tokenism. There is no room for coequal collaboration within the author function.[17]

In the Yup'ik tradition, the ideas most valued are those which have been contributed by others, each with the benefit and unique perspective supplied by his or her own experience. When one has something innovative to say, one references it to the authority of oft-repeated wisdom. The English-language proverb states that one should not hide one's light under a bushel. The Yup'ik equivalent states that one should keep one's rustling noises to oneself. Using the former style with a Yup'ik audience may sound presumptuous; using the latter style with an academic audience, one may be overlooked.

For Elsie Mather, the ground particularly shakes when she adopts the conflicting stance of both researcher and informant. As a researcher, she becomes curious to ask inappropriate questions and knows that older cultural contexts need explication for current audiences (both local and distant). As an informant, she is often in the position of emphasizing things which culture bearers intentionally do not explicate. Providing a metacommentary on the difference does not solve the problem, since such an explicit discussion is unwelcome to many Yup'ik members of the audience. Since we often work with recordings of tales made by other collectors (ranging from radio-show hosts to students), as well as those where Elsie Mather was part of the audience, it is not always possible for her to avoid making generalizations by choosing the option of describing the personal context and meanings of a story for her.

My own comprehension of these difficulties grew slowly as I began to realize some of the implications of my own cultural tradition. A series of anecdotes shows the progression in my awareness. One day my nine-year-old son came home from school and told me a story he had made up. For this assignment, he said, each child in the class had to create a "legend." The teacher had posted a chart, with columns conveniently prelabeled—they included categories such as "trickster" and "human-animal transformation." Each third-grade folklorist was to match appropriate motifs or character types with those he had "invented." The effective point, I suppose, was to demonstrate to each child that he or she bears a considerable folk tradition. But there was something less conscious going on here. Never mind that these looked more like folktales (as I found myself ironically explaining), my son was insistent that they were legends. It seemed typically Western: what was consistently highlighted was genre, individual invention, categorization, and analysis.

I juxtapose this anecdote to some of my earliest experiences learning about Yup'ik preferences. I remember, for example, practicing grammatical patterns with the help of a tutor. I was translating a series of words with third-person absolutive endings: "He goes; she speaks; it is big," I intoned. "How do you know it's a 'he'?" snapped my tutor. She could be a difficult person to get along with, and this pickiness seemed the last straw in a degenerating teacher-student relationship. "Because it's awkward to say 'he, she, or it' every single time," I replied, wondering why I had to tell her again that I knew gender is not grammatically marked in Yup'ik.

Some years later, my absolutives no longer in question, I began collaborative efforts to write language-learning materials and to transcribe and translate Yup'ik folklore. By this time, my main concern was to "get it right." I understood the resentment that came from seeing poor translations in print, accompanied by inaccurate commentary. Now, however, another problem emerged. The non-Yup'ik writers on the team wanted to include sociolinguistic information, an area not considered in the existing teaching grammar. The Yup'ik members of the group supported the idea but were uncomfortable with most of the sociolinguistic observations that were made. "No, it's not wrong," one person said; "in fact it's very accurate. It's just that we're not sure we want people to know about it." Again I thought I understood. Inaccurate information was harmful, but accurate information could be, too, since it violated the protective boundary between insider and outsider. In the past, outsiders had done a lot of harm with what they had learned, suppressing a variety of customs.

The final anecdote is a current one. Elsie Mather and I recently readied a story for publication (Morrow and Mather 1995); since it was meant for a general audience, the introduction carefully explained some of its cultural context. The well-known story told about a woman who returned from the afterlife and informed people how to "improve" their ceremonies for the dead. We explained something about the historic ceremony for the dead and the naming customs which perpetuate relationships among the living and dead. We also wrote about a metaphoric value of the story, its reminder that people should not remain aloof to the needs of others. I thought that this time the problem had been solved. Someone passed on to me the comments of one Yup'ik reader, however, who said he wished that he had not read it. He thought he'd rather not know why his people did the things they did.

Reflecting on these incidents, I find myself facing a serious dilemma. The last three interactions can be seen as progressive steps toward an impasse. Each demonstrates a basic distress associated with specifying meaning. The grammar lesson overtly recognizes a Whorfian distinction between Yup'ik, where gender is contextually implicit, and English, where speakers have to specify gender even when they cannot know which one to specify. My teacher's annoyance was not with my lack of grammatical knowledge but with my ignorance of a cultural preference for expressing the ambiguous as ambiguous. The situation with the materials development project underscores the dangers of making generalizations that may become truths. It is related to the first interaction in that both represent an untoward blending of the descriptive and the prescriptive (for in some ways, saying makes it so). This can be related to the protection of cultural boundaries, but the incident with the recent article suggests a more inclusive understanding.

This incident is the most problematic of all, for here a work was produced collaboratively, with an awareness of cultural differences between the collaborators and the need to create a text informative to non-Native readers and accurate and acceptable to Native ones. In fact, the piece described some of the cultural differences I have just mentioned. Yet the response of that Yup'ik reader was not "I do not want you outsiders to know why we do things," but "I do not want to know why we do these things myself."[18]

Amidst these constraints, Elsie Mather and I straddle the author function and the oral tradition. We remain awkwardly aware that suggesting one explanation rather than another results in a kind of harm and providing none may produce another. It is interesting to note that Phillip Charlie, who told the story in which the man becomes a walrus, also felt the need to offer explanations, since his story was addressed to an unseen radio audience. For these listeners, he provided one level of decontextualization, moving the oral performance from an immediate and interactive context to a delayed and distant one. What he chose to explain were practices and items related to material culture and subsistence; he did not explicate other meanings. He was comfortable with this stopping point, closing his narration with a traditional formula: "There are no more words to the story." In transmitting stories in a print medium, in another language, to another audience, we are never so sure when to stop.

It seems that with collaboration, the best we can hope for is that truths will prevail. If the Yup'ik reader feels that we have already said too much, and the non-Yup'ik reader is hungry to know more, then we have left you with the tension that we feel. It is an honest compromise; we satisfy our consciences as best we can and leave the rest of the meaning making to you. To the extent that we can maintain the betweenness of our dialogue, we reduce Foucault's question, "What difference does it make who is speaking?" if not to "the stirring of an indifference" (1984: 120), then at least to a more muffled roar.

In collaboration, we have foregrounded what may be essential incompatibilities between frameworks of meaning. At the same time, however, collaboration has taken us in important new directions, by mixing up the "our" and the "other" of our knowledge about other cultures and letting friction develop between different ways of conceptualizing discourse. Collaboration, I would argue, tends to entangle, untangle, unravel, and enrich dialogue between Native and non-Native collaborators, tradition-bearers, listeners, and readers— and it shows us that these apparently contrasting categories of people overlap and intertwine, especially in these media-shared times. To presume to know anyone's meaning is to stand on shaky ground, but only in looking for meaning are we learning that . . . and, of course, much more.

Notes

1. The paper was written for a forthcoming special edition of *Oral Tradition*, edited by Barre Toelken and Larry Evers, on collaboration.

2. Representation on paper is necessarily different from the situated performance of an oral form. Characteristics of orality such as repetition, formulaic phrasing, and nonverbal signaling are inherently difficult to render or appreciate on paper, and reducing the oral to a written format unavoidably obscures and distorts any given performance. It also has the effect (equally true for audiotape and film) of focusing the attention of a removed audience on one telling amongst the many that any given person normally hears throughout his or her life in many personalized contexts. Readers interested in orality and literacy in relation to the verbal arts will find a useful bibliography in Finnegan (1992). Dennis Tedlock and ethnopoets such as Jerome Rothenberg (1968, 1972) have particularly focused on poetic devices for rendering oral performance and have effectively shown how inseparable form is from content. Scollon and Scollon (1981) offer a relevant discussion in relation to cross-cultural communication.

    In my experience, Yup'ik storytellers and translators have not thought the idea of "fixing" fluid, interactionally responsive oral forms in writing to be a major problem per se. There is widespread interest in recording, broadcasting, and printing oral narratives since people have less opportunity to hear and enjoy them in more spontaneous contexts. Narratives are seen as a good focus of cultural preservation as long as permissions are obtained, qualified people are involved, and distribution plans are approved. The problems, as I will discuss, arise at other levels of interpretation.

3. Foucault gives Freud and Marx as the prime examples of such authors of discursive possibility.

4. Actually, as he points out, this is no simple task, either.

5. Unlike Tlingit storytellers, Yupiit do not recount a detailed genealogy that establishes their right to tell a story. Fewer relationships are mentioned in a Yup'ik narration; typically, they include the name of the person from whom the narrator heard it, the narrator's relationship with that person, and perhaps the narrator's or an earlier teller's relationship with his or her listeners. There are no ownership rights for Yup'ik tales. Anyone who has been "lucky enough to catch a tale" may retell it.

6. Both unpublished writings and mission publications may be found in the Archives of the Moravian Church in Bethlehem, Pennsylvania, and the Oregon Province Archives of the Catholic Church in Spokane, Washington.

7. Lynn P. Ager (now Wallen) wrote a master's thesis on this topic in 1971, and an article in 1974.

8. See Robin Barker's essay in this book, "Seeing Wisely, Crying Wolf," for an example of the contemporary persistence of this view of lore.

9. The cultural heritage effort was modeled on Eliot Wigginton's *Foxfire* approach. Ann Vick, who had been associated with early *Foxfire* publications, came to Bethel to work with local teachers and eventually edited some of their students' writing into a book (Vick 1983: 269–344).

10. For the elders framing their recollections, "we lived in mud houses" was probably a key phrase to evoke "the old days" for their youthful listeners. The move from those "real houses" (*nepiat*) to nuclear-family-based, above-ground frame houses was contemporaneous with, and related to, many major cultural shifts in the early twentieth century.

11. At another point (47–49), Alice also gets to briefly enjoy the freedom that namelessness permits. In the nameless wood, she is able to befriend a fawn. Because neither remembers that they are human and fawn, the animal is not afraid, and Alice is not surprised at their co-equal relationship. Here Carroll plays with something like the delicious but dangerous idea of the democratization of the fictive.

12. Although manifest in culturally specific ways in Yup'ik expression, this relational quality is a general feature of oral traditions. See Narayan (1989) for examples from India and Cruikshank's essay in this book, "Pete's Song," for the Yukon. After reading this essay, Elsie Mather commented that Yup'ik stories are "usually recalled or remembered by some action, rather than by some abstract expression or idea. Since

a story can apply to different situations and is often recalled by something happening at the moment, labelling may also confine it to only a certain time and place" (personal correspondence with the author, May 1994).

13. See, for example, Tennant and Bitar (1981), which was compiled from materials originally collected as part of Bethel Regional High School's cultural heritage project.

14. When Woodbury arrived in southwestern Alaska, I was working in the Yupik Eskimo Language Center with Elsie Mather and other language specialists, just beginning a major folklore transcription and translation effort. He helped us in our search for a format that would better reflect the richness of oral performance.

15. For a term project in one of my classes, Allison Kinyon-Coggins read this tale to a variety of individuals and recorded their reactions. She found that this detail so preoccupied many listeners that they had little else to say about the story.

16. We know too well that the transcription and translation processes in themselves are interpretive.

17. This is true when the coauthors are both academics as well. Coauthored publications do not count as much for tenure, and it seems to matter very much who is listed as senior or first author.

18. Elsie Mather thought that others might also feel this way. Compounding what I regard as Yup'ik cultural feelings about analysis is the more general issue of being written about at all. I recall the comment of the schoolmaster who had read Nancy Scheper-Hughes's ethnography of his village: "It's not your science [i.e., your accuracy] I'm questioning, but this: Don't we have the right to lead unexamined lives, the right not to be analyzed? Don't we have a right to hold on to an image of ourselves as 'different' to be sure, but innocent and unblemished all the same?" (1979: vi; brackets are Scheper-Hughes's). Unlike Scheper-Hughes's ethnography, our writing has never concentrated on revealing the darker side of life, but arguably being written about at all involves a loss of innocence or at least a loss of the ability to take things for granted.

References

Ager, Lynn Price. 1971. "The Eskimo Storyknife Complex of Southwestern Alaska." Master's thesis, Anthropology Department, University of Alaska Fairbanks.

———. 1974. "Storyknifing: An Alaskan Eskimo Girls' Game." *Journal of the Folklore Institute* 11(3): 189–98.

Barnum, Francis P. 1901. *Grammatical Fundamentals of the Innuit Language As Spoken by the Eskimo of the Western Coast of Alaska*. Boston: Ginn.

Carroll, Lewis. [1896] 1946. *Through the Looking-Glass and What Alice Found There*. Reprint, New York: Random House.

Clifford, James. 1986. "On Ethnographic Allegory." In *Writing Culture: The Poetics and Politics of Ethnography*, edited by James Clifford and George E. Marcus, 98–121. Berkeley: University of California Press.

Fienup-Riordan, Ann, ed. 1988. *The Yup'ik Eskimos As Described in the Travel Journals and Ethnographic Accounts of John and Edith Kilbuck, 1885–1900*. Kingston, Ont., Canada: Limestone Press.

Finnegan, Ruth. 1992. *Oral Traditions and the Verbal Arts: A Guide to Research Practices*. London: Routledge.

Foucault, Michel. 1984. "What Is an Author?" In *The Foucault Reader*, edited by Paul Rabinow, 101–20. New York: Pantheon.

Geertz, Clifford. 1988. *Works and Lives: The Anthropologist As Author*. Stanford, Calif.: Stanford University Press.

Gillham, Charles E. 1955. *Medicine Men of Hooper Bay, or The Eskimo's Arabian Nights*. London: The Batchworth Press.

Henkelman, James W., and Kurt H. Vitt. 1985. *The History of the Alaska Moravian Church 1885–1985: Harmonious to Dwell*. Bethel, Alaska: Moravian Seminary Archives.

Himmelheber, Hans. 1951. *Der gefrorene Pfad: Mythen, Marchen und Legenden der Eskimo*. 3d ed. Eisenach, Germany: Erich Roth-Verlaq.

———. 1953. *Eskimokunstler*. Stuttgart, Germany: Strecker and Schroder; reprint, Eisenach, Germany: Erich Roth-Verlaq. (Published in English as *Eskimo Artists*. Fairbanks: University of Alaska Press, 1993).

Kaliikaq Yugnek (later *Kalikaq Yugnek*) (Lower Kuskokwin School District, Bethel Alaska). 1974–77.

Lantis, Margaret. 1946. "The Social Culture of the Nunivak Eskimo." *Transactions of the American Philosophical Society* 35: 153–323.

———. 1953. "Nunivak Eskimo Personality As Revealed in the Mythology." *Anthropological Papers of the University of Alaska* 2(1): 109–74.

Morrow, Phyllis, and Chase Hensel. 1992. "Hidden Dissension: Minority-Majority Relationships and the Use of Contested Terminology." *Arctic Anthropology* 29(1): 38–53.

Morrow, Phyllis, and Elsie Mather. 1995. "Two Tellings of the Story of Uterneq: 'The Woman Who Returned from the Dead.' " In *Coming to Light: Contemporary Translations of Native American Oral Literature*, edited by Brian Swann, 37–56. New York: Random House.

Narayan, Kirin. 1989. *Storytellers, Saints, and Scoundrels: Folk Narrative in Hindu Religious Teaching*. Philadelphia: University of Pennsylvania Press.

Nelson, Edward W. [1899] 1983. *The Eskimo about Bering Strait*. Reprint, Washington, D.C.: Smithsonian Institution.

O' Connor, Paul, S.J. 1947. *Eskimo Parish*. Milwaukee: The Bruce Publishing Co.

Oswalt, Wendell H. 1963. *Mission of Change in Alaska*. San Marino, Calif.: Huntington Library.

Oswalt, Wendell H. 1964. "Traditional Storyknife Tales of Yuk Girls." *Proceedings of the American Philosophical Society* 108(4): 310–36.

Rothenberg, Jerome. 1968. *Technicians of the Sacred*. Garden City, N.Y.: Doubleday and Co.

———. 1972. *Shaking the Pumpkin: Traditional Poetry of the Indian North Americas*. Garden City, N.Y.: Doubleday and Co.

Scheper-Hughes, Nancy. 1979. *Saints, Scholars, and Schizophrenics: Mental Illness in Rural Ireland*. Berkeley: University of California Press.

Scollon, Ronald, and Suzanne B. K. Scollon. 1981. *Narrative, Literacy and Face in Interethnic Communication*. Norwood, N.J.: Ablex Publishing Corp.

Tedlock, Dennis. 1983. *The Spoken Word and the Work of Interpretation*. Philadelphia: University of Pennsylvania Press.

Tennant, Edward, and Joseph Bitar, eds. 1981. *Yuut Qanemciit: Yupik Lore*. Bethel, Alaska: Lower Kuskokwim School District.

Vick, Ann. 1983. *The Camai Book*. New York: Anchor Press.

Woodbury, Anthony C. 1984. *Cev'armiut Qanemciit Qulirait-llu: Eskimo Narratives and Tales from Chevak, Alaska*. Fairbanks: Alaska Native Language Center.

Angela Sidney with Julie Cruikshank, 1980. Photo by Jim Robb.

"Pete's Song"
Establishing Meanings through Story and Song

Julie Cruikshank
in collaboration with Angela Sidney

Mrs. Angela Sidney, the Tagish and Tlingit woman whose multiple tellings of one story are highlighted in this essay, passes on an oral tradition that is both good to "think with" and a useful part of the "equipment for living." These ideas echo Elsie Mather's point that stories are a part of everyday life, recalled by events that cast them in variable lights at different times for each individual.

Both Elsie Mather and Mrs. Sidney recognize that oral traditions are of the present as much as the past. In the following article, however, the emphasis is not so much on the ways that events enlighten us about stories as on the ways that stories enlighten events. For Cruikshank, this is apparent in Mrs. Sidney's differing uses of the Ḵaax̱'achgóok story to mark specific occasions in her family and community life. In this weaving of present and past events through narrative, folklore and oral history constitute a unified cultural framework for making meaning; they are inseparable.

This article speaks eloquently to issues of telling and listening to oral traditions, so its placement in the first section of the volume, "Writing," may at first seem puzzling. There is, however, an important point made here about relationships between tellers and transcribers/commentators. When Mrs. Sidney had Cruikshank write down her story for different publications and audiences, it was one way to legitimize her tellings in relation to specific historical events. She used writing as a supplement to telling and a way of approaching a diverse but literate audience.

Whereas Mather and Morrow highlight the ambivalences in this process, Cruikshank demonstrates that a storyteller may sometimes use writing as an extension of voice. Mrs. Sidney not only told Cruikshank when and how to record her tellings but also patiently taught her the way to "mean" with stories. That Cruikshank so successfully conveys these layers of understanding

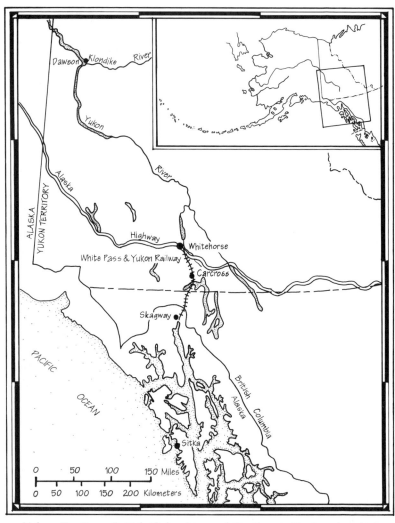

Yukon Territory, British Columbia, and Southeast Alaska, showing places mentioned in the text. Map by Robert Drozda.

to readers is a testimony to both of them and suggests a way that Mather's "monster" of literacy may at least be slightly tamed.

Ethnographies always begin as conversations between anthropologists and our hosts, who are, in turn, in conversation with each other. If we are fortunate, some of these conversations take unexpected turns, develop into genuine dialogues, and continue over many years. Dialogues open the possibility that we may learn something about the process of communication, about how words can be used to construct meaningful accounts of life experience. In this way, they differ fundamentally from structured interviews, where one of the participants claims rights both to pose the questions and interpret the responses.

It was my good fortune to have an ongoing dialogue with Angela Sidney, an elder from the Yukon Territory, Canada, for more than seventeen years. Our conversations began at our first meeting in 1974 and continued until the end of her life in 1991. Even though she is no longer able to participate actively in our dialogues, they continue whenever her words surface unexpectedly while I am puzzling about some problem, just as she undoubtedly hoped they would.

Angela Sidney described herself as a Deisheetaan (Crow) woman of both Tagish and Tlingit ancestry.[1] Born in 1902 near the present village of Carcross in the southern Yukon to Ła.oos Tláa (Maria) and Ḵaajinéek' (Tagish John), she was given the Tlingit name of Stoow and a second Tagish name, Ch'óonehte' Má. Her lifelong interest in passing on the knowledge she had acquired about the relationships between her mother's Tlingit and her father's Tagish ancestry brought us together. We began our conversation with a simple contract: I would record her life history for family members, and in return she would become my teacher—a role which intrigued her because it tested her pedagogical skills in new ways.[2] As well as a brief life history prepared for family members in 1975, she was able to publish several booklets of narrative, family history, and place names which have been widely circulated in her community (Sidney 1980, 1982, 1983; Sidney, Smith, and Dawson 1977).

A witty, warm, and thoughtful woman, one of her chief intellectual pleasures was trying to convey, across cultural boundaries, the subtle lessons about human behavior she had learned during her lifetime. Since she was born shortly after the Klondike gold rush, her life experiences encompassed almost a century of startling institutional changes—the brief but turbulent influx of prospectors at the turn of the century, the establishment of ecclesiastical residential schools, the involvement of indigenous trappers in an international fur market, the construction of the Alaska Highway, the development of an unstable mining economy, and the expansion of government infrastructure. But she was also intensely interested in changes that had occurred during the previous century. Her parents and grandparents had been involved in the flourishing trade between coastal Tlingit and interior Tagish peoples during the late nineteenth century, when Tlingit customs, clan names, and language were introduced inland. Her understanding of all these changes came from her lifelong attention to oral tradition. In our dialogues, she defined her task as one of teaching me how oral tradition continues to explain not just the past but also contemporary issues.

In this essay, I want to try to convey something of the process by which she used oral history to teach, because it so completely confounds any simple definitions of what oral history is or does. The central thesis guiding her work was that while oral tradition can indeed broaden our understanding of the past, it tells us even more about the present. Her concern about the importance of communication through storytelling underscores the value of performance theory in studies of oral tradition.

When Angela Sidney and I began working together, my own understanding of the term *oral history* was fairly superficial. I was delighted by our collaboration because it seemed to me an ethically sound way of doing research—it possessed a clear set of issues for me to investigate and a substantive product for Mrs. Sidney and her family. I assumed that I would be documenting details of social history as it had affected indigenous people in northwestern Canada, a perspective lamentably absent from most of the written records. My earliest questions were framed with reference to the Klondike gold rush, the Alaska Highway construction, and their impacts on the lives of indigenous people in the Yukon Territory.

Mrs. Sidney responded patiently but firmly, in each case suggesting that I begin by recording a particular story—perhaps one about a boy who stayed with the Salmon People, or a girl who married a star, or one about the woman stolen by Grizzly. Eventually, we recorded dozens of narratives in which a protagonist traveled under the water, beyond the horizon, or to the skies in order to learn about other dimensions of reality. Despite my initial sense that we were moving farther and farther from our shared objective of preparing an orally narrated life history, I gradually came to realize that Mrs. Sidney was consciously providing me with a kind of cultural scaffolding, the broad framework I needed to learn before I could begin to ask intelligent questions.

One of the stories she told me was about a Tlingit man named Ḵaax̱'achgóok. This essay will focus on her retellings of his adventures in different contexts because she was very explicit about the way a single rich narrative can be used to convey a range of messages. Angela Sidney understood, as only the most talented storytellers can, the importance of performance—that it involves not simply a narrator but also an audience, and that narrator and audience both change at different points in time and in different circumstances, giving any one story the potential range of meanings that all good stories have.

It is important to hear the story of Ḵaax̱'achgóok in Mrs. Sidney's own words.[3] Briefly, Ḵaax̱'achgóok was one of the famous Tlingit ancestors of the Kiks.ádi clan. One autumn he went hunting sea mammals with his nephews, only to receive a sign that hunting was now dangerous for him and that he should return home. Reluctantly, he destroyed his spears and returned to his winter village, but eventually it became unbearable to him that his wives should have to beg for food and be treated with disrespect. Setting out to sea once again with the same nephews, he was blown off course and became lost. Eventually, they washed ashore on a small island. Ḵaax̱'achgóok spent the following months devising ways to feed himself and his nephews and perfecting a kind of sextant which could plot the sun's trajectory as it moved north to the point of summer solstice. At precisely the day it reached its zenith, he set sail for home, using the sun as a navigational guide to chart his way. Despite his successful return, he faced the difficult business of acknowledging how much life had changed during his absence.

This narrative journey conveys some of the same power as Homer's *Odyssey*, but to interpret its content solely in terms of the written text would overlook meanings conveyed by different tellings in varied situations. Mrs. Sidney told me her version of the Ḵaax̱'achgóok story in 1974. Once she was sure that I had mastered the narrative and understood the content, she didn't ever actually tell the full story again in my presence. Instead, she made regular mention of it in our conversations in the same way that she referred to other stories she was teaching me. She used it as a point of departure both to discuss her own personal development and to interpret and connect a range of events that might otherwise seem unrelated.

After presenting the story in Mrs. Sidney's own words, I will discuss (a) her original telling of the narrative to me in 1974; (b) her account, several years later, of how and why she first told the story publicly; (c) her subsequent account of why she had the right to tell the narrative; and (d) her much more recent use of that narrative to commemorate a specific event in 1988. Her various tellings vividly reveal the way a skillful storyteller is able to use what appears to be the "same" story to convey a range of meanings. Each performance is historically situated, and the teller, the audience, and the intended meanings shift to meet the occasion.

First, then, the story as Mrs. Sidney told it to me in 1974:

This is a true story.
It happened on salt water, maybe near Sitka.
It goes with that song I sing—I'll tell you about it.

This man, Kaax'achgóok, was a great hunter for seal.
He was going hunting at fall.
He has eight nephews on his side, his sisters' sons.
Kaax'achgóok is Crow and so are those boys.
They all went out together in a boat.
Early in the morning, they left.
Fog was down low on the ocean.
He's captain: He sat in the back, guiding that boat.

He heard a baby cry that time, "Wah, wah."

"Stop. Listen. Stop that, baby, now!
Don't you know this is Kaax'achgóok's hunting ground?"
He listened quite a long time.
Here it was baby seal crying.
That's bad luck.
That voice even called his name, "Kaax'achgóok."

So he told his nephews, "That's bad luck.
Let's go back."

They came back that same evening.
He brought up his boat, paddles, spears, and he tells those boys to
        chop it all up.
"I'll never hunt again."

He knows it's something. It's bad luck to hunt now.

After that, he just stayed home, I guess.
Anyway, he didn't hunt anymore that one year—
Stayed home all year until fall.
Maybe he goes out a little bit, but he never hunts.

Finally, someone else killed sea lion.
They invited both those two wives of Ḵaax̱'achgóok.
When those wives of Ḵaax̱'achgóok came back, he asked the
     youngest one,
"Did they give you any fat? Any fat left over they give you to bring
     home?"

"No, just meat," she answered.

Then he asked his older wife,
"Did they give you any fat to bring home? Any left over?"

"No, no fat, just all meat."

"How come they're so stingy to not give you women any fat!"
He thinks maybe his luck will change.

Next morning he asks his older wife,
"Go ask your brother if I can borrow his boat.
I want to go out just a little ways.
Want to borrow boat, spear, hunting outfit.
I'm lonesome—tired of staying home."

She goes to her brother.
"I want you to lend my husband your boat, spear, your hunting
     outfit.
He wants to go out just a little ways.
Not far."

"Okay," he says.
"The boys will bring it over later this evening."
He's got eight boys too—
That's Ḵaax̱'achgóok's wife's people, Wolf people—they call them
     Killer Whale on the coast—

That evening they packed over a brand-new boat—dugout.
Spears, oars, everything in there already.

Ḵaax̱'achgóok tells those wives,
"You girls better cook up meat in saltwater for us."
Next morning those boys get water ready in sealskin,
Cook things.

Then, when they are ready, Ḵaax̱'achgóok goes out again.
Not far, north wind starts to blow.
You know north wind blows in fall time?
Ḵaax̱'achgóok thinks,
"Gee, we should go back while it's not too rough.
Let's go back," he tells his nephews.
They turn around.
Right away, that wind came up—they row and row.
Soon waves are as big as this house.

Ḵaax̱'achgóok is captain: What he does, the rest of the boys do.
He throws his paddle in the boat.
Those boys do that, too.
Ḵaax̱'achgóok pulled up a blanket and went to sleep.
Those boys, too, they sleep.
They went the whole night and the next day like that.

Toward the second morning, Ḵaax̱'achgóok woke up.
He feels the boat not moving, but he hears waves sucking back.
He pulled the blanket down and looked.
By gosh, they drifted onto an island—
Nice sandy beach.

"Wake up, you boys. What's this I hear?"
It sounds like when the wave goes out, goes back.

Next-oldest boy looks up, too.
"Yes, we're on land," he said.
"Well, might as well go on shore."

Those boys run around.
They see a leaf like an umbrella—
It's a stem with a hole that is full of rainwater.

"Frog leaf," they call it.

"Eh, save that [fresh] water."
Each has his own sealskin water bag.
He looks around.
"Take your time.
Go back and see if there's a good place to make a fire."
They found a good place, sheltered from the north wind.

"Let's go there."
Big trees around there.
They make brush camp out of bark.
They carry that bark with them in boat.
Just that quick, they had camp put up.
Look for wood—lots of driftwood.
"You boys are not to run all over. We'll check all around first."

On the south side of the island, there's a rocky point.
All kinds of sea lions, seals, all kinds of animals.
When they're on rocks, the tide is out.
He thinks that's the best time to club them.
That's what they did.
Each boy made a club.
They killed off as much as they needed—
Sea otter, sea lion, seal.
Not too much—just what they can handle.
He told them to look after that meat good.

Some people say he was there over a year—
Some say 'til next spring.
He dreamed he was at home all the time.
"I gave up hope, then I dreamed I was home."

That's the song I sing for you.
I'm going to tell you about it and tell you why I can sing it,
And why we call it "Pete Sidney's Song."
I'll tell you that when I finish this story.

That man, Ḵaax'achgóok, he always goes to north wind side every
      day.
He goes out on the point—never tells anyone.

He marks when the sun comes out in the morning—
Marks it with a stick.
In the evening, he goes out again,
Marks a stick where the sun goes down.
He never tells anyone why he does this.
He just does it all the time.
Finally, that stick is in the same place for two days.
He knows this marks the return of spring.
Then the sun starts to come back in June, the longest day.

In the meantime, he said to the boys,
"Make twisted snowshoe string out of sealskin.
Dry it; stretch it.
Make two big piles.
One for the head of the boat, one for the back of the boat."
Finally, when the sun starts back in June,
He sees it behind the mountain called Tloox, near Sitka.
In June, that sun is in the same place for one, two days.

He tells those boys just before the end they're going to start back.
Tells those boys to cook meat, put it in a seal stomach.
Once they're out on the ocean, there's no way to make fire,
So they've got to cook first.
They prepare ahead.
Sealskin rope is for anchor.
When the sun goes back again on the summer side, they start.

"Put everything in the boat."
He knows there's a long calm time in late June when the sun starts
    back.

No wind—
They start anyway.
They think how they're going to make it.
Those boys think, "Our uncle made a mistake.
We were okay on the island, but now we are really lost."

Row, row, row.

Finally, sun came out right in front of the boat.
Evening, goes out at the back.

Ḵaax̱'achgóok anchors the boat, and he tells those boys to
    sleep.

I used to know how many days that trip took—it's a long time,
    though.
I was ten when I heard this story first—
My auntie, Mrs. Austin, told me the story first time.
Later I heard my father tell it to the boys.

Sundown.
They anchor the boat when it goes down on the steering side.
Next morning, the sun came out same way at the head of the boat.
He knows what is going on—
They're right on course.
They keep doing that I don't know how long.

Finally one time, just after the sun goes down,
He sees something like a seagull.
When the sun comes up, it disappears.
Evening sundown, he sees it again.
Four days, he sees it.

The second day he sees it, he asks,
"What's that ahead of our boat? Seagull?"
They think so.
Where could seagull come from in the middle of the ocean?

They camp again.
It gets bigger.
Finally, it looks like a mountain.
They don't stop to rest anymore!
Four paddle all day—four paddle all night.
Their uncle is their boss: He sleeps all day, I guess. Don't know.
Finally, they see it.

Early in the morning, Ḵaax̱'achgóok's oldest wife, comes down to
    cry for her husband.
That youngest wife, they already gave to another husband.
Finally, all of a sudden, she sees boat coming.
She quits crying—she notices how her husband used to paddle,
Same as the man in the boat.

She runs back to the house.
"It looks like Ḵaax̱'achgóok when he paddles!
Get up! Everybody up!"

"How do you expect that?
It's a whole year now.
You think they live yet?"

Then he comes around the point—
People all pack around that boat.
They took him for dead—already made potlatch for him.
So he gave otter skin to everyone who potlatched for him.
Sea otter skin cost one thousand dollars, those days.

Then he sang songs he made up on that trip.
He made one up when he gave up the oars.
"I gave up my life out on the deep for the shark."
That song he gave to Ḵaanax̱.ádi people.

Then he made up a song for the sun who saved him:
"The sun came up and saved people."

He made that song during winter
And he sang it when he made a potlatch.
Then that song he sang,
"I gave up hope and then I dreamed I was home."

That's the one I sing.
Deisheetaan people, we own that song,
Because long before, our people captured Ḵaax̱'achgóok's brother.
When they started to make peace, he sang that song and gave it to
        us for our potlatch.
Then we freed his brother. That's how come we own it.
That's why we claim that song.

Layered Tellings

Narrative as Text

Angela Sidney's story of Ḵaax̱'achgóok can indeed be written
down and read as a text, one of many she told me in the course

of preparing her life history. When she first told me the story in 1974, her primary objective was to have it tape-recorded and transcribed in her own words. We read over the written text carefully and made the minor changes she suggested. At her request, it appeared in a booklet of narratives by three Yukon elders, *My Stories Are My Wealth*, printed for use in Yukon schools (Sidney, Smith, and Dawson 1977: 109–13). Once an orally narrated text is printed, though, it is open to a range of interpretations by readers as well as listeners.

There is no shortage of ways to approach the K̲aax̲'achgóok story if we regard it simply as a self-contained narrative. For example, because of the thematic attention to the sun in Mrs. Sidney's version,[4] it has sometimes been highlighted in Yukon classrooms at the end of June, presented as an example of indigenous perspectives on the summer solstice, a significant day north of the sixtieth parallel. Mrs. Sidney was pleased by this acknowledgment and even agreed to tell the story and be interviewed by a local radio station on June 21 one year near the end of the 1970s.

Given the structural parallels with the *The Odyssey*, the story might also be seen as an example of powerful epic narrative. The hero's journey, constructed around disappearance, extensive suffering, and eventual return, dramatizes a theme common to much world literature. Like all good literature, the story addresses fundamental human problems. The psychological dimensions of returning home after prolonged absence were certainly on Mrs. Sidney's mind in other versions she tells, discussed later in the essay. The story of K̲aax̲'achgóok undeniably constitutes a work of literature: bilingual texts of another version of this narrative, in both the Tlingit language and in English, have been presented in exquisite detail by Richard and Nora Dauenhauer in *Haa Shuka/Our Ancestors* (1987: 82–107, nn., 323–33), their first volume in a series entitled *Classics of Tlingit Oral Literature*.

Alternatively, we might ask whether this narrative incorporates historical events from "real time." K̲aax̲'achgóok was a famous ancestor of a named clan, the Kiks.ádi Crow clan, and it is conceivable that his journey might be traced to an actual historical figure. The possibility of incorporating orally narrated accounts into ethnohistorical analysis seems to give oral history rather elastic promise, particularly when so much northern scholarship rests exclusively on written records. Yet exclusively literal interpretation of the events in the story would be too narrow.

Such diverse possibilities suggest good reasons for paying attention to the story of K̲aax̲'achgóok as text, with a range of conventional avenues for hearing its content—as a reflection of mythology, history, ethnology, language use, psychology. Too frequently, though, textual analyses begin and end with these questions. As Paul Ricoeur reminds us, there is a difference between what a narrative *says* and what it *talks about* (1979: 98). Had Angela Sidney not referred to the story again herself, I might simply have regarded it as just one among other fine examples of oral narrative from northwestern North America.

Narrative as Gift

Some years later, in 1981, Angela Sidney and I were firmly engaged in the process of recording her life story. By then, I understood that the dozens of narratives we had recorded and transcribed really did provide a kind of framework to which she could refer when she talked about her own experiences. Repeatedly, she explained choices she had made or advice she had given with reference to narratives learned from parents, aunts, and uncles—narratives exploring the subtle relationship between human and superhuman domains. Her narrative allusions and interpretations always added another dimension to whatever event we were discussing.

She talked about Kaax̱'achgóok again on July 6, 1985, this time in a very different context. Her son Pete, then in his seventies, was visiting one afternoon, and although he had obviously heard the story many times before, she took the opportunity to explain, with him present, why it had such significance in his life. Pete was one of many First Nations men who served overseas during World War II, and she talked, this day, about how difficult his absence had been for her. "Five years he's gone—just like that Kaax̱'achgóok story I told you."[5]

During his absence, she said, she and her husband had bought their first radio, "so we could listen to where they're moving the troops so we would know where he is." When the war ended, her son sent her a telegram from Europe announcing his imminent return: "DEAR MOM, I'M BOOKED FOR CANADA. TOMORROW I'M LEAVING." With a map, she and her husband calculated how long it would take to cross the Atlantic by ship. When he arrived in New York, he sent a telegram. "LANDED SAFELY IN U.S." They estimated that it would take four days for him to cross the continent by train to Vancouver. She allowed another four days to travel up the west coast of the country by ferry, and an additional day to ride inland on the narrow gauge White Pass and Yukon Railway to his home in Carcross, Yukon. "From the time he got on the boat from Vancouver, we're counting the days again. Well I'm counting the days—I don't know if the rest do!"

As the excitement mounted, her husband asked her how they should celebrate the occasion of his return. She described the feast she planned to give, the people she planned to invite. " 'And then,' I told him, 'I'm going to sing that Ḵaax̱'achgóok song!' And my old man said, 'Gee, I didn't know you were so smart to think like that! That's a *good* idea.' " When Pete arrived home, then, his gift—the greatest gift she could give him—was the song sung by Ḵaax̱'achgóok when he returned home. "That's why we call that 'Pete's song': 'I gave up hope, and then I dreamed I was home.' "[6]

But the story does not end there, because her right to sing the song was immediately challenged. Her narrative about how her clan had acquired rights to use that song, and hence her own decision to make a gift of it to her son, forms an integral part of the next version of her story.

Narrative as Settlement

Tagish people in the southeastern Yukon adopted Tlingit-named clans sometime during the nineteenth century. As on the coast, rights to use songs and stories remain firmly grounded in clan membership, which is traced through the maternal line. Angela Sidney, like her mother, was born into the Deisheetaan Tlingit clan, and her son, Pete, also belonged to her clan. Her father's cousin, Koołseen (whose English name was Patsy Henderson), was the senior living member of her father's Daḵl'aweidí clan, and he challenged her right to sing the song at this celebration. As a relatively young woman in her early forties at the time, this put her in a vulnerable position. She recalled, "[He] told my mother, 'It's not you fellows' song, that song. You can't use that song!' He asked Johnny Anderson about it, and Johnny Anderson said, 'No, it's not a Deisheetaan song.' "

Mrs. Sidney explained how she demonstrated that the song had actually been given to Deisheetaan by the Kiks.ádi clan and that she really was using it in an appropriate way. Ḵaax̱'achgóok, she explained, belonged to the Kiks.ádi clan (which, like Deisheetaan, is grouped with Crow or Raven clans). Sometime in the past, a dispute arose between the Deisheetaan and Kiks.ádi clans. A Kiks.ádi man—"Ḵaax̱'achgóok's [clan] brother"—was taken by Deisheetaan clansmen as a slave in payment for an offense committed against them. As hostilities escalated, the two clans met and negotiated a conventional settlement. An exchange was worked out so that the Kiks.ádi man was returned to his kinsmen, and they, in turn, gave the Deisheetaan clan the Ḵaax̱'achgóok song. Because songs are among the most important property owned by clans, the dispute was considered settled.

To confirm that as a Deisheetaan woman she was acting appropriately, Mrs. Sidney said, she did further research. She traveled down to the coast, to Skagway, Alaska, to meet with Tlingit elders there. She told two senior elders, Maggie Koodena and Bert Dennis, what had occurred and asked them to judge whether she had acted appropriately.

> I told [Maggie Koodeena] all about how I sang that song when Peter came back and when I made that dinner for him. I called everybody from across the river to his welcome dinner, and I sang it before we started out that dinner and I said that Ḵaax̱'achgóok song was our song. And Uncle Patsy didn't believe it. So I went to Skagway, too, and I asked Maggie Koodena, and she told me all about it. She told me about the war we made, and that's how come he gave us that song. Ḵaax̱'achgóok made lots of songs. He made songs for the sun and he made songs for when he shoved his paddle in their boat, and *that* song he gave to Ḡaanax̱.ádi. And that sun song, I don't know who he gave it to. He just kept it for himself, I guess.
>
> He [Ḵaax̱'achgóok and his clan members] gave that Ḵaax̱'achgóok song to *us* in place of his brother. That's why we use it. That's why *I* use it. That's why I gave it to Pete when he came back from the army, because he just went through what happened to Ḵaax̱'achgóok. He drifted away in the ocean, but he finally came back. I asked all about that, too [before I used the song].[7]

Narrative as Commemoration

Angela Sidney was forty-three years old when she first performed the Ḵaax̱'achgóok story and song in 1945. More recently, at the age of eighty-six, she decided to use this story again, this time in a very different public setting. By now, she was acknowledged as a senior elder storyteller in the Yukon Territory. She was in great demand as a storyteller in schools and had performed at the Toronto Storytelling Festival in 1984. She was widely credited as the inspiration for the annual Yukon Storytelling Festival.[8] She had been awarded the Order of Canada by the governor general in 1986 for her linguistic and ethnographic work. At this stage in her life, no one was going to challenge her right to tell whatever story she chose.

When the new Yukon College complex officially opened in Whitehorse in 1988, she was invited to play a formal role in the ceremonies
and to give the college a Tagish name. Although I was now living outside the territory and was unable to attend the opening celebrations,
Angela Sidney and I met several weeks later, and she described her
performance. To commemorate the event, she told me, she had sung
the K̲aax̲'achgóok song because it conveyed her feelings about what
Yukon College could mean to young people in the territory.

Her audience was a very mixed one this time, including hundreds of non-Native as well as First Nations people from throughout
the Yukon. It is not at all clear that the meaning of her story was
self-evident to her listeners, but she was single-minded in her commitment to present them with something they could "think with" if
they so chose. Because she could not be sure that her audience would
understand her reasons for telling the story, we discussed the idea of
distributing the text with some additional commentary so that others
could recognize why she had chosen it. And so we did.

> The reason I sang this song is because that Yukon College is going
> to be like the sun for the students. Instead of going to Vancouver
> or Victoria, they're going to be able to stay here and go to school
> here. We're not going to lose our kids anymore. It's going to be
> just like the sun for them, just like for that K̲aax̲'achgóok. (Sidney
> 1988: 9–16)

Commentary

With the growing discussion about indigenous knowledge, indigenous perspectives on history, and comanagement of natural resources
in northern Canada and Alaska, there is sometimes a tendency to treat
orally narrated accounts as collectible "texts" which can, in turn, be reduced to "sources" from which "data" may be extracted. Researchers
pose questions about landscape, flora and fauna, history, ethnography, language, psychology, and social behavior. In their search for
answers, they may look to orally narrated accounts, sometimes going directly to living elders, other times searching archival collections
for material recorded in the past.

The implication is that oral sources are somehow stable, like written sources, and that once spoken and recorded, they are simply
there, waiting for interpretation. Yet anyone who has been engaged

in ethnographic fieldwork knows that the content of oral sources depends largely on what goes into the questions, the dialogue, the personal relationship through which it is communicated. Oral testimony is never the same twice, even when the same words are used, because the relationship—the dialogue—is always shifting (Portelli 1991: 54–55). Oral traditions are not natural products. They have social histories, and they acquire meaning in the situations in which they are used, in interactions between narrators and listeners. Meanings shift depending on the extent to which cultural understandings are shared by teller and listener.[9]

The persistent idea that oral testimony can be treated as data is not so different from Boas's conviction a century ago that the actual telling of narratives remained relatively uninfluenced by the observer and that the "native point of view" could be gleaned from recorded texts of myth and folklore. Two problematic practices have emerged from this assumption. First, as Dell Hymes (1985) points out, the words of a single speaker have often been glossed over in the name of an entire community, as though that person were merely some kind of information conduit. Secondly, ethnographers have normally gone on to assume full authority for these ethnographic products (Sanjek 1993).

If we think of oral tradition as a social activity rather than as some reified product, we can view it as part of the equipment for living rather than a set of meanings embedded within texts and waiting to be discovered. One of the most trenchant observations of contemporary anthropology is that meaning is *not* fixed, that it must be studied in practice, in the small interactions of everyday life. These meanings are more likely to emerge from dialogue than from a formal interview. In her retellings of this one story, Mrs. Sidney shows how she is able to communicate meanings that are both culturally relevant and highly personal. She readily acknowledges that her interpretation could be contested by other community members. She claims only that she has made every effort to present her interpretation as she understands it from her own research.

Angela Sidney's use of the story of Kaax'achgóok actually demonstrates the way she uses narratives as a kind of cultural scaffolding on which to construct the story of her own life. It is one of many complex narratives she asked me to record after she had expressed interest in the project of documenting her life experience. As our work progressed, she repeatedly referred back to specific stories, interrupting her narrative with comments like, "You remember that story about _____? Well, I told you that one already. That's the one I'm talking about now.... " And then she would proceed to show how that story could illuminate some event which had occurred during her own life. Her construction of her life story relied heavily on this full range of narratives as points of reference (Cruikshank et al. 1990). Such stories, then, can be both culturally specific and highly personal.

Angela Sidney's various tellings of the Kaax̱'achgóok story remind us that there is more involved than textual analysis when we approach oral tradition. Her point, in her various retellings, is to show that oral narrative is part of a communicative process. First, she demonstrates, you have to learn what the story *says*. Then you learn what the story can *do* when it is engaged as a strategy of communication. Unless we pay attention to the reason a particular story is selected and told, we will understand very little of its meanings. Her point in retelling stories about Kaax̱'achgóok is precisely to show that a good story, well used, does not merely explain but also can add meanings to a special occasion.

Her tellings raise questions about the stability of story, narrator, and audience over time. After establishing the Kaax̱'achgóok story as one full of possibilities for interpretation, she made it central to three other narratives several years later. One of her stories referred to an event that had occurred more than a century before; another was tied to an important event in her own life, one which had happened forty years earlier; a third commemorated an event with significance for the future. In her tellings, there is no simple analogue between the narrative and a reified "oral history."

But if stories are historically situated, so are narrators. Mrs. Sidney was very aware of the way her own evolving role as performer changed on different occasions. In 1945, she was a relatively junior woman speaking in front of elders who challenged her right to tell the story. The point of her next version, referring back to the late 1800s, was to establish her emerging ethnographic authority as she conducted research in conversation with her elders. In 1974, as a woman in her early seventies, she saw herself as a teacher, both of me and the "schoolkids" who might read her narrative. At her fourth telling, in 1988, she was positioned as an acclaimed senior storyteller in the Yukon, unlikely to be challenged by anyone, but also less likely to be understood by her heterogeneous audience. The net effect of her bringing the four versions together in recording her life history (Cruikshank et al. 1990: 35, 136, 139–45, 360 n. 9) was to demonstrate how she had established the authority to tell and attribute meanings to one story during the course of her lifetime.

Listeners change too, and Angela Sidney always had a careful eye for her audience. Because she took seriously the goal of demonstrating her communicative competence (Bauman 1977), she assumed responsibility for ensuring, at each telling, that her audience understood what she was saying. The 1974 telling was for novices—for me and "the schoolkids" who needed to learn the story outline. This was very different from the 1985 version, told in the presence of her son to invoke an event from 1945, his arrival home from military service in France. Her son was an interactive audience; after all, he knew the story well, but he also had his own version of the events. He kept trying to interject and add details about his own journey. On that occasion, though, Mrs. Sidney saw this as *her* story, and she intervened firmly whenever he stopped to breathe. No one was going to interrupt her telling this time! Giving him the gift of the Ḵaax̱'achgóok story had been a pivotal event in her emerging role in her community. Her husband's delight with her intelligence ("Gee, I didn't know you were so smart to think like that! That's a *good* idea.") was countered by her paternal uncle's disapproval ("It's not you fellows' song, that song. You can't use that song!").

Her account about how she gave this song the name "Pete's song," then, illustrates both the consensus by which cultures celebrate their sense of collectivity and the oppositional process by which difference and boundary are maintained (see Abrahams 1992: 48). The fact that a culture is shared does not mean that all individual interpretations will be the same, but it does guarantee that conflicting interpretations will be significant (Siikala 1992: 212). Publicly challenged, Angela Sidney conducted her own ethnographic research with Tlingit elders, who confirmed her legitimate, inherited clan right to tell the story, sing the song, and give such a gift. Part of her reason for insisting on retelling the story in 1985 was to show her son (and me) that an audience of elders, who themselves assumed the role of cultural experts about questions of Tlingit oral copyright, had publicly endorsed her choice in 1945. Her various audiences—those elders, her son, myself—could appreciate and understand the role of narrative and song as statement about clan identity.

In 1988, her audience changed again, this time to a very diverse gathering attending formal ceremonies commemorating the opening of the local college. Although Angela was pleased with her choice of the Ḵaax̱'achgóok story to represent the symbolic importance of the college for the community, she was quite sure that many members of this audience, hearing the story for the first time and lacking a context for recognizing it, would fail to understand her meaning. She recognized that effective communication of oral tradition requires more than performers and performances—it also demands an expressive community sharing similar expectations (Abrahams 1992: 47). She puzzled later about how to make her point in a different way; in other words, how to demonstrate her communicative competence to this very mixed audience. Eventually she concluded that it would be appropriate to extend our dialogue, reproducing in printed form the narrative she had originally recorded with me and adding a short explanation. We arranged for its publication in *The Northern Review*, a journal published at Yukon College (Sidney 1988).

In conclusion, Angela Sidney's story draws on a traditional dimension of culture to give meaning to a range of contemporary events. During the years we have worked together recording events from her life, she has repeatedly demonstrated that she thinks and processes information with reference to the narratives she learned as a young woman. She has shown that she organizes, stores, and transmits her insights and knowledge of the world through narratives and songs describing the human condition. Her narrative is as much about social transformation of the society in which she lives as about individual creativity. Her point is that oral tradition may tell us about the past, but its meanings are not exhausted by that reference. Good stories from the past continue to provide legitimate insights about contemporary events. What appears to be the "same" story, even in the repertoire of one individual, acquires multiple meanings depending on the location, circumstance, audience, and stage of life of both narrator and listener.

Angela Sidney spent much of her life demonstrating the way this process works, and today younger women and men in her community continue to draw insights from the methods she used to teach. The words she used to end one of our dialogues one winter afternoon say it most clearly: "Well," she concluded, "I've tried to live my life right, just like a story."

Notes

Angela Sidney and I worked together for many years. This paper reflects our dialogues about one of the many narratives we discussed in the course of compiling her life history. It is discussed briefly in *Life Lived Like a Story: Life Stories of Three Yukon Elders* (Cruikshank et al. 1990).

1.   In the southern Yukon, social organization was profoundly influenced by two matrilineal moieties: Wolf (Ägunda) and Crow (Kajìt). In those parts of the southern Yukon where there was considerable coastal Tlingit influence, these moieties were further subdivided into clans. Three clans named in this essay are Deisheetaan and Kiks.ádi, both Crow clans, and Dakl'aweidí, a Wolf clan.

2.   I had already been living in the Yukon for several years by 1974 and had heard about Mrs. Sidney from her children, grandchildren, and numerous friends. Consequently, we already knew about our shared interest in oral history when we first met.

3.   This narrative was also recorded by Swanton (1909, nos. 67 and 101, pp. 225, 321) and in Dauenhauer and Dauenhauer (1987: 82–107, and notes, 323–33).

4.   In the version told by Mr. Andrew P. Johnson and recorded by the Dauenhauers, Kaax'achgóok relied on his knowledge of the stars and planets to find his way home (Dauenhauer and Dauenhauer 1987: 95, 330).

5.   To learn how she incorporated this into her life story, see Cruikshank et al. (1990: 135–36).

6.   Oral copyright of songs, like stories and artwork, remains vested in clans; however, issues surrounding ownership of songs continue to be particularly sensitive. In their 1987 publication, the Dauenhauers note that Mr. Johnson specifically asked that the words to Kaax'achgóok's song not be transcribed.

7.   Compiled from discussions on June 4, 1981 (tape no. 387); June 22, 1981 (tape no. 390); and July 6, 1985 (tape no. 559). The tapes are located at the Yukon Native Language Centre, Whitehorse, Yukon.

8.   This festival has grown each year and is now called the Yukon International Storytelling Festival, drawing performers from the circumpolar North and elsewhere.

9.   See Siikala (1992) for a discussion of similar concerns as they relate to oral traditions from northeast Asia and the South Pacific.

References

Abrahams, Roger D. 1992. "The Past in the Presence: An Overview of Folkloristics in the Late Twentieth Century." In *Folklore Processed: In Honour of Lauri Honko on His Sixtieth Birthday*, edited by Reimund Kvideland, 32–51. Helsinki: Studia Fennica Folkloristica 1.

Bauman, Richard. 1977. *Verbal Art as Performance*. Prospect Heights, Ill.: Waveland Press.

Cruikshank, Julie. 1990. In collaboration with Angela Sydney, Kitty Smith, and Annie Ned. *Life Lived Like a Story: Life Stories of Three Yukon Elders*. Lincoln: University of Nebraska Press.

Dauenhauer, Nora Marks, and Richard Dauenhauer, eds. 1987. *Haa Shuka, Our Ancestors: Tlingit Oral Narratives*. Vol 1 of *Classics of Tlingit Oral Literature*. Seattle: University of Washington Press.

Hymes, Dell. H. 1981. "Breakthrough into Performance." In *"In Vain I Tried to Tell You": Essays in Native American Ethnopoetics*, edited by Dell Hymes, 79–141. Philadelphia: University of Pennsylvania Press.

———. 1985. "Language, Memory, and Selective Performance: Cultee's 'Salmon Myth' As Twice Told to Boas." *Journal of American Folklore* 98: 391–434.

Portelli, Alessandro. 1991. *The Death of Luigi Trastulli and Other Stories: Form and Meaning in Oral History*. Albany: State University of New York Press.

Ricoeur, Paul. 1979. "The Model of the Text: Meaningful Action Considered As a Text." In *Interpretive Social Science: A Reader*, edited by Paul Rabinow and William M. Sullivan, 73–101. Berkeley and Los Angeles: University of California Press.

Sanjek, Roger. 1993. "Anthropology's Hidden Colonialism: Assistants and Their Ethnographers." *Anthropology Today* 9(2): 13–18.

Sidney, Angela. 1980. *Place Names of the Tagish Region, Southern Yukon*. Whitehorse: Yukon Native Languages Project.

———. 1982. *Tagish Tlaagú/Tagish Stories*. Compiled by J. Cruikshank. Whitehorse: Council for Yukon Indians and Government of Yukon.

———. 1983. *Haa Shagóon/Our Family History*. Compiled by J. Cruikshank. Whitehorse: Yukon Native Languages Project.

———. 1988. "The Story of K̲aax̲'achgóok." *The Northern Review* 2: 9–16.

Sidney, Angela, Kitty Smith, and Rachel Dawson. 1977. *My Stories Are My Wealth*. Compiled by J. Cruikshank. Whitehorse: Council for Yukon Indians.

Siikala, Anna-Leena. 1992. "Understanding Narratives of the 'Other.'" In *Folklore Processed: In Honour of Lauri Honko on His Sixtieth Birthday*, edited by Reimund Kvideland, 200–13. Helsinki: Studia Fennica Folkloristica 1.

Stahl, Sandra Dolby. 1989. *Literary Folkloristics and the Personal Narrative*. Bloomington: Indiana University Press.

Swanton, John. 1909. *Tlingit Myths and Texts*. New York: Johnson Reprint Corp.

Map by Robert Drozda.

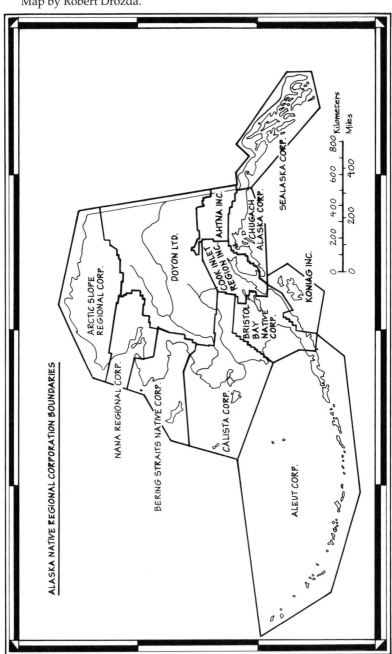

ALASKA NATIVE REGIONAL CORPORATION BOUNDARIES

ARCTIC SLOPE REGIONAL CORP.

NANA REGIONAL CORP.

BERING STRAITS NATIVE CORP.

DOYON LTD.

CALISTA CORP.

COOK INLET REGION INC.

AHTNA INC.

CHUGACH ALASKA CORP.

SEALASKA CORP.

KONIAG INC.

BRISTOL BAY NATIVE CORP.

ALEUT CORP.

0   200   400   600   800 Kilometers
0   200   400 Miles

PART II

HEARING

Maggie Lind in her birdskin parka in the summer of 1976, just a couple of months before she died. Photo by James H. Barker.

Seeing Wisely, Crying Wolf

A Cautionary Tale on the Euro-Yup'ik Border

Robin Barker

The previous two essays emphasize that interpretations of a story are at best incomplete and raise the problem of whether writing can be informative without becoming authoritative. In this piece, Robin Barker demonstrates that interpretations, whether based on oral or written accounts, can simply be wrong. They can, however, be wrong in ways that tell us, if we listen to ourselves and each other carefully, something basic about the role of interpreters and the process of interpretation. "How Crane Got His Blue Eyes" is a Yup'ik tale that has been used for the classroom instruction and entertainment of Alaska Native and non-Native children for at least twenty-five years. Among such schoolchildren, in fact, it is perhaps the best-known of all Alaska Native tales. It is a moral tale, but how it is moral is open to . . . interpretation.

In attempting an interpretation, Barker comes face to face with her personal and cultural assumptions. Drawing on her understanding of teacher-student relationships, her personal experiences in the Yup'ik region, and her discussions with Alaska Native listeners and tellers, she traces her evolving comprehension of the crane story. She makes us listen repeatedly and carefully to different tellings and understandings. Each time she reaches a new provisional conclusion, we learn more about the ways that meaning is contingent and relational.

Increasingly, classrooms provide a primary context for adults to tell and children to listen to stories from a variety of cultures. Multicultural classrooms invite the use of materials that celebrate cultural diversity. Yet such materials tend to be adopted as if they automatically conveyed the essence of their sources. Teachers set out with specific objectives, intending children to receive certain messages from stories. These may or may not be messages which accurately reflect the cultural traditions in question; the teachers bring their own preconceived notions to this process, especially when they are representing unfamiliar cultures.

In either case, the children are generally treated as passive recipients of meaning: they either "get the point" or they do not. Teachers rarely see the children as active participants in the coconstruction of individualized and culturized meanings. Barker drives this point home with an anecdote illustrating that even when teachers are in fact telling stories from their own personal and cultural backgrounds, their listeners may come away with surprisingly varied messages. In the end, "How Crane Got His Blue Eyes" becomes a cautionary tale about the use of cautionary tales.

What follows is a description of the evolution in my own thinking about a Yup'ik tale known as "How Crane Got His Blue Eyes." The tale is popularly used throughout Alaska in elementary classrooms; it is presented simply, without much thought about the complexities of investigating its meaning. As an educator who worked in the Yup'ik region for twelve years, I have come to recognize that folklore must be treated in ways that take these complexities into account. Overcoming linguistic and cultural bias is not easy, however. For example, my own first interpretations of the story were strongly influenced by European oral and literary conventions. As I thought about the story, examined alternate texts, and talked with Yup'ik friends, however, I became increasingly aware of the ways that meaning is coconstructed in general, and particularly in cross-cultural interaction. Using myself as a foil, then, I will juxtapose differing interpretations of this story to offer glimpses of the ways meaning is negotiated between speaker and audience.

The discussion does not lead ultimately to an internally coherent interpretation of the tale; rather it is meant to show, through one example, how complex the use of folklore is. Clearly, the way in which Euro-American, Yup'ik, or other audiences of schoolchildren negotiate the meaning of stories with the teachers they encounter is an important matter.

The Teller and the Tale

Maggie Lind of Bethel was the most well-known, popular storyteller in the Kuskokwim region. Her tellings of "How Crane Got His Blue Eyes" have appeared in a variety of forms, oral and written, Yup'ik and English. Published and audiotaped versions may be found in classrooms throughout the state and are widely known to the Alaska public through radio broadcasts.

I have included two versions of the story here. The first I transcribed from a record made by ethnomusicologist Lorraine Koranda in 1966.

"How the Crane Got Blue Eyes"

One time the crane was walking along. He was going to eat some berries, so he took his eyes off and put them on a stump. And he said, "If someone comes along, you must holler to me and tell me that somebody's coming."

So he went out and started eating berries, and after a while, while he was eating berries, the eyes said, "Master, somebody's coming, and they are going to take us away!"

So the crane quickly ran down to the river and put on his eyes and looked; and it was only a piece of wood drifting along. So he put them back on the stump again and said, "Don't you tell me any more stories after this."

So the crane went back and ate some more berries, but after a while the eyes called again, "Master, somebody's going to take us away." And they got farther and farther away. So after a while he went down and looked for his eyes, and somebody had taken them away.

The crane went back into the tundra and he found cranberries and put them in for his eyes. But everything was too red.

And he took blackberries and put them for his eyes. And everything was too dark.

So he found blueberries, and he put them on. And everything was just nice.

And ever since, the crane has blue eyes. (Koranda 1966)

Maggie Lind told the second version to Gladys Fancher for publication in a volume of stories from all over Alaska "primarily for use in schools and in homes of schoolchildren" (Frost 1971: dust jacket notes).

"How Crane Got His Blue Eyes"

A long time ago Crane lived by himself on the tundra near Bethel, on the Kuskokwim River.

Crane knew where some good, juicy berries grew.

One morning he awoke very hungry for some berries.

He arose, stretched his long legs, and flapped his big wings.

Up, up, up he flew, on his way to the berries.

Soon Crane found the berries.

He flew down to the ground.

Then he took out his eyes, and put them on a stump.

Crane: "Eyes, you watch for me. If you see anything coming, call me. I will not go far away."

Eyes: "Yes, Master, I will watch for you."

Crane went fast to get to the berries.

He ate some of the sweet, juicy berries.

Then Crane's eyes began calling him.

Eyes: "Master, Master, I see something coming this way. Please hurry, Master, before it gets me."

Crane tried to run fast to his eyes.

He put them on and looked all around.

All he saw were some willows.

He took out his eyes again and put them on a stump.

Crane: "Don't fool me again. Just call me when you really see something coming."

Crane went back to eat more berries.

My, they tasted so good.

They tasted so very, very good.

Again his eyes called him.

Eyes: "Master, Master, hurry, hurry! I see something coming."

Again Crane tried to run fast to his eyes.

He put them on to see what his eyes had seen.

All he saw was a log floating down the river.

Crane: "Eyes, you fooled me again! Be more careful before you call me."

Crane took out his eyes again and put them on the stump.

He went back to eat more berries.

My, how sweet they tasted!

Again his eyes called him.

Eyes: "Master, Master, come! Someone is taking me away. Hurry! Come and get me!"

Crane tried again to get to his eyes.

When he got back to the stump, he could not find them.

His eyes were gone!

Crane: "Oh, my! How will I see now? My eyes are gone. I must find new eyes!"

Crane picked up two blackberries to use for his eyes.

Everything looked black.
Crane: "Oh, my! I can't see at all."
Crane took out the blackberries.
Then he picked up two cranberries to use for his eyes.
Crane: "Oh, my! Everything looks red."
Crane didn't like that at all.
He took out the two cranberries.
Crane then found two blueberries to use for his eyes.
He liked them.
Everything was so very pretty.
He saw blue sky and blue water.
Crane: "I'll use these blueberries for my eyes. I like them!"
That is how Crane got his blue eyes. (Frost 1971: 23–26)[1]

The differences between these two popular versions are immediately noticeable and invite comment. The playscript format of the Fancher text is obviously not characteristic of spoken narrative. As a schoolteacher, Fancher very likely decided that the importance of using "culturally relevant" material in classrooms justified considerable revision in the interest of making the story more understandable and fun. In her author's notes, she says that the stories are meant to be used in classrooms, possibly in dramatic presentations. She may have anticipated the creation of costumes and scenery and imagined hearing the tale in children's voices. In this case, what is altered along with the text is the adult/child relationship of teller and listener. In the playscript, the children are cast as the speakers, while normally the tale would be told by an adult to children. Generally, unlike in Western schools, Yup'ik children are not expected to "perform" for adults but to listen to them respectfully.

Although these changes most likely were made by Fancher, Lind probably adjusted her telling specifically for schoolchildren as well. There are two reasons for thinking this. One has to do with Lind's history, and the other with what we know about the way she framed her stories for general audiences of children.

Maggie Lind was raised at the Moravian children's home in Bethel, but she told me that she spent considerable time with her grandmother, who told her many stories. Lind was bilingual in Yup'ik and English. A picture of her at the children's home at about ten years of age places her birth close to 1905 (Lenz and Barker 1985: 41). She must have been approaching seventy when these stories were collected; she died in 1976. Fancher was a non-Native teacher who lived in Bethel for over a decade in the 1950s and 1960s. Although the book does not specify, it is likely that Lind told this story to Fancher in English as she often did when addressing a wide public, for example on the radio.

Maggie Lind was known for her particular interest in storytelling, the preservation of tradition, and the education of children. Lind was vocal in her defense of traditional lands and ways (Barker 1975: 10). Another photograph in the Bethel history (Lenz and Barker 1985: 114) shows her telling and illustrating traditional girls' storyknife tales in 1936 (see Ager 1971; Oswalt 1964). Her grandson, John Active, characterized her as a woman with a driving commitment to teaching young people and passing Yup'ik culture to coming generations. She often voiced the need for young people not to forget (Active 1992).

Raised by white missionaries and married to a man whose mother was Yup'ik and whose father was a white trader, she grew up in the midst of Bethel's mixed Euro-American and Yup'ik cultures. One might speculate that although Lind was always very upbeat about her life with the Moravians, her preservation activities were important to her as a way of recapturing experiences lost by her upbringing as well as a marker of ethnicity (for a discussion of outmarriage and ethnic markers, see Hensel 1992).

At any rate, Lind consciously (and probably unconsciously as well) worked to bridge the cultural gap in her tellings of Yup'ik tales, sporadically incorporating certain European elements. For example, in another story she told, the stock character of the unmarried Yup'ik girl becomes, in her translation, a princess, and the married couple lives "happily ever after" (Lind 1972).

She also made changes to the crane tale. Many traditional Yup'ik stories begin with a statement placing them in an unspecified, distant past—"a long time ago"—but in a specific place (for examples, see Nelson 1899: 457–99). Lind follows this formula in the Fancher version. However, the summary sentence at the end—"That is how Crane got his blue eyes"—is less characteristic and may derive from European patterns. (Alternatively, it may be another adaptation by Fancher, since the Koranda recording ends, "And ever since, the crane has blue eyes.") Yup'ik legends that explain natural phenomena usually finish with a statement about the way things are today without making cause and effect explicit (again, see Nelson 1899: 457–99). This shifts the stance of storyteller from expert to observer and models for the young listener a socially appropriate narrative style. The Fancher version ends with a clear pronouncement about a fact, very uncharacteristic in Yup'ik narrative.

I also find it interesting that, for the musicologist, the eyes cry for help twice, but for the schoolteacher, they cry out three times, the magical number in European folktales. Is this an accommodation on Lind's part? Perhaps because she knew that the story was to be used in school, she unconsciously adjusted the form to sound like the "school stories" that she had heard at the Moravian orphanage. After all, the colloquial "holler" in the Koranda recording is transformed to a more formal "call me" in the school version. In general, the language of the Fancher version has the feel of the basal schoolbooks of the time. Phrases like, "up, up, up he flew," could have been lifted straight out of *Dick and Jane*. Is this Lind or Fancher? The use of the designation "Master" for Crane in both versions draws from the language of fairy tales and shows Lind's ability to connect Yup'ik stories with European literary convention. Some of these modifications may be Fancher's, but this version of the story has clearly been adjusted to fit in to school.

A First Interpretation

The first time I heard this story, my interpretation was almost completely determined by European associations. The degree to which such cultural assumptions can distort interpretation is delightfully illustrated in Laura Bohannan's classic essay, "Shakespeare in the Bush" (1966). As a diversion from her fieldwork, Bohannan tried and failed to prove the universality of *Hamlet* in a lively and confusing discussion with a group of Tiv tribesmen in West Africa. Just as the Tiv were able to construct a coherent, if incorrect, interpretation of *Hamlet* based on African witchcraft, so I constructed an interpretation of "How Crane Got His Blue Eyes" in terms of cautionary tales familiar to me.

To begin with, I envisioned the mysterious something that stole the eyes to be a wolf. For Euro-Americans like myself, the wolf is the prototypical threat that lurks just outside of civilization, ready to destroy the unwary. This image anticipated my later association of the story with the European tale, "The Boy Who Cried Wolf," an Aesop's fable as ubiquitous in Euro-American elementary classrooms as the crane story is in Alaskan ones (Reeves 1962: 59). In my experience of the story, the two tales paralleled one another; the fable cast a shadow on the Alaskan tale and outlined its meaning in my unconscious.

In the European story, a boy is assigned to watch a flock of sheep for the village. Bored, he pretends a wolf is approaching and calls for help. This is repeated once or twice, and the villagers, disgusted with his foolery, refuse to come on the final summons. This time the wolf really has appeared, and, depending on the version, either the boy or the sheep are killed.

In my mind, both stories were obviously meant to teach children that it pays to do what your superiors tell you, thereby reinforcing the social hierarchy. I suspect that other white schoolteachers would be likely, as I was at first, to understand Lind's message to be that "lying does not pay."

I started by unconsciously visualizing a lurking threat (a wolf, which could be a threat to children and the social order) which greatly affected my understanding of possible themes. I drew on literary convention to do this (Aesop and the wolf genre of fairy tale), and then I tried to adjust my interpretation according to my perception of Lind's intentions. Given her background, the message that lying does not pay seemed plausible. However, an attempt to relate the story to Yup'ik culture was to lead me to quite a different conclusion.

A Second Reading: Attempting a Yup'ik Interpretation

Any attempt at a Yup'ik reading of the story, one that takes Yup'ik cultural themes and beliefs into account, will of course still be limited by my outsider's perspective. In fact, I realize that even if I were Yup'ik, my understanding of the story would still be relative to my individual experience. However, as I tried to extend my thinking to account for a Yup'ik cultural perspective, themes that emerged included the importance of vision, reciprocal relationships in the natural world, characterization of ideal hierarchical relationships, and finally, some concrete details about the natural world.

Although I tried my best to "see" as Yupiit might, drawing on my own experiences with them, Aesop continued to foil my speculation. I could shift my thinking about the story *content*, but the influence of my culture on the *process* of analysis remained. Rather than edit these "failures" out of subsequent drafts, I have left them in to support my argument that cultural context is everything when it comes to listening.

In retrospect, the process would have pleased the forgotten elementary teacher who taught me about fables. In most fables, I reasoned, the animals represent prototypical humans. Here's some-body out berry picking (must be a female since berry picking is mostly a female endeavor). There is also a subordinate character, the eyes, ordered to stay put. This must be a child. Any Bethel child could im-mediately identify with the familiar experience of being taken out on the tundra during berry-picking season. Furthermore, the eyes, like a child, come from the body of the crane.

For very small children, berry picking is not always a wonder-ful experience. The spongy tundra is very difficult to move around on and does not offer much entertainment. In addition, mothers are unenthusiastic about children eating a lot of berries. In short, berry picking is potentially boring, and the adults are too busy and having too much fun to want to be disturbed. In the story, Lind makes it lip-smackingly obvious that the crane is having all the fun.

Crane's solution to this problem is characteristic of Yup'ik parents. He gives the eyes (child) a job, in this case the responsibility to look for danger. It should be noted here that by Yup'ik standards, it is a compliment and a privilege for a younger person to do something for an elder. As in "The Boy Who Cried Wolf," perhaps we are being told that the child's responsibility is critical for the group as a whole. However, the eyes then fail in this assignment.

The interpretations of the two stories, though parallel up to this point, diverged radically with the meaning of the failure. The Eu-ropean boy fails because he is dishonest and unmindful of the time and energy he is demanding of adults. Importantly, he also fails to anticipate the reactions of the adults. The nature of the failure of the Yup'ik "child" is less explicit. Crane does accuse his eyes of "fooling" him, but he does not refuse to come at the third call. This immediately eliminates the conclusion that adults will mistrust unreliable reports.

In addition, the word *fooling* may carry a moral impact for Euro-Americans that did not exist for Lind. In Yup'ik, there is only one verb, *iqlu-*, which can mean either lying or joking. Given the lighthearted, trickster quality of the story, the fact that the crane consistently heeds the eyes' calls, and the focus of the ending on the satisfaction of the crane, I could only conclude that this tale is not about the dangers of lying.

"Then what *is* it about?" I asked myself, as I wondered at how easily I had associated the story with the Aesop fable. I thought of myself on the tundra or looking out across a huge expanse of the frozen Kuskokwim River, puzzling over some mysterious and am-biguously distant object. I remembered how hard it is to be sure about

Helen, Shirley, and Maggie Wasuli picking salmonberries near Kotlik in late July 1983. Photo by James H. Barker.

what one sees. Perhaps the story recognizes that one's own eyes are very quickly fooled on the tundra, that learning to see accurately is not easy. I wondered whether the eyes had actually been seeing something all along. The storyteller leaves this question unanswered, another clue that weakens the idea that lying is a central theme. In any case, unlike the adults in Aesop's fable, Crane is not willing to take the risk of ignoring the warning. For a Yup'ik audience, I concluded, the interpersonal dimension of lying must be incidental.

What I then decided is that the story is not about lying, about the importance of using words wisely. Instead, it is about vision and the importance of using one's senses wisely. The fact that the eyes can be understood either as a separate character from the crane or as part of a single creature allows the story to be heard on two levels. If the story is understood in the first sense, as a drama between parent and child, then the child suffers a terrible fate for lack of acuity; he or she disappears and is replaced by another child. The importance of learning to use one's eyes wisely in order to keep (or take) one's place in the social sphere is amply demonstrated. The theme of obedience to one's superiors is still a central value, but it revolves not around honesty but around paying visual attention.

In the other sense—with Crane and his eyes as a single character whose acuity fails—the story shows simply that vision is essential for personal survival. The crane's panic at the loss of his vision and his care in replacing his old eyes with better ones reveal how important this is.

These themes of the importance of vision and learning to use one's vision well are ubiquitous in Yup'ik culture. Fienup-Riordan's essay, "The Mask: The Eye of the Dance," details many ways in which sight is socially restricted or put to beneficial use because of its power (1990: 49–67). Another legend collected by Fienup-Riordan, "The Boy Who Went to Live with the Seals," outlines a young hunter's education. As part of his training, he is admonished many times not to fall asleep, which is, of course, to keep one's eyes open (1983: 177). This same admonition is repeatedly echoed in Lantis's collection of descriptions by older men of their traditional education (1960). That Yup'ik children should hear cautionary tales about vision makes sense. Within Eskimo social hierarchies, vision is to be used in circumscribed ways for the protection and benefit of all (Burch 1975). Conventions of gaze and eye contact are related both to maintaining the social hierarchy and ensuring hunting success.

Stories featuring removable eyes that explore themes of vision, blindness, and power are not uncommon in other Native American folklore. Many of them, notably the coyote stories, contain elements of trickery as well. Examples can be found in Rothenberg's Nez Perce coyote tale (1972: 102) or the Winnebago hare cycle collected by Radin (1956: 79–80). Morrow's essay, "The Loon with the Ivory Eyes," cites variants from several Eskimo groups of a story in which a loon gives sight to a blind boy (1975: 146–47). Interestingly, Morrow associates these stories with artifacts and ritual practices that draw connections between birds (loons in particular), powerful vision, clairvoyance, shamanistic powers, and removable eyes.

These ethnographic readings gave me an expanded literary context for the crane story which, coupled with my long experience with Yup'ik parents and children, prompted revised interpretations. I know what it is like to see and move about on the tundra. I know what berry picking is like for adults and children, men and women. These experiences contributed greatly to my growing understanding of the story.

Even so, I was drawing on an interpretive convention from European fable (animal symbolizes human) to create a picture of mother and child on the tundra. I had also glossed the gender of the crane, substituting female for male following European symbolic conventions. Would this be possible, or even relevant, for Yup'ik listeners? Lind consistently refers to Crane as "he," but I was able to overlook this, knowing that Yup'ik pronouns do not specify gender and bilingual speakers often substitute "he" for "she." Translation forced Lind to make a gender choice that put my interpretation in question.

Although I felt a little closer, I still did not think that I had been able to understand the story as a Yup'ik might. In spite of my exposure to Yup'ik folklore and my experience in the Kuskokwim area, the effects of my schooling in European literature were hard to shake. Given the mix, it is difficult to say that I had done any more than make the story mine. At this point, cumulatively, I thought the story was about both honesty in adult-child relations and the importance of using vision wisely.

It is very possible, given her mixed history, that the story carried both messages for Lind, one about honesty and obedience and another about vision, just as it did for me at this point. In any case, as an instructional tale for the mixed community of children in Bethel, the message is likely to be quite dependent on the listener.

Up to this point, the thrust of this process of interpretation has been to decide what the story was "about." This search for the message in a tale is a part of listening that has been reflexive for me since elementary school. I have been taught to figure out what "the point" is, particularly in the case of fables, which are so clearly constructed around a moral lesson. The explicitly stated moral of the Aesop story is "liars are not believed even when they tell the truth" (Reeves 1962: 60). Morrow's article in this book suggests that morals should be left open to individual interpretation. Thus, there are no stated morals in Yup'ik stories, a fact that continues to frustrate non-Native students as they read folklore. Whatever messages may be embedded in the crane story, it is characteristic that they are implied. Implicitness is highly valued in Yup'ik culture (Morrow 1990), so it is not surprising that one needs to look to the context to understand the intentions of the speaker.

Conversations: Yup'ik Readings

Having carried my interpretation as far as reading and personal experience would take me, I finally shared my ideas with two Yup'ik women who were interested in the progress of my essay. Nastasia (Cugun) Wahlberg of Bethel, a literature student at the University of Alaska Fairbanks, had heard the story from her mother as a child and now tells it to her young daughters. Rhona Nanalook, a young teacher from Manokotak, had heard the story in primary school (probably the Fancher version).

Some important differences in interpretation existed between us. The parent-child symbolism had never occurred to either woman. After some conversation, we decided that this stemmed from my having related the crane's behavior to berry *picking*. Wahlberg pointed out that the crane had simply gone out on the tundra to *eat*, something just as likely to be done by either a man or a woman. Both women saw the character as somewhat foolish, not at all parental. Nanalook felt that Crane was careless in his "gluttony." Wahlberg added that the story ends too positively to carry a heavy moral message.

Both agreed, however, that vision is a central theme in the story. Nanalook's reading was that Crane did not look carefully enough (perhaps because he was foolish in removing his eyes). Wahlberg felt that Crane was resting his eyes and that they were too "flighty" and "fearful" to make wise judgments about "what is truly danger-ous." Interestingly, their interpretations differed as to who errs and whether the eyes and Crane are seen as one or separate characters.

However, both women strongly supported the idea that the story communicates the social importance of using one's eyes correctly and that circumscribed use of vision has moral overtones.

Wahlberg and Nanalook both made reference to another broad theme of Yup'ik culture, the reciprocity of plants, animals, and humans as equal elements in the natural world. Many Yup'ik myths describe actual transformations, and most teach the importance of proper interspecies treatment for mutual survival. The representation of humanlike animals very simply reinforces the close relationship between animals and humans. In addition, Wahlberg pointed out that "nature [berries] and animal spirits are one" in this story, and the use of berries for eyes reinforces the idea in a very literal way. She also observed that by "manipulating nature," trying out different berries to use as eyes, Crane may not have demonstrated a completely correct stance toward the natural world. She suggested that this lapse adds to the comic quality of the story.

Both Wahlberg and Nanalook stressed the entertainment value of the story, and I was reminded of the first time I had heard it on the Bethel radio, a very funny rendition by Lind. Wahlberg mentioned that her mother's version was hilarious, that her description of the crane eating berries, losing his eyes, and especially trying out new ones was great cause for laughter. Wahlberg said that she tries to recapture that spirit when she tells the story to her young daughters.

Interestingly, she mentioned that she has introduced a change in these tellings. Although she likes delighting the children with the comedy, she also uses the story to teach the colors of the various berries, important details in the natural world. To do this, she has added salmonberries. This alteration demonstrates flexible use, and by implication, Wahlberg's understanding that stories can vary in purpose. That a story is changed in its rendition hints at an underlying belief that meaning lies as much with each successive listener as with the "original" storyteller. This idea contrasts with the general Euro-American view, which tends to see literature as more static in rendition and purpose.

For each speaker and listener in this sequence—Lind, Fancher, Koranda, myself, Nanalook, Wahlberg, and her daughters—ideas about the purposes of storytelling are determined by culture, context, and personal experience, and for all of us, purpose certainly affects meaning. Among many possibilities, Fancher's purposes might have been literacy development and cultural awareness. Lind's could have been teaching values, developing cultural pride, and entertaining. With her children, Wahlberg uses the story for didactic and entertainment purposes. For Nanalook, Wahlberg, and myself, the story became a departure point for a series of conversations about values, literacy convention, child rearing, and pedagogy in both Yup'ik and Euro-American cultures.

As a result of these conversations, I identified main themes that seemed essentially Yup'ik: the importance of right behavior (if not obedience), the role of vision in the social sphere, and the essential importance of clear sight for personal survival. Ultimately, the message that seemed clearest to me after our conversation was that reciprocity in the natural world must be practiced by both parties with the utmost care, or disaster will result.

A Classroom Event

Now that I have reached this point in my evolving interpretation of the crane story, it should be increasingly clear that the ways in which an individual speaker and listener construct meaning are exponentially variable as the story interacts with cultural context, narrative conventions, and perceived storytelling purposes. The two crane stories are examples of a tale collected in interviews. How would Maggie Lind have told it to second graders in Bethel, or how does Rhona Nanalook tell it to her Athabaskan preschool children in Fairbanks? For that matter, how would I tell it?

In my current work instructing beginning teachers, I often have the opportunity to see how they use folklore in school. A storytelling event that I observed in a classroom not long ago illustrates how difficult it can be for teachers and schoolchildren, speakers and audiences, not to mention education instructors, to mutually negotiate meaning. What is particularly wonderful about the case in question is that it involved an Alaska Native teacher telling a story of her own to non-Native children. As her white supervisor, I found that I was in a position to understand the response of her students and explore with her how it differed from the meanings she thought were being communicated. In this situation, I benefited in turn from the lessons I had learned from Maggie Lind's crane story.

The teacher was Linda Evans, an Athabaskan woman in her thirties, and the schoolchildren were students from white and African-American military families. In the middle of a lesson on Athabaskan subsistence living, Mrs. Evans decided to tell a story from her experience as a child. She set the stage, telling the children that she and her parents and grandmother used to set snares for rabbits. The snares needed to be checked each day, and sometimes she was assigned to the chore. The children listened with rapt attention as Mrs. Evans described the beauty of the trail and snowy trees, the way the snare worked, that the rabbits were dead and frozen when they were collected, and how they lay stiffly in the sack as she carried it along the trail. These last details prompted looks of discomfort.

Then Mrs. Evans described coming around a bend to find a live rabbit in one of the snares. Aloud, she remembered looking at the creature, knowing that she was supposed to kill it and bring it home. She told how she had searched for exactly the right stick to club the animal, how she had raised the stick and then hesitated. The expressions on the children's faces showed intense interest at this point. An audible exclamation of relief and appreciation went up as the teacher reported that she had lowered the stick and released the rabbit. They smiled as she described its bounding escape through the snow.

From this point in the story on, Mrs. Evans's delivery intensified, but the children's interest appeared to wane. The teacher described walking back home with dread and her relief at not being asked too many questions about her expedition. She then related that her mother had checked the snares the following day and returned to confront her about the missing rabbit. Both her mother and grandmother had been angry with her, and she described the scolding she had received.

During these last details, Mrs. Evans looked expectantly at the students as if she was reaching the climax of the story. What she saw were fidgety children, some with hands raised. Clearly they felt the story was over and it was their turn to talk. She lamely added that she had been disobedient and had not been able to escape the consequences.

When the teacher then called on the students for their comments and questions, they generally expressed their admiration for her good deed in saving the rabbit's life. They objected to the scolding and sympathized with her. No one asked how Mrs. Evans's mother had found out about the rabbit. No one commented on her misconduct. The more the students talked, and the more Mrs. Evans reiterated the position that she had done wrong, the more a feeling of impasse set in. Both the students and teacher began to falter in their assertions and look frustrated and confused.

Later, when I asked Mrs. Evans how she felt about telling the story, she expressed frustration that the children had not "got the point." After deeper probing, it became clear that she felt that the mystery and interest in the story lay not in the events surrounding the escape of the rabbit but in her mother's detection of what had happened in the footprints that revealed the child's search for the stick and the animal's escape. Although this part of the story was not told, Mrs. Evans thought that this point should have been self-evident. Additionally, she was frustrated that the moral of the story had been missed. The children had actually acclaimed what she felt was a breach of proper behavior. For Athabaskans (and for Yupiit), game which offers itself must be taken, or the species will be seriously offended. Worse yet, her respected mother and grandmother had ended up the villains of the tale.

This incident perfectly exemplifies the way that speaker and audience, each bringing to a story a set of values, conventions, and purposes, can fail to negotiate meaning. In this case, everyone involved seemed aware that a discrepancy of interpretation had taken place. In other instances, teacher and students might have adjusted and agreed on a negotiated meaning without knowing they had done so. Or they might have decided on quite different interpretations without becoming aware of the discrepancy. My sense is that the incident in Mrs. Evans's classroom was the exception in that an obvious impasse was reached.

More often, I believe that speakers and audiences (teachers and students especially) are inclined to think that communication has taken place when discourse flows smoothly according to the conventions of the setting. Since these conventions are ritualized and explicitly practiced at school, special dangers exist when materials (like folklore) that allow highly variable interpretation and yet are supposed to definitively represent cultures are used.

Conclusion

The varied interpretations of Maggie Lind's story that I have presented here should complicate the picture enough to give teachers a healthy appreciation for the process of telling and listening in a cross-cultural context. On the levels of concrete content, structure, genre, symbolic convention, purpose, and analytic convention, to name only a few, the mutually constructed meanings of a story remain subject to cultural context. Meaning seems about as substantial as a wolf's shadow when it falls across the unconscious assumptions that dwell within the safe fold of cultural conventions.

In raising these questions, I do not intend to discourage adults from using folklore in classrooms. Instead, I urge caution about easy, one-sided interpretation. I also suggest that teachers consider audiences of children; they need to pay close attention to the variability of meaning that can lie between speaker and audience. The idea of telling the story to children and predicting the way my telling and their hearing would emerge is daunting, given the difficulty I encountered sorting out my own understanding of the tale and deriving a Yup'ik interpretation. Crane's message—that reciprocity must be conducted with care—seems relevant. I encourage adults to open the doors of complexity to children. A group of students working together to construct alternate meanings gains a valuable appreciation for the variability of interpretation.

Sometimes, in spite of all these points of difference, a bit of common ground can be found as well. If pressed, I would have to say that the story teaches all of us about observation. Even for non-Yupiit, this message seems to come across. As a preschooler, my own son heard the story on the radio and was fascinated by one tiny detail: the eye color of the crane. Was it true? Only looking carefully will tell.

Notes

This paper benefited greatly from conversations with Phyllis Morrow, Nastasia Wahlberg, and Rhona Nanalook.

1.   Maggie Lind's stories in this volume are not credited to her. Her grandson, John Active, confirmed that she told them to Fancher for the Frost collection.

References

Active, John. 1992. "Funny Words." In *Sharing Our Stories and Traditions: The 18th Annual Bilingual Multicultural Education Conference,* edited by Anne Kessler and members of the Alaska State Board of Education, 29–30. Juneau: Alaska Department of Education.

Ager, Lynn Price. 1971. "The Eskimo Storyknife Complex of Southwestern Alaska." Master's thesis, Anthropology Department, University of Alaska Fairbanks.

Barker, James. 1975. *"I Feel Like I'm Just Wasting My Breath": Testimonies Spoken by Western Alaskans to the Bureau of Land Management.* Bethel, Alaska: Association of Village Council Presidents, Nunam Kitlusisti.

Bohannan, Laura. 1993. "Shakespeare in the Bush." In *Anthropology: Contemporary Perspectives,* edited by Phillip Whitten and David E. D. Hunter, 162–66. New York: Harper Collins College Publishers.

Burch, Ernest S. 1975. *Eskimo Kinsmen: Changing Family Relationships in Northwest Alaska.* St. Paul: West Publishing Co.

Fienup-Riordan, Ann. 1983. *The Nelson Island Eskimo: Social Structure and Ritual Distribution.* Anchorage: Alaska Pacific University Press.

──────. 1990. *Eskimo Essays: Yupik Lives and How We See Them.* New Brunswick, N.J.: Rutgers University Press.

Frost, O. W., ed. 1971. *Tales of Eskimo Alaska.* Anchorage: Alaska Methodist University Press.

Hensel, Chase. 1992. "Where It's Still Possible: Subsistence, Ethnicity and Identity in Southwest Alaska." Ph.D. dissertation, University of California, Berkeley.

Koranda, Lorraine D. 1966. *Alaskan Eskimo Songs and Stories.* Seattle: University of Washington Press.

Lantis, Margaret. 1960. *Eskimo Childhood and Interpersonal Relationships: Nunivak Biographies and Genealogies.* Seattle: University of Washington Press.

Lenz, Mary, and James H. Barker. 1985. *Bethel, the First Hundred Years, 1885–1985: Photographs and History of a Western Alaska Town.* Bethel, Alaska: City of Bethel Centennial History Project.

Lind, Maggie. 1972. *Bethel, Stories and Legends.* Audiotape no. H-91-12-163, recorded on 8/5/72. Oral History Collection of the Alaska and Polar Regions Department, Elmer E. Rasmuson Library, University of Alaska Fairbanks.

Morrow, Phyllis. 1975. "The Loon with the Ivory Eyes: A Study in Symbolic Archaeology." *Journal of American Folklore* 88(348): 143–50.

──────. 1990. "Symbolic Actions, Indirect Expressions: Limits to Interpretation of Yupik Society." *Etudes/Inuit/Studies* 14(1–2): 141–58.

Nelson, Edward W. 1899. *The Eskimo about Bering Strait.* Eighteenth Annual Report of the Bureau of American Ethnology to the Secretary of the Smithsonian Institution. Washington, D.C.: Bureau of American Ethnology.

Oswalt, Wendell H. 1964. "Traditional Storyknife Tales of Yuk Girls." *Proceedings of the American Philosophical Society* 108(4): 310–36.

Radin, Paul. 1956. *The Trickster: A Study in American Indian Mythology.* New York: Schocken Books.

Reeves, James. 1962. *Fables from Aesop.* New York: Henry Z. Walch, Inc.

Rothenburg, Jerome. 1972. *Shaking the Pumpkin: Traditional Poetry of the Indian North Americas.* Garden City, N.Y.: Doubleday and Co.

Yup'ik translator Vernon Chimegalrea records place names with Tuluksak elders Edward Wise, Peter Waskie, and Peter Napoka, July 1988. Photo by Robert Drozda.

"They Talked of the Land with Respect"

Interethnic Communication in the Documentation of Historical Places and Cemetery Sites

Robert M. Drozda

If it is difficult to hear the voices of oral tradition in a classroom, where the educational system turns meaning making into lesson learning, it is perhaps even harder to hear them in the goal-directed confines of an agency. Bureaucrats may cast tradition bearers as information givers, people from whom one can get answers to predetermined questions in a recognizable form. In such a situation, tradition bearers may assert what is important to them in ways that go unacknowledged by their interlocutors.

In this essay, Robert Drozda discusses the communication which evolved between anthropologists and Yup'ik elders in the course of fulfilling a federal mandate to document historical places and cemetery sites. Working with Yup'ik people in their traditional lands, the federally employed researchers encountered beliefs and cultural insights that differed dramatically from their own. Distinct cultural differences and contrasting ideologies about the relationship between human beings and the landscape became apparent. Yup'ik elders characterized federal site documentation as a system of "laws which are written down and ... have numbers," bounding parcels of land "like floor tile." They contrasted this with a Yup'ik's (a genuine person's) sense that land had always been used "without saying something about it."

In fact, some elders had a lot to say about it, often through stories associated with places. Over time, they also demonstrated an understanding of site investigators' perspectives, while continuing to answer in ways that communicated something of their worldview. The site investigators, on their part, began to rework their approach and learned to listen in different ways to what they were being told. The inseparability of form and content made this a delicate process. (Does the question, "What does this place name mean?" presuppose an English translation of the word or a story about the place?) Both Barker's and Drozda's essays force us to confront the difficulty of passing traditions on to strangers through negotiated encounters.

Under the provisions of section 14(h)(1) of the Alaska Native Claims Settlement Act (ANCSA) of 1971 (Public Law 92-203), the secretary of the interior was authorized to withdraw eligible lands as Native historical places and cemetery sites. Most Alaska Native regional corporations established under the act filed applications for the properties, and the Bureau of Indian Affairs created an office in 1978 to investigate these sites.[1]

Although the land entitlement under this section of the act is relatively small—less than one-tenth of 1 percent of the entire forty-million-acre land settlement (Bureau of Indian Affairs ANCSA Office n.d.)—historic and cemetery sites hold great significance for the Native people of Alaska beyond their specific acreage. As historical and cultural resources, the lands are (or should be) important to non-Native Americans as well. However, the degree and scope of their significance to the two groups are in contrast and reflect dissimilarities in cultural views and basic assumptions toward the land and its historical resources. The development and implementation of this section of the settlement act has been a complicated process. The very nature of the act, with its involvement with ethnic societies on the periphery of mainstream American culture, immediately created problems of cultural misunderstanding, including, but not limited to, difficulties of interethnic communication.

In this essay, I will discuss some of the complications encountered by federally employed, non-Native researchers of historical and cemetery sites in predominantly Yup'ik-speaking southwestern Alaska (see the map, "Native Languages of Alaska and Yukon Territory," p. x). Contrasting cultural definitions will be identified and accented with specific examples excerpted from tape transcripts and recordings made with Natives from Yup'ik villages in the Calista corporate region.[2]

Cooperation between site investigators and Yup'ik villagers was absolutely essential for the documentation of the historical properties applied for by Calista. Since the overwhelming majority of applications involved sites from the historic or late prehistoric periods (Pratt 1992), Native elders were crucial, not only to provide historical information about places but also to assist investigators in locating sites. The majority of elders we employed for this purpose were monolingual Yup'ik speakers. This certainly complicated matters for researchers (none of whom were Yup'ik speakers) and required us to employ competent bilingual interpreters.

Throughout the course of the documentation project, the obstacles encountered by Native and non-Native participants served as experiential lessons to both groups. Many of these problems resulted from vast differences in language, communication styles, worldviews, and individual personalities. The lessons that were learned form the basis of this essay. In addition, I will suggest some solutions to basic interethnic communication problems based on the mutual growth and understanding that has occurred over the span of this project.

Although some of the problems and remedies discussed may seem apparent, surely others remain to be discovered. They are perhaps less conspicuous due to the complexities and multifaceted nature of language (including the bureaucratic and legal language of the act), culture, personality, and intercultural communication. These are factors that we often respond to beneath the conscious level of individual awareness. Lastly, one must understand that this essay is not a collaboration and therefore reflects a particular perspective, based on the experience of its non-Native, English-language author.

ANCSA 14(h)(1): History and Assumptions

Before I discuss specific interethnic communication situations encountered during the documentation of these historical places and cemetery sites, it is necessary to give a brief background into the history and assumptions which led to this section of the settlement act. These initial assumptions form a framework or context for later communication difficulties and misunderstandings. This background represents only a general overview and is by no means complete.

In the process of negotiating Alaska Native land claims, many groups met in order to reach a compromise settlement. The primary parties involved were representatives from the federal government and Alaska Native groups. Commonly, when people from divergent cultural backgrounds come together to reach a compromise, the view of the dominant culture takes precedence over any others (Morrow and Hensel 1992). This appears to have been the case with ANCSA, a system of law grounded in the cultural assumptions of the dominant American society, which has now been superimposed onto the Yupiit

and other Alaska Natives, whose history and current cultural viability
rest on distinctly different ethical rules and concepts of law.

Although Yup'ik and other Alaska Native leaders were actively
involved in the development of the settlement act and in fact pushed
for it, many Yup'ik villagers remain critical of this participation. They
cite the lack of consideration of their law as their reason and a basic
concern. Paul John, a Yup'ik elder from Toksook Bay, addressed this
issue during a 1984 interview (translated from Yup'ik):

> The Kass'aqs [white people] seem to feel that what they call "the
> law," the law that they made, is a powerful aspect. The Kass'aqs
> used to think that we don't have laws. They didn't seem to try to
> understand our culture first; they seemed to just say, "Here's your
> land." Our ancestors had laws. It's not that they didn't have any
> laws. The Kass'aqs' laws are written down and they usually have
> numbers relating to specific laws. The sites shown on the map (the
> ones the surveyors are doing now) are not the only ones; there are
> many rivers with names, many lakes with names, and many hills
> with names. Everything seems to bear some name that was passed
> on down, generation to generation, from our ancestors. And then
> when they tell us about things we should follow, like if we were to
> go out to the wilderness or to a place that has a name, they'd tell us
> that the place is a place for so and so, like for hunting, fishing, or
> trapping. In telling us so, they are telling us about their law. They
> do have laws.
>
> The Natives as a group seemed to treat the land as one allotment.
> They used to at one time use the land without saying something
> about it. Where anyone went to be, he never heard or was to hear
> someone speaking of a land that belongs to him alone. The whole
> land to the north or wherever has no measurement. A person went
> wherever he wished to go, however far he can go; even if he went
> as far as a bullet can reach, he would have no limitations. That is
> how they seem to use the land.
>
> It happens that who and what they [Bureau of Indian Affairs
> surveyors] work for did not tell us more [instruct us more], al-
> though they should have. But their workers were all or mostly
> Kass'aqs; they hardly had Native workers. Because of that, they
> couldn't tell us more, communications were poor. If they had
> Yup'ik workers, we'd have a better understanding. I'm speaking
> of what I myself know and understand. I've found that sometimes,

when it's too late, I begin to understand the situation. I also come
up with solutions when it's too late, it seems. (John 1984)

Mr. John added this telling narrative at the end of a taped interview
conducted to gather information about places specifically applied for
as historical or cemetery sites. The interviewer asked John if he had
any general comments he would like to make on a topic of his choice.
John's decision to speak about basic differences between Yup'ik and
Western law demonstrates a frustrated acceptance of the dominant
foreign set of laws and an understanding of both systems. Also, by the
very act of speaking out on this issue, he was exercising an important
aspect of traditional Yup'ik law.[3]

Those of us who were raised in Western society may find it difficult
to understand the depth of the difference between oral and written
law. We must realize that Alaska Native languages have been written
down for only a relatively short period of time, yet rules and laws
have always been observed and respected by the Yupiit. What the
Yupiit are saying, it seems, is that Western laws cannot be trusted
because written laws can and often do change, whereas oral law, as
presented by the Yupiit, contains the history of the people and reflects
the integrity of the orator. One's word does not change. When the law
can only cross a person's lips by way of a written document, a basic
trust in fellow humans is sacrificed.

In his narrative, John repeatedly makes reference to the oral—to
names, to telling, to hearing and speaking—as a means of codifying
Yup'ik law. Yupiit used the land "without saying something about it,"
as compared to the white people's laws, which "are written down and
. . . have numbers." Words—especially in writing—have been used to
change relationships with the land as well as between inhabitants of
the land (see Morrow 1990).

Several other points made by John are worth summarizing: First,
the Yupiit had laws which were superseded by the law of the federal government. Second, the Yup'ik laws and principles of land use
contained a different concept of ownership and no arbitrary idea of
boundary. In fact, according to traditional Yup'ik ethics, discussing
the land or boundaries (in the Western sense) could even be viewed
as disrespectful and potentially harmful. Third, non-Natives did not
try to understand the Yup'ik ways ("communications were poor").
Fourth, the Yupiit regret that they did not understand all of the
implications of the settlement act until it was too late.

Rules and Regulations

The development of section 14(h)(1) definitions and rules and regulations (43CFR2653.5) closely followed those established under the National Historic Preservation Act of 1966 (NHPA). Under this act, the establishment of a National Register of Historic Places allowed for the evaluation of sites according to a set of criteria which addressed issues of significance (Tainter and Lucas 1983). Although the eligibility criteria in this case were modified to address Alaska Native rather than national significance (Utley 1980), the determinants are heavily couched in Western concepts. *Historical site* is defined as

> a distinguishable tract of land or area upon which occurred a significant Native historical event, which is importantly associated with Native historical or cultural events or persons, or which was subject to sustained historical Native activity, but sustained Native historical activity shall not include hunting, fishing, berry-picking, wood gathering, or reindeer husbandry. (43CFR2653.0-5)

Two key terms in this definition which immediately jump out are *significant* and *importantly associated*. The cultural relativity and ambiguity of these terms becomes apparent when one considers Yup'ik testimony such as that from Mr. John. He includes rivers, lakes, hills, and named places as "importantly associated" sites, worthy of documentation and preservation. The law does not allow for these. John is by no means alone in this feeling. There are, in fact, thousands of named places which serve not only as physical markers in the landscape but also comprise an inseparable aspect of a larger, cohesive, interrelated matrix of Yup'ik law, land, culture, and livelihood.

Likewise, for historical places and cemetery sites, as defined by the settlement act, significance criteria are culturally ambiguous and have generally been interpreted in Western terms. Native historical significance is described as present

> in places that possess integrity of location, design, setting, materials, workmanship, feeling and association, and:
>
> (1) That are associated with events that have made a significant contribution to the history of Alaskan Indians, Eskimos or Aleuts, or
>
> (2) That are associated with the lives of persons significant in the past of Alaskan Indians, Eskimos or Aleuts, or

(3) That possess outstanding and demonstrably enduring symbolic value in the traditions and cultural beliefs and practices of Alaskan Indians, Eskimos or Aleuts, or

(4) That embody the distinctive characteristics of a type, period, or method of construction, or that represent the work of a master, or that possess high artistic values, or

(5) That have yielded, or are demonstrably likely to yield information important in prehistory or history. (43CFR2653.5[d])

The Yupiit traditionally had their own rules and regulations regarding land use (Fienup-Riordan 1988: 20). In a 1988 interview printed in the Bethel newspaper *Tundra Drums*, Yup'ik educator Cecilia Martz described some of the basic differences between Native and Western rules and regulations:

> Through thousands of years of living here, native people developed all these rules and regulations to maintain that harmony. You could see this in how we view the land. Animals are important, plants are important, old gravesites, old hunting grounds. All these things are important and are imbued with spiritual quality. In the Kass'aq [white] culture ... there are little compartments, and you have time for each of them, but it's not whole, holistic. These native people, even when they're fishing, there is spirituality involved. When you're eating. When you're doing anything, there's a spiritual connection. [The compartmentalizing aspect of white culture] was uncomfortable because it made things less meaningful and less attached to each other. (1988: 25)

A great rift exists between the Native perspective and the federal rules for determining significance. In the traditional Yup'ik order, nurturing harmony is essential in keeping places significant. That is, places are significant in relation to other places and to the individual and collective Yup'ik psyche and worldview. In the Western way of thinking, places are reduced to separate things which "possess" qualities that can be observed and rated in terms of significance. This Western land tenet serves to sever Yup'ik harmonizing ties, thus removing places from their greater context of reflection and association.

The idea of "feeling and association" contained in the Code of Federal Regulations fails to take into account the varied ways in which other cultures, in this case the Alaska Natives, view their environment. The Yup'ik assertion is that all lands may be considered historically significant, that they do not contain qualities in and of themselves but are reflections of personal feelings and associations. This view leads to their frustration with the compartmentalization inherent in the Western mechanistic, reductionist, scientific paradigm. Yup'ik elder Joshua Phillip of Tuluksak compared the two views (translated from Yup'ik):

> When I went to the Lower 48, I saw that the land there was like floor tile. We have nothing like that here in Alaska. Since the time of our ancestors there have been names for rivers, ponds, lakes, hills and trees. In my area, I know the names of the mountains and waters. By naming everything those who came before us marked the land . . . it would be beneficial to us if we could implant markers for our rivers, hills and trees. . . . The markers will also show the people from outside that this land has always been ours. (Alexie and Morris 1985: 7)

Here Mr. Phillip demonstrates again the importance of indigenous place names. Names are not applied to places arbitrarily. The very fact that a place is named often establishes or reveals its significance. Furthermore, Yup'ik place names are enduring—passed down from generation to generation. Here, too, the contrast between the verbal and the written is emphasized. In order to legitimize Yup'ik land claims to non-Yupiit, Phillip suggests physical markers to augment the well-known mental markers (names) which have long been in place.

Subsistence: A Significant Activity?

Rules and regulations for determining historical place and cemetery site significance do not consider subsistence, in and of itself, to be a valid activity for determining site eligibility. Yet it is difficult for one to imagine what could be more important, as it is impossible to separate Alaska Native historical places and cemetery sites from hunting and gathering ones. The location of one was and is completely dependent upon the other. Here again, the Western concept seems to isolate and categorize living areas as somehow distinct from livelihood, whereas to the Yupiit, such a division is entirely illogical.

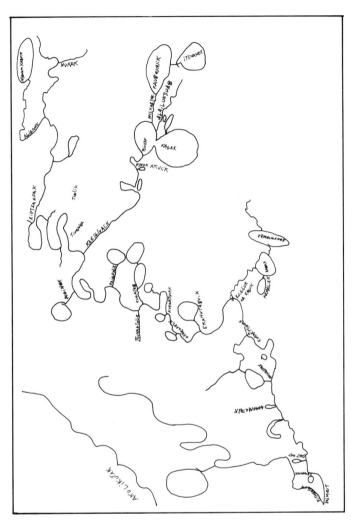

Sketch map of the Elaayiq River drainage, a tributary of the
Kuskokwim River, drawn from memory by Joshua Phillip in
1982. It includes names of historical villages and campsites
written in an old Yup'ik orthography. Mr. Phillip provided
this map to assist in locating historical places and cemetery
sites. It covers roughly four hundred square miles. USGS
maps of the same area record seven names; six are incorrect.
Mr. Phillip recorded thirty-three place names and numerous
hydrological features not shown on official maps. During
a more in depth survey in 1988 elders recorded over one
hundred place names in the same area. *North is to the left of
the map.*

Oral-history interviews conducted specifically to gain information and understanding about historical use of sites are replete with indirect references which illustrate the significance of place to sustenance. Indeed, as village elders have become more familiar with Western concepts of division and separation, their testimonies begin to address the problem directly, again combining understanding of the opposing view with their frustration with basic Kass'aq assumptions. Joshua Phillip provided the following information about the significance of the historical place named Qemirrluar (translated from Yup'ik):

> Those guys can also tell about the uses of that area, Qemirrluar, since they have been using it during the fall and spring. They are brothers from the village of Akiacuaq [Akiachak]; they are the last ones to have built a house there. They have even wintered there. They also know the streams in the surrounding area that have fish, and also in the spring they hunt in the area. They had it as their hunting area just like one would do in the [other] hunting areas; that is how they hunted in these fall camping areas. They'd hunt in the whole area surrounding a place. They didn't just go to one place; they'd hunt in the whole area, and even though they'd encounter other people, they never said anything; they'd just choose any area of land and hunt in the area. They'd have it as their harvesting area. That is how those ancestors were; they'd hunt in the whole area surrounding a settlement. And they never said that it belonged to someone else elsewhere, and they never said that it had a boundary; there were no boundaries, no lines; they just used the whole area surrounding them as a harvesting area, as hunting area, and there were no lines whatsoever! That is how Qemirrluar was used. And that is the *meaning* behind Qemirrluar [emphasis added]. (Phillip 1988)

When Mr. Phillip tells the "meaning behind Qemirrluar," it is like a story—a history in itself. The meaning does not rest in the literal translation of the Yup'ik name but rather in the knowledge and memory of events that people have about their ancestors, who have used the same area for hundreds of years or longer. Notwithstanding the fact that Qemirrluar and other places can be specifically delineated as sites, their meaning extends beyond any precise boundary to include all lands necessary to support the population.

Although researchers contend that the Yupiit of southwestern

Alaska did indeed have "boundaries" (Fienup-Riordan 1983, 1984; Pratt 1984)—that is, specific areas which individuals or groups traditionally identified as theirs—here I believe Phillip is speaking of boundaries in the Western sense, where (to the Yupiit) culturally meaningless and insignificant lines and boxes ("like floor tile") are marked out around pieces of land and transferred to paper. In a parallel to the Yup'ik attitude toward written laws, here the authenticity of the land is detached from the landscape and conveyed to paper, where it can be further divided and legally manipulated.

Along with the delineation of boundaries comes the concept of land ownership, and with this the Western notion of trespass, which is foreign to the basic Yup'ik ethic of sharing the land and its resources. Once again, in the Yup'ik cosmology, everything is connected. More than once when I attempted through questioning to determine probable boundaries for sites, comments such as "the whole river is a historical site!" were evoked from Natives. Some sense of inherent right to land use probably did exist among Yupiit; however, it was ownership of a different sort, part of an unspoken agreement which Phillip describes as using the land without saying anything about it.

Site Investigations

Based on the rules and regulations contained in the Code of Federal Regulations, teams of federally employed researchers (generally archaeologists and anthropologists) were responsible for investigating sites applied for by Alaska Native regional corporations. Following the investigators' completion of individual site reports, Bureau of Indian Affairs claims examiners evaluated the research findings and made site eligibility determinations. Claims examiners were "never archaeologists, historians or the like" (Pratt and Slaughter 1989); thus, the determination of significant Native historical places was left to individuals far removed both from site investigation and Yup'ik views about the land.

Researchers conducted site investigations in the Calista region each year from 1981 through 1991. More than 80 percent were concentrated in the Yukon-Kuskokwim area. Investigations typically involved locating sites, identifying surface features (structural remains, artifacts, graves), describing and mapping cultural features, determining the extent of sites, and surveying boundaries. Archaeologists sometimes performed limited subsurface testing, in which case organic samples may have been prepared for analysis.

In order to locate sites and supplement knowledge gained from physical investigations, researchers necessarily relied on the cultural, geographical, and historical knowledge of Yup'ik elders. As a result, approximately twelve hundred oral-history tape recordings were made with over four hundred Calista region elders. The recordings comprise a detailed record which treats many diverse aspects of Yup'ik history and culture, including subsistence resources and activities, land use, technology, traditional arts, social organization, religious and ceremonial life, language, and culture change.

Oral-History Recording

The remainder of this essay concentrates on basic interethnic exchanges between site investigators and Yup'ik elders in the documentation of specific sites applied for by the Calista Corporation. Most of these exchanges were made through an interpreter. Adaptations were made as each group (non-Native site investigators, Yup'ik elders, and interpreters) increased its understanding of the others' communication patterns. This process advanced Bureau of Indian Affairs field methodologies and interviewing techniques because researchers needed to respond to a variety of problems relating specifically to differences in communication styles, languages, concepts of land use, ideas of land ownership, and worldviews.

In order to put this process in its proper perspective, one must first consider that no project of this type or scope had ever been undertaken by the federal government. Therefore, virtually no amount of expertise or training could have adequately prepared researchers for the realities of the field. Arguably, anthropological or archaeological training or "book knowledge" could even have acted as a hindrance, especially since very little contemporary work existed on culturally appropriate methods for communicating with Yupiit.

Certainly, training in sociolinguistics and cross-cultural studies would have been beneficial by making researchers more aware of cultural differences. However, sources of information for improving interethnic communication between Alaska Natives and non-Natives were largely unknown.

Another complication worth mentioning involves the antagonistic and distrustful relationship between the two organizations which initially shared site investigation responsibilities: the Bureau of Indian Affairs ANCSA Office and a former division of the National Park Service known as the Anthropology and Historic Preservation/Cooperative Park Studies Unit (AHP/CPSU). The term *shared* is used here in its loosest sense, since the relationship between the two organizations was adversarial from the beginning. They "rarely worked together to fulfill their respective obligations on [the] project" (Pratt and Slaughter 1989), to the extent that field researchers often received conflicting information regarding the scope of their duties.[4]

The important point is that the conflicts at project management levels between the National Park Service AHP/CPSU and the Bureau of Indian Affairs ANCSA Office often translated to a lack of cooperation and confusion about the roles and responsibilities of members of field crews. This in turn resulted in, among other things, low morale among field researchers, a lack of consistency in fieldwork, an inability to develop a reasonable strategy for entering villages, and a lack of organization when conducting oral-history interviews. After the Bureau of Indian Affairs gained full control of the project in 1983, problems associated with logistics and lack of focus substantially lessened. This marked a turning point when field researchers and supervisors were able to concentrate on the task at hand, redefine their research objectives, and work toward improving field methodologies.

In spite of the transition, tensions remained between expectations set by project management at the Bureau of Indian Affairs and realities in the field experienced by researchers.[5] Fortunately, by this time veteran researchers could fall back on several seasons of practical field experience to supplement their own professional ethics. They realized that it was up to those directly involved in fieldwork to learn the most efficient methods for completing their tasks. Much of this learning was to take place through trial and error.

The realities of fieldwork involving Native villagers increased researchers' knowledge and led to alterations in information-gathering techniques. However, Bureau of Indian Affairs project management was frequently slow in responding to the needs of both Natives and researchers. This ongoing tension between management's constraints and fieldworkers' needs continued to affect the interaction between researchers and villagers. The researcher was in the awkward position of trying to function within unrealistic but powerful bureau-cratic restrictions while at the same time striving to understand and adjust to the reality of Yup'ik daily life and communicate with people from a vastly different culture.

Through time, experience, and numerous personnel changes, the ethnographic process improved at the Bureau of Indian Affairs. Much of this improvement can be seen by analyzing their oral-history col-lection. Probably the most extreme example of how not to do things involves an interview which was conducted at a historical site during the first season of field investigations in the Calista region. The tape recording registers, in addition to a Yup'ik elder and an interpreter, no less than six non-Native interviewers, including representatives from three federal agencies and a helicopter pilot, all of whom are asking the elder questions (Akelerea 1981). As might be expected, the record-ing contains only bits and pieces of useful information, interspersed with interviewers vying for the floor (or in this case, tundra).

Here priority was clearly not given to proper consideration for the interviewee and his potential to provide pertinent information about the site. It is doubtful that any of the questioners intended to offend, but rather disrespectful behavior resulted from both their lack of understanding and lack of control. In any case, the situation was grounded in a ridiculous field policy which required a member of each agency (the Bureau of Indian Affairs and the National Park Service) to be present during an interview.[6] In retrospect, this mauling of the interviewee seems inexcusable; however, it is representative of situations that arose due to the mutual distrust which existed between managements at the two agencies.

Still, mistakes and misunderstandings cannot be blamed wholly on management. Individual researchers were inexperienced and often naive. Even after the project was taken over by the Bureau of Indian Affairs, a common mistake was to have two or more researchers in-terviewing one elder. This may have resulted from the insecurity of being a conspicuous minority in any Yup'ik village. In addition, at both AHP/CPSU and the ANCSA office, there seemed to be an atti-tude among some researchers (primarily trained in archaeology) that the collection of oral history was everyone's right and "the fun part of the job" (Kenneth L. Pratt, conversation with the author). It meant "visiting with the Natives" and perhaps reflected a belief that oral history should not be taken seriously since the information could not be verified or relied upon for accuracy. Around this time in the early 1980s, Arctic anthropologist Ernest S. Burch observed,

Most of my colleagues still do not believe what Natives have to say about their own histories. "Narrative history," "oral history," "memory culture"—these phrases commonly are used as pejoratives by representatives of the social science disciplines in Alaska. Archaeologists refuse to believe anything that is not manifested in stone tools or middens. Historians will not believe anything that was not recorded on paper. And cultural anthropologists will not believe anything that they have not seen with their own eyes. Some anthropologists have actually boasted to me that they do not believe what Alaska Native historians have told them. They are blinded by a combination of cultural arrogance, personal bias and the limitations of their professional specialties. (1981: 16–17)

Surely this bias and skepticism existed among some project investigators. Further, some also assumed interviewing Native elders did not require any special skills beyond those of normal conversation.

Despite researchers' inexperience in communicating with Yupiit and poor interview techniques, some very high-quality information emerged from interviews in the early years of the project. These instances occurred, however, as a result of the cooperation and understanding between the individuals involved and had little to do with project management. The other side of this, of course, is that all the experience and training in the world cannot prevent a bad interview. However, learning some basic communication rules with the other culture cut down the chances.

In addition to demonstrating cultural insensitivity, this fortunately isolated, worst-case example of six interviewers brings up several problems which are compounded by having too many people involved in an interview:

(1) There is no real way for the interviewer to develop rapport with the elder or interpreter. In more recent years, the general policy has been to assign one interviewer to each elder and ideally, to each village as well. When the communication is direct and personal, an interview becomes less formal and the interviewer, interviewee, and interpreter can become accustomed to one another (see Scollon and Scollon 1980).

(2) The desire for information (or perhaps entertainment) overlooks the proper way to request and obtain it in the other culture. A serious problem for field researchers is that direct questioning is considered disrespectful in Yup'ik society, especially toward elders. The following excerpt from a 1988 interview records the words

of a translator who, anticipating a problem, explains the Yup'ik questioning ethic to the Bureau of Indian Affairs anthropologist:

> In their time, we weren't allowed to ask our parents or we weren't allowed to ask our elders. That's how they were. They [didn't] bother to ask them. Even to this day, I cannot ask him [the interviewee] what existed. Once in a great while I might if I get real curious. But a general practice for the male members [is] not to ask anybody.[7] If they want to let you know, they'll tell you. 'Cause some of the things we do are rather awkward, entirely different from your way of doing things. But it is [an] accepted way of life; it's acceptable in our way. It may not be acceptable in other societies. (Andrew 1988)

This practice of not questioning is basic to the traditional Yup'ik method of informal instruction, which is characterized by watching, listening, paying attention, and learning from mistakes. Interestingly, it was predominantly through this experiential method (however unconsciously it may have operated) that field researchers managed to obtain oral histories without offending people.[8]

(3) Researchers' complete unfamiliarity with the Yup'ik language created a problem, particularly when interpreters were difficult to find, as when summer fieldwork conflicted with fishing or berry picking. This led to many problems. For instance, interviewers often relied on phonetic English spellings of Yup'ik place names written by previous researchers or on official government topographic maps. Invariably, attempts by non-Natives to pronounce names were either met with amusement or more often simply added another layer to the confusion.

During later years of field research in the Calista region, Bureau of Indian Affairs investigators spent a great deal more time lining up translators who could work consistently, demonstrated personal interest in their history, and had training in the current standardized Yup'ik writing system. Some researchers also enrolled in Yup'ik language classes.

In 1986, the Alaska Native Language Center (ANLC) at the University of Alaska Fairbanks was contracted to provide professional translation and transcription of oral-history tapes. Previously, researchers had essentially relied on direct oral translations, which could vary widely, depending on circumstances and the skill of the interpreter. ANLC involvement in the project allowed researchers to focus on conducting more interviews entirely in the Yup'ik language. The most positive benefit of this approach is that an elder's narrative can continue uninterrupted without breaks to accommodate English translation.

In some cases, especially when rapport had been established between researcher, interpreter, and elder, questions were translated prior to the start of the interview. In effect, the interview was really conducted by the interpreter, who would write down translated responses as they were given by the elder. This method afforded the researcher the opportunity to relax a bit, listen closely to the rhythms and nuances of the Native language, and concentrate on making sure the equipment was functioning properly. This approach, however, requires a very skilled interpreter/translator and a commitment by the researcher to devote time to developing a sound working relationship.

Communication Strategies

Many of the interethnic differences that outside researchers need to be aware of when working with Yupiit, especially elders, relate to basic rules of courtesy. Some of them have been learned by project researchers and may prove beneficial to others in their interactions with Yupiit and perhaps other Native Americans. Although these differences can be itemized individually, they all interrelate in a variety of ways. Many were reemphasized to the author by staff members (especially Sophie Barnes and Gerald Domnick) of the Yupik Language Center, Kuskokwim College, in Bethel during the spring of 1988.[9]

(1) What may appear to non-Natives as "wandering" narrative is an integral part of Yup'ik conversational style. Especially with elders, one should let their train of thought continue so as not to lose anything. Sometimes an interviewer may become confused and think the question is not being answered. Be patient and do not interrupt.

(2) Generally questions are not answered directly in Yup'ik; likewise, researchers should try not to ask direct questions. Yup'ik elders Noel Polty of Pilot Station and Ben Fitka of Marshall (translating) provide an example:

Noel [in Yup'ik]: They say that regarding this tradition of asking favors indirectly, people were reluctant to say things, things such as, "Please give me a bit of sugar." They weren't able to make the direct request. When they wanted things, they'd ask for favors indirectly.

Ben [in Yup'ik]: Another Yup'ik way of asking for things.

Noel [in Yup'ik]: Yes, it was another way that Yupiit used for asking for things.

Ben [English translation to Bureau of Indian Affairs interviewer]: Okay, like they can't pronounce, they can't say to people when they have potlatch [a traditional gathering], "Give me sugar," like, you know, for instance, even maybe fish or something. They can't ask for it by name from the person, so they have to call on other names so that person whom they asked for will supply it. That's their custom among the old time people. (Polty 1982)

(3) Self-reference should be avoided. One should refrain from putting another person in the position of referring to himself or herself directly, as this violates cultural rules of modesty.

(4) Definitive statements are generally not made about the future. For example, when one is going out hunting, he may state, "I am going out to have a look around." In this instance, a strong definitive statement would be arrogant and likely cause the hunter to suffer some misfortune. Lott Egoak of Akiak illustrates (translated from Yup'ik):

[A man was killed by a brown bear.] They told that man not to go by himself! He said, "Oh, it's okay, I have a gun"; but still he was killed because he was saying that he was ready to defend himself! (1988)

(5) When planning or making appointments, an answer of "maybe" can indicate a positive intention, close to a definite "yes" in English. Yes is a sign of arrogance, as if mortals have control over their destiny. Maybe realistically allows for unforeseen circumstances to alter plans.

(6) One should respect pauses in speech and not interject prematurely:

One big thing a lot of people don't know is the length of the pause. The pause that you have in between is one of the big causes of mis-communication. Kass'aqs have a shorter pause than native people. Native people are taught at a young age that you're not supposed to rush in and answer whatever you're asked, or whatever you're talked to about. You're supposed to sit there and listen and think about it before you answer. So they develop a longer pause than Kass'aqs do. It's a little thing, but it causes a lot of problems. (Martz 1988: 25)

(7) One should accept silences, which are an integral part of Yup'ik communication. Often it is more effective to sit and "do nothing," to relax and allow time for people to get to know you. It takes more time initially but will pay off later as people become comfortable with you. In time, you will be rewarded with more complete information. Generally Yupiit get to know strangers by watching, whereas Westerners do it by talking.

(8) The concept of time is especially vital to understand. Different concepts of time are a root cause of many communication problems between non-Natives and Yupiit. It is important for non-Natives to relax the time constraints that they may carry with them from their usual daily lives in more urban areas.

(9) Direct eye contact indicates attentiveness in Westerners; to the Yupiit, it may be seen as disrespectful or challenging. This is likely to be truer with elders than with younger people, who are more accustomed to interaction with non-Natives.

(10) To the Yupiit the power of the word, gaze, and thoughts can make things happen.[10] Therefore, thoughtful action is necessary in realizing and maintaining the harmony of the system. Respectful thought and behavior is essential not only toward other humans and animals but also toward the land. George Moses of Akiachak states (translated from Yup'ik):

You know when you're going to use someone's belongings you have to ask first. That is how it is with the land. Let us not drag our minds but use our minds in respect for the land. Don't be empty-headed (1988).

Concluding Remarks

For all of us, specific places evoke images, thoughts, and feelings which become part of our sense of being. One place can hold many meanings for many individuals. Historical-place and cemetery-site delineation in terms of boundaries and acreage fail to capture the rich Yup'ik essence of the places and simply reflect Western concepts of land ownership. Through the living memories expressed in actions, words, and songs, places become vibrant, and some essence of that deeper meaning can be shared by those who choose to listen.

Despite the difficulties surrounding section 14(h)(1) of the settlement act and its implementation, the historic and cemetery sites project has had many merits. Chief among them is the vast oral-history collection, which, among other things, is a fairly comprehensive record of the interethnic communication at the heart of this massive federal project, errors and all. The value of this collection to the Native people of Alaska will surely increase with time. Several of the elders quoted in this essay have passed away. Those of us who remain have much to gain from the memories of their lives, the examples they set, and the words they left behind.

Finally, I would not have been able to write this essay if I had not also been guilty of the ignorance and naïveté I discuss in it. Rather than find fault and blame others, I choose to accept my own actions and experience, judge only myself, and be thankful for the patient (and impatient) teachers and lessons that have helped me along the way.

I will close with a long excerpt from a letter written by Marie Meade, a teacher, artist, and friend who has worked as an interpreter, translator, and cultural consultant for both the Bureau of Indian Affairs and the Alaska Native Language Center on Yup'ik oral history for ANCSA 14(h)(1) since 1988. The letter was originally addressed to project lead archaeologist Dale Slaughter and submitted as an editorial to the *Tundra Drums* following field investigations in the Yukon-Kuskokwim Delta area in 1988. It illustrates the value of pursuing this important preservation work in the face of large and small obstacles, some of which have been discussed in this article. Meade expresses feelings and values that those of us who have worked on the project, as members of another culture, cannot completely understand or share. Yet she adds a dimension which extends across cultures and contrasts to the starkness of mere physical description. Perhaps such experiences and values, as expressed by Meade, truly reflect the deeper meaning inherent in Native historical places and cemetery sites and emphasize the importance of oral documentation.

> Throughout the summer I accompanied your staff to several Kuskokwim villages on occasion. We met with elders in groups and on an individual basis studying maps and marking sites and identifying place names for many, many lakes and rivers,

landmarks and sacred places.... It gave me an insight and more appreciation for my elders' knowledge and wisdom as I listened to them talk about the land and water. The land that sustained their lives both physically and spiritually. It was refreshing and enlightening for me to become aware and to be provided a reminder of the real connection they have with the land and water as they remembered their past experiences. The spirit was still there and alive. They talked of the land and water with much respect as though they were referring to another human being. We also took some elders flying in the helicopter in locating sites that were identified on the map. I especially will not forget the thrill and joy of my uncle Nickolai Berlin when we took him to his birthplace. It was wonderful to watch as he spoke of his first years of life on that land. I sensed that spark as he traveled back in time and remembered. I will not forget the beautiful words of gratification he expressed as we departed the land.

The time I had with the elders listening to their life experiences and listening to the stories and legends that relate to the land we studied was valuable teaching for me. Sometimes it was overbearing when I think of all the information entering into my head. But the tape recorder was there, fortunately. As they told their stories, they shared with eagerness and willingness. I sensed their love, compassion and longing to pass on their valuable lessons, teachings, stories and songs they learned from their elders. I felt their pain in losing the connection they have with many of the old ways they once knew and lived. I also was very grateful for the opportunity to be there and for them to pass on their knowledge to me. (Meade 1988)

Notes

1. Thirteen regional corporations were created as a result of the passage of ANCSA. One of these corporations, known as the Thirteenth Corporation, represents Alaska Natives residing outside of the state. This corporation was not eligible to make site selections. Of the remaining twelve corporations, only Arctic Slope Regional Corporation chose not to make any selections. See the map on p. 78.
2. The Calista region encompasses over fifty-six thousand square miles in southwestern Alaska. The majority of the region is made up of the

large coastal floodplain delta created by the Yukon and Kuskokwim rivers. Nelson and Nunivak islands in the nearby offshore waters of the delta are included. Bethel, a town with a resident population in 1990 of about 4,700 (of which 3,000 or 64 percent are reported to be Yupiit), is the governmental and commercial center of the Yukon-Kuskokwim Delta. The reported population in 1990 for the entire Calista region is 19,447, of which 16,775 or 86.3 percent are Natives (Calista Corporation 1991).

3. In her essay, "The Yupiit Nation: Eskimo Law and Order," anthropologist Ann Fienup-Riordan rebukes the commonly reported belief (which Paul John also refers to) that Eskimo peoples traditionally had no formal laws or system of governance. Fienup-Riordan was repeatedly informed by Yup'ik elders that they did have laws, and the most important means of conveying these laws was through speech. She states that "what governed the group must be continually restated." Elders who were especially outspoken about the rules for living were highly regarded as leaders. The written record (on Yup'ik governance) compiled by Fienup-Riordan and presented to Yup'ik elders was criticized by them because it "did not contain enough information on the aspect of Yup'ik governance that they considered most important—its emphasis on speaking out" (1990: 96).

4. This is a complex topic with a convoluted history. The law clearly stated that the National Park Service was to act as a consultant to the Bureau of Indian Affairs on each site investigated. However, exactly what this involvement entailed was open to question. Differences in interpretation of the rules and regulations by the two agencies created an aura of distrust which carried over into the field and affected fieldwork. For more details on this professional relationship, its development, and the eventual withdrawal from the project by AHP/CPSU, consult Pratt and Slaughter (1989) and Pratt (1992).

5. Pratt (1992) makes the point that the Bureau of Indian Affairs ANCSA management viewed the project as "simply one part of a massive land transfer process (that is, a real estate exercise)" (76). With this conviction, they did not seem particularly concerned with the fact that documentation of sites involved sensitive issues within Native villages as well as complicated interethnic communication which warranted special consideration.

6. In this case, the third agency was the U.S. Fish and Wildlife Service, which has management responsibilities for federal lands in the Yukon-Kuskokwim Delta.

7. This is true for women as well.

8. Due to the circumstances of project research, Yup'ik elders appeared to be understanding and tolerant of non-Natives' continual questioning. Once, after working closely with a young interpreter who had written Yup'ik translations of my questions in preparation for an interview, I

suggested that he might be able to conduct it without me. He assured me that it would not be proper. This man was very interested in the history and traditional tales told by the elders, and he stated that although he was not allowed to ask the questions, it was acceptable for him to translate. He also said that he was grateful that we were there to ask the questions. Despite outside influences such as television and schools, which are changing the ways in which information is transmitted among Yup'ik elders and youth, the interpreter's respect for the elder compelled him to observe the questioning ethic. Later, when I was reviewing transcripts, I saw that my presence allowed him to ask questions by repeatedly prefacing them with phrases like "this one here would like to know" and "now he is curious about...."

9.   Further examples of some of these same points are found in "Recommendations for Improved Interethnic Communication" in *Interethnic Communication* (Scollon and Scollon 1980: 43–45).

10. A more in-depth analysis relating specifically to indirect language, self-reference, and the power of words among Yupiit is presented in Morrow (1990).

References

Akelerea, Dan. 1981. Taped interview. Bureau of Indian Affairs ANCSA Office, Anchorage, Alaska.

Alexie, Oscar, and Helen Morris, eds. 1985. The *Elders' Conference 1984*. Bethel, Alaska: Orutsararmiut Native Council and Kuskokwim Community College.

Andrew, Wassillie, and John Andrew. 1988. Taped interview. Bureau of Indian Affairs ANCSA Office, Anchorage, Alaska.

Burch, Ernest S., Jr. 1981. "Studies of Native History As a Contribution to Alaska's Future." Special lecture presented to the thirty-second Alaska Science Conference, Fairbanks, Alaska, Aug. 25, 1981.

Bureau of Indian Affairs ANCSA Office. n.d. *Cemetery Sites and Historical Places*. Anchorage, Alaska.

Calista Corporation, and Natural Resources Department. 1989. *The Calista Region: A Gentle People, A Harsh Life*. Anchorage, Alaska.

Egoak, Lott. 1988. Taped interview. Bureau of Indian Affairs ANCSA Office, Anchorage, Alaska.

Fienup-Riordan, Ann. 1983. "The Past As Prologue: Regional Groupings and the Cultural Significance of Harvest Disruption on the Yukon-Kuskokwim Delta." Paper presented at the tenth annual meeting of the Alaska Anthropological Association, Anchorage, Alaska, March 12, 1983.

Fienup-Riordan, Ann. 1984. "Regional Groups in the Yukon-Kuskokwim

Delta." Paper presented at the eleventh annual meeting of the Alaska Anthropological Association, Fairbanks, Alaska.

Fienup-Riordan, Ann. 1988. "A Problem of Translation: Animals As Infinitely Renewable or Finite Resource?" Paper presented at the fifteenth annual meeting of the Alaska Anthropological Association, Fairbanks, Alaska, March 26, 1988.

_____. 1990. *Eskimo Essays: Yupik Lives and How We See Them.* New Brunswick, N.J.: Rutgers University Press.

John, Paul. 1984. Taped interview. Bureau of Indian Affairs ANCSA Office, Anchorage, Alaska.

Martz, Cecilia. 1988. "Yup'ik Teacher Gives Clues to Communicating." *Tundra Drums,* 30 June (Bethel, Alaska).

Meade, Marie. 1988. "Grasp, Hold on to Culture." *Tundra Drums,* 20 October (Bethel, Alaska).

Morrow, Phyllis. 1990. "Symbolic Actions, Indirect Expressions: Limits to Interpretations of Yupik Society." *Etudes/Inuit/Studies* 14(1–2): 141–58.

Morrow, Phyllis, and Chase Hensel. 1992. "Hidden Dissensions: Minority-Majority Relationships and the Use of Contested Terminology." *Arctic Anthropology* 29(1): 38–53.

Moses, George. 1988. Taped interview. Bureau of Indian Affairs ANCSA Office, Anchorage, Alaska.

Phillip, Joshua. 1988. Taped interview. Bureau of Indian Affairs ANCSA Office, Anchorage, Alaska.

Polty, Noel. 1982. Taped interview. Bureau of Indian Affairs ANCSA Office, Anchorage, Alaska.

Pratt, Kenneth L. 1984. "Yukon-Kuskokwim Eskimos, Western Alaska: Inconsistencies in Group Identification." Master's thesis, Western Washington University, Bellingham.

_____. 1992. "Documenting Alaska Native Cultural History: ANCSA and the Role of the Bureau of Indian Affairs." *Arctic Research of the United States* 6: 74–77.

Pratt, Kenneth L., and Dale C. Slaughter. 1989. "Archeological Research and the ANCSA 14(h)(1) Program." Paper presented at the sixteenth annual meeting of the Alaska Anthropological Association, Anchorage, Alaska, March 3, 1989.

Scollon, Ronald, and Suzanne B. K. Scollon. 1980. *Interethnic Communication.* Fairbanks: Alaska Native Language Center, University of Alaska Fairbanks.

Tainter, Joseph A., and G. John Lucas. 1983. "Epistemology of the Significance Concept." *American Antiquity* 48(4): 709.

United States. 1994. "Alaska Native Selections." Title 43 Code of Federal Regulations, Part 2650, Subpart 2653.0–5

Utley, Robert M. 1980. Letter to Wendy Arundale, Cooperative Park Studies Unit, National Park Service, Fairbanks, Alaska, 30 October.

A Bright Light Ahead of Us
Belle Deacon's Stories in English and Deg Hit'an

James Ruppert

James Ruppert leads us to consider the encounter between tradition bearer and audience in a rather different (bright) light than the preceding two authors. He suggests that the communication between teller and audience begins long before the two actually meet. Scholars, for example, bring standards of authenticity to their "listening" so that they may simply not hear some tellings. Given a choice between a Native language telling and one in English, they often assume that the former is richer and more genuine and simply discount the English telling as a secondary artifact.

By comparing Belle Deacon's stories as told in English with the translations of her Deg Hit'an tellings, Ruppert very effectively demonstrates that the English renditions are worth hearing. For one thing, they evidence the teller's consciousness of her anticipated audience, what Ruppert terms the "implied listener." The telling, Ruppert suggests, is shaped by the implied listener prior to, and in addition to, the actual audience at a given performance.

Ironically, by preferring the Native-language telling, the scholar denies his or her own listening experience as a non-Native. The scholar's presence, too, implies a wider non-Native audience to whom the teller addresses her stories. While we want to understand how Belle Deacon thinks about and consequently addresses a community of Deg Hit'an speakers, it is equally important to hear what she wants to tell a monolingual English audience.

Are the stories, then, different? Belle Deacon insists that they are all "part of the same thing." Ruppert explores what she may mean by this, using Toelken's concept of "culturally moral subjects" (1981). Ultimately, Ruppert's essay suggests that using a performance approach may prevent us from considering the imagined construction prior to any given performance. Most importantly, he reminds us that we should listen to whatever a storyteller tells.

Belle Deacon at work making baskets. Photo by Rose Atuk Fosdick, courtesy of the Institute of Alaska Native Arts, Inc.

They said this about the way my stories go.
In the time of long ago [they would tell us this]:
"If you don't fall asleep, you can obtain the old wisdom" that was
    being told to us when I was a child.
"Even if you are sleepy, you should try to stay awake.
And you shouldn't fidget.
You should just think about everything.
Then you'll get the old wisdom that was told to us in the past."
After we'd thought about it a little,
"Tell it to us," they would say to us.
When we start to tell it, [a story] is like a bright light ahead of us,
    just as though it were written as we speak.
                                    —Belle Deacon (1987: 3)

So begins the collection of stories by noted artist and storyteller
Belle Deacon, *Engithidong Xugixudhoy: Their Stories of Long Ago* (1987).
Eight examples of her movement toward the bright light are transcribed into Deg Hit'an (Ingalik), with an English translation facing
the Native-language text. However, one of the unique things about
the volume is that versions told in English follow five of the tales. I
would like to open with a question: How does the English telling of
a Native tale by a Native-speaking storyteller differ from the original
version and its translation. Furthermore, I would like to suggest that
the English version may actually add to our understanding of the
way the tale functions as well as our appreciation of the creativity of
the storyteller.

First, I should acknowledge that my comments will be based on
the English translation of the Deg Hit'an. That is obviously a tenuous
position from which to start, but let me add two points that give me
hope that there may be some value in my discussion. First, I do not
intend to discuss the linguistic conventions of Deg Hit'an storytelling.
I would like to deal with macro questions of value and meaning in the
stories with a full understanding that much contemporary discussion
has tied meaning to form and context. Second, the unquestionable
expertise of James Kari and the close involvement of Belle Deacon in
these translations may lend reliability not inherent in others. As an
accomplished artist in several fields, Deacon is intent on representing
Deg Hit'an cultural material to a non-Native world.

Some scholars may feel that English tellings of Native tales are inferior in numerous ways. As all recording and transcription removes us
from actual performance, storytelling in English modifies the texture

of the Native telling. Often the assumption has been that the English version is something like a synopsis of the tale, since there are no Native linguistic contextualization cues, no audience interaction (except for Kari and Deacon's husband). I'm not sure this is the case with Belle Deacon's English stories.

Clearly reading the English tellings against the translations reveals that many elements have been eliminated. There seem to be no examples of indirect address, but these are not frequent in Belle Deacon's stories anyway. We lose the influence on the listener of what has been called "high language," with its archaic words and elaborate metaphor, eliminating part of the frame and form that establish the performance of the story. In at least one English telling, Deacon condenses a section dealing with instructions (1987: 38). The most obvious change is that she drops sections of the stories, especially ones concerning travel (39, 59, 79). Perhaps these sections are keyed into words in specific formulas in Deg Hit'an. Once those words are not there, the mnemonic devices that hold the telling together are undermined, and sections drop out.

There are a few instances in the five stories where Deacon seems to delete references to a mystical sense of knowing about people's actions, as if censoring information about shamanistic activity (60). She even drops one reference to urine (40). These omissions may be due to her sense of what is appropriate to talk about in English. As an accomplished storyteller, she naturally assesses the English-speaking audience's interpretative role. Since she realizes that the target English audience is not present, she must create an imagined one. In literary studies, Wolfgang Iser (1978), following Wayne Booth (1961), has called this conception "the implied reader." I would alter that to suggest that Deacon creates an implied listener. Thus she can project the listener's role, his or her interpretive standpoint, onto the telling of the story. This is, of course, also true of her telling of the story in Deg Hit'an and may be characteristic of all collected and recorded narratives. The implied listener's contribution to meaning is embedded in the narrative before the actual listener's collaborative contribution and is modified by the storyteller's interpretation in performance.

In other ways, the English telling continues some significant elements of her art but in a less comprehensive manner. We lose some of her emphasis on sensory detail, but much remains. There is less dialogue in the English version, though it is still an important part of the telling. Her provocative use of questions posed to the listener, both in the voice of characters and her own voice as storyteller, is retained, but there are fewer instances of it. Questions still form a significant stylistic element designed to create audience participation as well as introduce a level of interpretation, in Tedlock's sense of the word (1983). While the English tellings are dynamic, there appears to be less dramatic tension between the characters. There is significant switching from past to present tense as Deacon tries to find an English analog for the Athabaskan verb's ability to create the feel of a continuing past in the stories.

While many formal and stylistic elements carry over into English, Deacon seems also to be searching for new contextualization clues. In the English version, she seems more likely to mention contemporary items like marbles and chain saws that would be difficult to explain in Deg Hit'an. As is to be expected, she also seems more inclined to explain the cultural significance of actions. At one point, she interrupts the telling with a comment about her lack of knowledge about a part in the story. This list of differences ought to be enough to make problematic any analysis that wishes to point out the value of an English-language telling. Yet there may be something we can learn from these English versions.

Perhaps my position will become clearer if we look at a story told in Deg Hit'an and translated into English as "The Old Woman Who Lived Alone." In it, an old woman living alone ingeniously kills a bear who comes into her house. As she puts up the meat, Raven unexpectedly comes to stay with her. She feeds him and then wants him to leave, but of course Raven doesn't go. He stays, pretending to work, all the while stealing her food. Eventually, as part of a plan to get rid of him, she offers to clean his head and stabs him in the ear with her awl. She throws him over the riverbank onto the ice. He regenerates the next day, and she does the same thing again, only the second time she cuts off his claws and pushes him into the water hole and under the ice. Soon after this, two of Raven's wives arrive with their children. When one child finds Raven's claw, they attack her, and the old woman kills the wives and kids by drowning them in the water hole. Then she lives for a while without food until she goes out into the woods and hangs herself.

The cultural significance in the story seems to revolve around the main character's ingenuity and self-sufficiency in a situation that would normally offer no hope for an old woman without family and a hunter. Her good fortune in acquiring a great cache of meat is mixed with the misfortune of attracting a gluttonous raven, as well as the ambiguity of killing a bear and eating its meat.[1] The laws of hospitality are pushed too far until she must kill her guest. This provokes retribution by relatives whom she must also kill.

The suicide at the end is presented as an act of despair, since she is starving with no hope of reprieve. Deacon describes her situation, "Then her food ran out and she was without [food] for a long time / And then she went out into the woods and hanged herself. / That is all" (1987: 103). Suicide in traditional Deg Hit'an culture was highly unusual and a sign of insanity, though references to leaving old people to die are not unheard of (Osgood 1958: 148). While the ending might be intended as surprising, it seems to focus the implied listener on the complex of "culturally moral subjects," as Toelken (1981) calls them: on the old woman's too literal and too extensive compliance with the expectations of hospitality to the point where she exhausts even her normally meager food supply. It is only then that she acts to kill Raven. Her final suicide emphasizes the mental and personal results of such improper actions.

The English telling runs pretty much the same until the end, when the old woman laments that people have led her into living the wrong way. She has no food and says, "I don't want to live for what I done." Deacon says she goes into the woods and that she doesn't know what happens to the woman. At first glance, we might suspect this reflects a hesitancy to refer to an action like suicide that is forbidden by contemporary religious attitudes as well as an acknowledgment of the belief that one should be remorseful for killing. The ending could then be seen as a result of the storyteller's accommodation to the values of an implied English listener.

As a new mental representation of the same story, the storyteller's interpretive act fixes the position of the implied listener within a series of previously existing cultural contexts. This narrative, then, provides a new perspective on the dynamic totality of meaning which the story in all its versions generates. When the old woman kills Raven, his wives, and his children, she puts herself into the position of "someone who always kills people" and thus is ready to be killed herself, as often happens in oral narratives of western Alaska. As a killer of other beings, she has no place in the contemporary world, which must be rid of cannibals and other deadly obstacles to harmonious living. As the murderer of a powerful shaman, it is likely she will also die. Osgood has noted the Ingalik fear of those who seek out seclusion (1959: 67), but the old woman also takes on a male hunter's role to kill the bear. Even more seriously, she kills the powerful trickster/transformer Raven, who is responsible for much of the shape of the world. All of these actions bring about her separation from the normal human community. Indeed, as Osgood has observed, for the Ingalik, killing any woman is evil, even if the women are Raven's wives. And the murder of a shaman will cause the death of the killer (100).[2]

Her remorse and suggested suicide in the English version shift the focus from a more social consideration of mores such as hospitality to a deeper spiritual probing of an individual's response to unexpected bounty of a questionable nature. Such good fortune may lead to violence, as one must establish an appropriate relationship with a powerful spirit being which sometimes follows in its wake. This new interpretation proceeds from no change in audience except the implied listener. Could the story now be consciously or unconsciously directed to a spiritless society intent on gaining material prosperity at all costs? Or is the total sum of culturally moral subjects accessible to the storyteller from any one version of the story?

Now if we think that this version may help the English reader appreciate the story, the question still remains whether a Deg Hit'an listener would have any real appreciation of this other dimension or if the English telling really gives both audiences something additional. I'd like to delay my answer to that question until we've looked at two more stories.

In the story translated as "The Man and Wife," a couple work tirelessly every day and accumulate all the riches they need. The wife makes the hunter Indian ice cream every day, until one time when she doesn't feel well and decides not to make it. The hunter comes home and insists. She goes out to make the ice cream and disappears. The hunter laments her loss and wastes away until Raven comes and takes pity on him. He tells the hunter that a powerful giant from the world below has kidnaped his wife. Raven and the hunter make a giant fish out of a log and bring it to life. The man travels in the fish and brings the wife back. Raven instructs them on how to burn food and clothes to thank him and then leaves the two happy and reunited.

In the Deg Hit'an version translated into English, Deacon makes much of the dramatic interrelationship between the husband and wife. A conflict is developed between the husband's drive to hunt every day and the wife's desire to have him stay home sometimes. Deacon comments that he treats her like a doll, placing her on his knee when he returns. The husband's grief and guilt are emphasized as well as the happy reunion, and the latter is celebrated by the woman making Indian ice cream for the man and Raven. The culturally moral

subjects include the value of industriousness versus personal satisfaction, roles of men and women, the emotions of grief and remorse,
the willingness of the spirit world to help those who cry piteously,
and the establishment of a vehicle for communication with the spirit
world.

In the English version, Deacon adds some generalizations about
the woman and her accumulation of wealth. She says:

> I don't know for what, they just get so much ahead. Ahead to
> eat, you know. And that way they just have e——verything. And
> they kind of are well-to-do. And they have everything [that] they
> think of or know, 'cause this woman is just too smart, and she do
> too much work, you know. But her husband don't know it; her
> husband don't know that she's making so many things. (1987: 34)

Then Deacon adds a new detail not in the translated version: "Well,
when he wear out his clothes, she make another for him and they don't
use old clothes, mostly new things, because they have too many" (34).
She later observes that the giant takes the woman because she is "the
most beautiful and most handy worker" (36), and that the hunter so
enjoyed Raven's company that he didn't think about his wife. These
new details shift the focus from a discussion about social roles of men
and women and the creation of ritual connections to the spirit world
toward a more abstract discourse on the accumulation of wealth.

This shift becomes even more apparent when the English telling
emphasizes Raven's knowledge about the couple's extensively packed cache. The hunter appears not to know what the wife has placed
in the cache. In this telling, the wife also feels that there is a spiritual
force that is influencing her to become sick; perhaps she has done
wrong and something will now happen to her. Also when the couple
are reunited, wealth again comes to the foreground. They want to pay
Raven as if he were a mortal shaman. He refuses, emphasizing his
inability to breathe in this world and his need to return to the spirit
world. He asks them to burn the food and clothing for him on a fire.
The amassing of wealth has drawn the notice of the evil giant (as such
an accumulation drew Raven's attention in the earlier story), and it
is only by the dissipation of the excess wealth through the creation of
the fish, the visit of Raven, and the burning of the gifts for the spirit
world that a proper balance can be restored. Fortunately the couple
also has a spirit ally in Raven so that they can succeed.[3] The English language version gives Deacon the opportunity to reemphasize

meanings existing in the tale as an interpretive response to an implied listener.

The last story I want to talk about is one translated as "Polar Bear" (see the appendix). In it, a successful hunter is married to a jealous, strong woman who beats him up constantly. A grandmother and granddaughter live at the edge of the village, subsisting on the charity of the jealous wife. One day the hunter returns from an especially successful hunt. He is the object of much admiration by the village, and the jealous wife beats him up in front of everyone. Later in the *kashim* (community house), he decides to leave the village for good early the next morning. He paddles for three days across the water and reaches land. Meanwhile, the granddaughter, who has been in puberty seclusion, has gone out early and, contrary to instructions, has looked up and out to sea and glimpsed the hunter as he was leaving. She doesn't tell anyone. The jealous wife finds her husband gone and literally tears the village apart. She comes to the grandmother and threatens to kill them unless they tell her what the village has done to hide her husband. The girl reveals what she has seen. Over the objections of the community, which asserts the traditional taboo against a "corner girl" getting into a canoe,[4] the wife sets out after the husband, taking the girl with her.

Meanwhile, the husband has found an area rich in game, and another woman has invited him to stay with her. The new wife's spirit power lets her know that the jealous wife is coming. As the new wife and the jealous wife fight, the latter is torn to pieces. The hunter and his new wife prepare to burn the jealous wife's body and belongings. They find the corner girl and ask her to stay with them. They live happily until the hunter wakes one morning with his voice gone and the knowledge that they must return to the village. The new wife hesitates to go, but the hunter insists. She obeys but wants to use her own special paddle. He wants to use his. They start out over the water using his paddle, and a storm overpowers them. They are knocked into the water, and when they rise to the surface, the hunter and the new wife have been transformed into polar bears and the corner girl into a mermaid.

In the translation, Deacon elaborates on the details of the interaction between the woman and the village. Her domination of her husband is the first step in her mastery of the village. The village's and the husband's lack of control of the woman, her violence in wrecking the village, and her attack on the new wife are given detailed treatment, as well as the way she once again violates the community's traditional order when she makes the corner girl get in the canoe. As the woman vents her destructive jealousy, she disrupts personal, social, and spiritual values. All eyes are on her, and our pity is with the husband.

The English telling, on the other hand, emphasizes the hunter's experience of domination and seclusion. Deacon adds the detail that the jealous wife uses her husband's meat to win friends, while he sits alone at a party in the *kashim*. Deacon notes that he "had to look at his feet. Never look around nowhere because he's scared of her, because she's too powerful" (1987: 58). In other words, he must act exactly like a corner girl in puberty seclusion.

At the end of the English version, Deacon adds the detail that the new wife dresses up and looks beautiful. Deacon strongly emphasizes the wife's reluctance to go on the trip. She gives the new wife many additional lines of dialogue, explaining that she will acquiesce to taking the trip across the sea if it is her husband's will. The new wife explicitly predicts their death if the husband insists on using his paddle, but in the end, she goes along with his wishes. Foregrounded is the irony of the husband, who had no power to exert his will previously, now insisting on a tragic course. The new detail about the way the husband would walk around previously with his eyes downcast ties him explicitly to the girl in puberty seclusion.[5] His act of abandonment and the girl's offense are linked in such a way as to create serious doubt about the positive nature of his actions, especially in fleeing from his duty to restrain his wife. This English telling explores his choices and his failure to be a male role model with no little irony about when a husband should exercise his will and when he should listen to his wife. It appears that in this version of the story, the culturally moral subjects surrounding *his* actions are brought into focus.

It seems clear to me that the English tellings allow Deacon to explore new interpretations and representations of the narrative. However, without the influence of situational differences and audience interaction, we can hypothesize the existence of an implied listener who presages a performance interaction with an actual audience. While the performance elements of narrative art may be important, perhaps they have been overemphasized; they may not tell us as much about Deacon's art as we think. I am still left with the question of why an interpretation that emphasizes the male role should be emphasized for an English-speaking audience. Is there something more than just interpretation working here? Something more essential to the story?

When I asked Deacon about changes that might appear in telling a story to different audiences, she insisted that the stories are always told the same way every time, saying, "No, it's the same always; you tell the story from the beginning and go through to the end; nothing is added." I asked her about changes when she told her stories in English, and she replied, "No, it's the same story." I pushed on, asserting, "But you use different words; some characters say different things." A little exasperated, she concluded, "Yeah, but they're all part of the same thing."[6]

It seems that for Deacon it is the story that is important, not the audience, the context, or the language. Perhaps she perceives some level of deep structure that cannot be compromised in the telling so that various interpretations are latent. Indeed, much of the dramatic action and thematic interplay is the same in all the versions of the story. But the storyteller's interpretation seems to come from an already-existing dynamic of meaning embedded in the various culturally moral subjects in the narrative and only partly responds to an implied listener's influence. This dynamic is what I call the *field of meaning* which an oral narrative evokes. Deacon's "old wisdom" resides not in any one conclusion about the meaning or moral of a story nor in any one interpretation that she might give for any telling. The existence of an implied listener may evoke a particular rendition, but that possibility only exists because the narrative itself possesses a dynamic interaction of meanings that lies deeper than formal narrative structures. Each telling is a walk through that field. The same landmarks are there though we take new paths and linger at different spots on various days.

The English telling is still the same story, and it can reveal the old wisdom as it enters the arena of meaning in that story. It is clear to me that serious attention to the English versions can help the non-Deg Hit'an come to a more complete understanding of the fields of meaning in each tale. Ultimately, I cannot show that it will improve the appreciation of a bilingual Deg Hit'an audience, but as I think about the way utterance excites the dynamics of cultural value and artistic insight, it seems to me that each telling of a story foregrounds and advances one locus of the many ongoing cultural conversations from which understanding emerges. As such, each telling, even an English one, opens the possibility of a new excitement of meaning. I hope that folklorists, anthropologists, linguists, and other collectors of oral material will not automatically discount English tellings of Native tales and that when the opportunity presents itself, these will be found and preserved. Belle Deacon's job is to tell the story, to follow that bright shining light until it is reached. Our job is to listen to the story over and over in as many versions as possible until we grasp some of the old wisdom.

Notes

1.   Since she is past the age of menstruation, the taboo against eating bear meat no longer applies, but a certain amount of ambivalence remains. See Osgood (1959: 136).

2.   Raven's actions and functions are parallel to those of shamans in other Deg Hit'an stories and society generally. The killing of a raven is taboo (Osgood 1958: 136). It is a positive action to kill an evil shaman, but it is probable that the shaman's spirit will destroy the killer (149). Traditionally, the body of a shaman was cut up because otherwise both the body of the shaman and that of the killer would swell up (150).

3.   This emphasis on the ambivalence about accumulation of wealth is also apparent in a videotaped English version Deacon told at the State Museum in Anchorage, where she was demonstrating her craft. In this tape, she expands on the beginning of the story by elaborately describing the woman's various sewing accomplishments. Osgood also notes some cultural ambivalence about the female accumulation of wealth (1959: 69). If we believe with Melville Jacobs that the tales reveal areas of social tension, then we can see female material accumulation as an ambivalent social act, one capable of attracting notice by a spirit being (1959: 2, 4, 12).

4.   Kari notes that the term *corner girl* refers to a menstruating woman. It comes from the practice of sequestering these women in corners of houses.

5.   Osgood notes that it was considered shameful for a man to act like a woman (1959: 67). In discussing the Yup'ik, Fienup-Riordan also notes that a girl's violation of puberty seclusion taboos may result in destruction of the spirits of animals. When the woman breaks the taboo, she collapses the distinction between the animal and the human world. The place where the man is when the violation occurs determines where he will forever reside (1983: 216). The hunter in the story is out to sea when the violation occurs. He and the corner girl will remain in the sea world as opposed to the village one. VanStone also notes that such an act might cause a hunter to lose his skill (1979: 38).

6.   Deacon's comments are from a personal conversation with the author on March 23, 1992, in Fairbanks, Alaska.

References

Booth, Wayne. 1961. *The Rhetoric of Fiction*. Chicago: University of Chicago Press.

Deacon, Belle. 1987. *Engithidong Xugixudhoy: Their Stories of Long Ago*. Edited by James Kari, and translated by Belle Deacon and James Kari. Fairbanks: Alaska Native Language Center and Iditarod Area School District.

Fienup-Riordan, Ann. 1983. *The Nelson Island Eskimo: Social Structure and Ritual Distribution*. Anchorage: Alaska Pacific University Press.

Iser, Wolfgang. 1978. *The Act of Reading*. Baltimore: Johns Hopkins University.

Jacobs, Melville. 1989. *The Content and Style of American Oral Literature: Clackmas Chinook Myths and Tales*. Chicago: University of Chicago Press.

Osgood, Cornelius. 1958. *Ingalik Social Culture*. New Haven: Yale University Publications in Anthropology.

———. 1959. *Ingalik Mental Culture*. New Haven: Yale University Publications in Anthropology.

Tedlock, Dennis. 1983. *The Spoken Word and the Work of Interpretation*. Philadelphia: University of Pennsylvania Press.

Toelken, J. Barre, and Tacheeni Scott. 1981. "Poetic Retranslation and the 'Pretty Languages' of Yellowman." In *Traditional Literatures of the American Indian: Texts and Interpretations*. edited by Karl Kroeber, 65–116. Lincoln: University of Nebraska Press.

VanStone, James. 1979. *Ingalik Contact Ecology: An Ethnohistory of the Lower-Middle Yukon 1790–1935*. Chicago: Field Museum of Natural History.

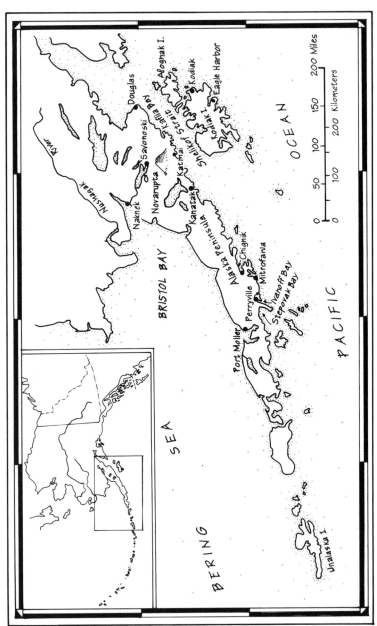

The Alaska Peninsula. Map by Robert Drozda.

PART III

REMEMBERING

Perryville with Chiachi Island across the channel, September 1992. Photo by Lisa Hutchinson Scarbrough, Alaska Department of Fish and Game.

The Days of Yore
Alutiiq Mythical Time

Patricia H. Partnow

Historians and cultural anthropologists have gathered increasing evidence that we all remember the past in ways that reflect present understandings of ourselves. This in no way discounts the value of oral history, which encodes specific and valuable historical and cultural details (as Robert Drozda, for example, documented in his interviews on Yup'ik historical and cemetery sites). Rather, it suggests that beyond the facts of oral history lies a symbolic dimension: history as self-definition.

In this exciting essay, Patricia Partnow captures a moment when the Alutiiq residents of Perryville began a process of ethnic self-definition that continues today. The cataclysmic eruption of Novarupta Volcano in 1912 forced the evacuation of Katmai and became a watershed in the lives of the survivors, who ultimately established the current village of Perryville. In the oral tradition of their descendants, the eruption sharply divides traditional from modern times, imbuing the past with Edenlike qualities, giving the eruption the symbolic force of an atomic explosion, and turning history into oral tradition. In the structural aftermath of Novarupta, the earlier Alutiiq distinction between two folklore genres collapsed, and Russian Orthodox symbols and folklore motifs blended with Eskimo ones. The synthesis provides a coherent basis for Perryville people to define themselves today.

As scholars of oral tradition, we are also at a watershed, contemplating the age-old question of how tradition can be at the same time conservative and ever-changing. Clearly, transmission of oral tradition requires a prodigiously accurate memory and a simultaneous contemporary act of re-creation. As we shift our understanding from the memorized to the rememberer, we no longer see tradition as a weight to be carried but as a set of ideas to be renewed and revitalized. When our words return, we make them ours indeed.

Introduction

On June 6, 1912, Novarupta Volcano in southwestern Alaska exploded in one of the largest eruptions in the history of the world. Ash and pumice buried the Alaska Peninsula villages of Katmai and Douglas and the seasonally operated fish-processing camp at Kaflia Bay and fell two feet deep on the city of Kodiak, 115 miles away. The explosion spawned continuous thunder and lightning storms and resulted in total darkness for more than forty-eight hours. Its roar was heard as far away as Juneau, 750 miles distant (Martin 1913: 131). This event was the cause of widespread displacement of the Alutiiq (Pacific Eskimo) population of the Alaska Peninsula. Katmai and Douglas villagers were rescued by Revenue Cutter Service ships and transported to a location far to the southwest, where they established the new village of Perryville.

The eruption became a nationwide media event, which resulted in the formation of Katmai National Monument. Many people, Native and non-Native, locals and visitors, recorded their experiences during those few days in the summer of 1912. Their accounts give a valuable picture of life on the Alaska Peninsula at the time. They also illustrate the process by which a witnessed event becomes part of oral tradition and exemplify the manipulation of symbols and history in ethnic self-definition.

In this essay, I explore the symbols attached to the Katmai story as contemporary Perryvillers tell it and consider the way their narratives cast the disaster in a mythic light. I also discuss three stories recorded in 1992 which describe life in Katmai before the eruption. These narratives illustrate the way that modern Alutiiq definitions of both folklore and history derive from the eruption.

Sources for the Katmai Eruption Story

Eyewitness Accounts

When I first visited Perryville in September 1990, I explained that I was interested in hearing "old stories and history." My hosts responded with brief descriptions of the Katmai disaster and Perryville's founding. They gave me copies of written accounts of the eruption by eyewitnesses Father Harry Kaiakokonok (a Russian Orthodox priest) and George Kosbruk. Kaiakokonok had been a five-year-old and Kosbruk a young man of eighteen at the time of the eruption. Both had lived all of their adult lives in Perryville.

In addition to publishing an account of the eruption in a 1956 issue of the Sitka Public Health Service newsletter, *Island Breezes* (Kaiakokonok 1956),[1] Kaiakokonok recorded two interviews in 1975 with National Park Service rangers (1975a, 1975b). These interviews are a mixture of firsthand memory and secondhand report. Kaiakokonok's memories contribute a child's perspective of playfulness and fearlessness but are limited by ignorance of who made decisions or the precise chronology of events, details which were filled in later. In describing events that occurred outside his own experience, Kaiakokonok was careful to differentiate what he knew firsthand from what he had been told. An obligatory postbase in his native Alutiiq language, *-uma*, indicates when the speaker did not personally see the events he describes but believes them to be true. Although Kaiakokonok's testimonies are in English, he uses the translation of this postbase, "must have been," to indicate the same careful attitude toward weighing evidence in his second language. A final account, represented as a verbatim rendering by Kaiakokonok to former Perryville resident Tom Jessee, is included in a letter Jessee wrote in 1961, although how the author obtained or recorded the story is not indicated.

George Kosbruk was also interviewed and recorded twice by National Park Service employees (1975a, 1975b). These testimonies reveal the perspective of an eighteen-year-old man who was fully aware of the danger the eruption posed but are incomplete because of Kosbruk's difficulty with English. A more reliable source is an unpublished translation of a performance recorded at an elders' conference in Dillingham in the late 1970s by linguist Jeff Leer of the University of Alaska Fairbanks (Kosbruk n.d.). Kosbruk's fourth account (Kosbruk 1976) appeared as a printed interview in the 1976 edition of Kodiak High School's student publication *Elwani*. This narrative is the product of several editorial steps. First Kosbruk told the story in Alutiiq to Effie Shangin of Perryville, who translated and transcribed it in English. She then sent the written English version to her son, who was attending school in Kodiak, where it was again edited, this time for printing. A fifth account attributed to George Kosbruk is included (with the description by Father Harry) in Jessee's 1961 letter.

Aside from differences attributable to individual experience, the accounts by the two men are quite similar. Jessee explains that they had recounted the story many times through the years to younger

Perryvillers: "He [Kosbruk] usually supplied skeletal details which Harry fleshened and brought to life" (Jessee 1961).

Father Harry Kaiakokonok's first published testimony (1956) was written forty-four years after the eruption, and his and George Kosbruk's 1975 interviews were recorded more than a half century afterward. During the interval between occurrence and telling, an inevitable metamorphosis occurred. The narrative's structure came to conform to indigenous literary conventions, characters and plot elements took on symbolic meanings, and the stories were imbued with particular messages for contemporary audiences.[2]

Contemporary Oral Traditions

Younger Alutiiqs,[3] who had not lived through the eruption themselves, also told me parts of the Katmai story. Most of these accounts focus on the search for a new home after the rescue from the coast. They reinforce the connection of today's Perryvillers both to their history and the village's current location and coincidentally validate claims to the land around Perryville.

I was also told a unique story by a woman who called herself a "Russian Aleut."[4] She had grown up in the village of Chignik Bay but now lives in Kodiak. She maintained that soon after establishing their new village, the Perryvillers had gone to the top of a hill and tossed the entire supply of flour given them by the Revenue Cutter Service into the air, watching it fall like snow. A common motif in contact-era stories involves Natives treating European food in ignorant and inappropriate ways (see deLaguna 1972: 259; Goodwin 1986: 168; Eliza Jones, personal communication with the author, May 1980; McClellan 1970a: 121–28.). The Katmai version of the motif establishes ethnic distance between the teller, a Russian Aleut, and the subjects of the story, Alutiiq Natives. It also declares, incorrectly, that the founding of Perryville was the first real contact between the people of Katmai and Westerners, emphasizing discontinuity in local attitudes between pre- and post-Katmai life.

Written Documents

Written sources, both official and unofficial, also describe the disaster. These include wireless messages and annual reports of the United States Revenue Cutter Service (USRCS), whose ships were instrumental in the rescue and relocation of the peninsula Natives after the eruption. Other witnesses, further removed, provide varied perspectives. Inhabitants of Kodiak whose homes were buried in ash

(Chichenoff 1975; Ellenak and Ellenak 1976; Erskine 1962); residents of Afognak, where the refugees were taken after their rescue from the Alaska Peninsula (Harvey 1991); and geologists (Martin 1913) all left recorded and written accounts.

Life at the Time of the Eruption

In the spring of 1912, Alaska Peninsula Alutiiqs lived in a handful of small villages on the Bering Sea and Pacific coasts. Those most directly affected by the eruption lay along the northeastern Pacific coast—the two former Alaska Commercial Company posts of Douglas and Katmai, along with Cold (Puale) Bay,[5] Wrangel,[6] and Kanatak. A sixth village to the southwest, Mitrofania, was a Creole, or "Russian Aleut," community. Perryville, where about a hundred Alutiiqs now reside, did not exist before 1912. Its beaches and rivers served Mitrofania residents as summer fish camps.

By 1912, the population center on the Pacific side of the Alaska Peninsula had shifted from the fur-hunting post at Katmai south to the fishing town of Chignik, which was populated primarily by seasonal cannery workers but also by a handful of resident Alutiiqs (U.S. Census Bureau 1910). Other commercial activities along the coast were confined to Cold Bay, which had long had a small store visited by residents of Katmai and the inland village of Savonoski[7] (Kaiakokonok 1975a, 1975b), and Kaflia Bay, the site of a seasonal saltery and store, where Katmai and Douglas villagers camped during the summer.

Most Alutiiqs in these villages lived in semisubterranean sod-covered dwellings, commonly referred to as *barabaras*. There were three log houses at Kaflia Bay which were inhabited by families who had recently moved there from Katmai and Douglas. Katmai residents hunted both land and sea mammals, some preferring to hunt one, some the other (Kosbruk 1975b). The men were experts at using bows and arrows as well as guns. Drift whales were eaten, and in fact, one had washed up on the Kaflia shore in the early summer of 1912, shortly before the eruption (Kaiakokonok 1975a). Fishing was one of the most important subsistence activities, and as in years past, those at Kaflia in 1912 beach-seined for salmon (Kaiakokonok 1956, 1975b). People collected and enjoyed seagull eggs. Some people still used seal oil in stone lamps, and everyone found it necessary at times to substitute it for kerosene in lanterns (Kaiakokonok 1975a). Alutiiqs regularly used tobacco, tea, and flour and made pan bread as a staple. Alcohol was used and sometimes abused by local inhabitants (AOM 1904: 14). People routinely traveled by both wooden skiffs or dories and sealskin kayaks. In fact, it was by kayak that three young men made a dangerous journey after the eruption to seek help in Afognak.

In 1912, there were Russian Orthodox chapels at Katmai, Douglas, Kanatak, Wrangel, Chignik, and Mitrofania (AOM 1912: 77; ARC, reel 180). No formal schools were located in peninsula Alutiiq villages before 1922, when the Perryville school was established, but a number of residents were literate in Russian. Vladimir Stafeev, Alaska Commercial Company manager at Douglas, notes that someone could read and write in every Douglas household in 1892 (Diary: July 12, 1892). Of the entire Alutiiq population of the Pacific side of the Alaska Peninsula in 1900, 30 out of 98 Native hunters, or 31 percent, were literate (U.S. Census Bureau 1900). Their literacy was closely tied with the Russian Orthodox Church, which had operated schools for Natives and Creoles in the larger settlements during Russian days. In the smaller villages on the Alaska Peninsula, it must be supposed that reading and writing were taught to children at home by their parents or church readers.

During the Russian days and the period of major fur trading after the Americans came, in fact up to the time when the Alaska Commercial Company closed its posts on the peninsula at the turn of the century, most able-bodied Alutiiq men had been involved in seasonal sea otter hunting for trade and sale.[8] They were accustomed to traveling great distances in this pursuit, and in fact whole families regularly went on long journeys. George Kosbruk describes one kayak voyage down the Pacific coast of the peninsula (1975a), and Harry Kaiakokonok notes that people made frequent portages over Katmai Pass to the village of Savonoski (1975b). Both Katmai and Douglas had long served as regional trading posts visited by Dena'ina, Yup'ik, and Alutiiq hunters, who brought otter, beaver, fox, wolf, and bear skins to trade.

The Story

Prologue

During June of 1912, most of the people of both Katmai and Douglas had congregated, as usual, at the Kaflia Bay saltery to earn money and put up fish for winter use. The few permanent residents of Kaflia, including the Kaiakokonok family which had recently moved there, inhabited the only substantial dwellings in the settlement. The seasonal visitors from Katmai and Douglas had pitched tents for the summer.

Most oral reports of the eruption begin with a description of the abundant fish and game at Katmai immediately before the event. Kaiakokonok explains,

> And this creek was so clean, crystal clear water—oh, summertime, and thousands and thousands of salmon go into that river. Every kind of a species of salmon; dogs, humpies, silvers, reds, mix up. Then springtime they say ... our rivers used to be plugged with those [candlefish]. . . . Springtime, front of that village, the flat used to be all black with geese, many kind of ducks, swans. . . . There was moose all the time, and caribou. (1975a)

Premonition and Preparation

The stories then tell of a premonition of disaster. The Savonoski people are said to have known that the volcano was going to erupt and hence moved to Naknek ahead of time. Kaiakokonok notes, "Several times, maybe more than several times, we used to notice the jerks. Not exactly a earthquake; big jerk and a big rumble from that volcano. And that's why this Savonoski people from way up there inland ... they know that eruption was coming" (1975a). Actually, Savonoski's residents moved to Naknek each summer for the fishing season. The summer of 1912 was probably no different from previous years (Hussey 1971: 329).

But according to the stories, the people of Savonoski were not the only ones to sense coming disaster: Land mammals had been especially scarce that spring and summer. People believed they had evacuated the area because of the impending disaster: "The animals must have known that something was the problem, and they go some other places where they can survive" (Kaiakokonok 1975a).

The Eruption

The people at Kaflia Bay first knew of the eruption when they heard a tremendous noise and saw a cloud coming out of the mountain. Everyone shouted, "*Puyulek! Puyulek!* [Volcano!]" One old man, called Apacaq, realized that the boats must be turned upside down and water gathered before all the streams were choked with ash.

The shape of the volcanic cloud has undergone an interesting change in the retelling through the years. Geologist George C. Martin, who journeyed to the scene with a National Geographic Society party several months after the eruption, was told that the cloud was "a beautiful illuminated funnel-shaped cloud, which rose straight into the air.... It afterward assumed different colors and dissolved into cloudbanks, being illuminated all the time. A similar cloud was observed from Iliamna ... the description different ... only in the statement that in losing its funnel-shape form it assumed the 'shape of a ship'" (1913: 161). In his written version (1956), Father Harry Kaiakokonok describes the cloud thus: "The mountain just come up something compare to a fountain; it's quite difficult to make a definite description concerning this erupting mountain. She must rose up something like a bread dough and flow over on all sides with what they might call pumice stone...." (1956). By the 1975 interview, the image has changed. Kaiakokonok then says, "It comes up like a mushroom. Like that, that—you see that atomic bomb when it exploded? It looks something like that. It comes up and flowing, flowing, flowing; red, black, just like rolling all around! And the man who was staying right by it, he made a picture of it, drawing with a pencil. And then he made it just like a atomic bomb explosion" (1975a). George Kosbruk, in his *Elwani* article, says, "Roaring thunder followed, then a mushroom-like cloud shot up real high. No difference from a bomb picture we see in magazines today" (1976: 17).

The image of the mushroom-shaped cloud, which would not have been meaningful before 1945, compares not just its shape to one generated by an atomic bomb but also the magnitude of the explosion to the disasters of Nagasaki and Hiroshima. The cloud's shape symbolizes the complete destruction of Katmai, Douglas, and the old way of life.

Judgment Day

Kosbruk's and Kaiakokonok's testimonies then discuss the long, dark, hot, noisy, smelly ordeal when pumice and ash poured down on the community for forty-eight hours (Kaiakokonok) or five days (Kosbruk). All the people gathered in the log cabins that had recently been built (Kaiakokonok 1975a). Kaiakokonok notes that he, as a child, was not afraid, but that the adults were. George Kosbruk states, "People believed in the Bible, and how it would be when the world came to an end. So we all thought this was it. We had no hope of surviving; we gathered this from older people. Prayer was our only hope. We gathered together and made a special prayer to the Virgin Mary" (1976: 18).

Messengers

The prayers were answered by a slight glimmer of light through immense clouds of ash. The people then decided to supplement prayer with human action. They sent three young men in kayaks to the village of Afognak across Shelikof Strait. Johnson reports that two of the messengers were Wasco Sanook and Vanka Orloff, a visitor from Afognak (1977: 171).[9] The third man remains unidentified, and in fact none of the three is named in accounts by Perryvillers. The kayakers' anonymity may be due in part to the fact that they were all young men, not yet suitable role models for other Alutiiqs. Their anonymity also serves a dramatic purpose in the Katmai story, for it lends a mythic element in emphasizing the *role* of messenger rather than individual identities. Further, this anonymity gives the impression that the story is very old, as if the events had occurred so long ago that names are no longer remembered.

Rescue and Exile

The kayakers' mission was successful. The Revenue Cutter Service was alerted, and a ship steamed to Kaflia Bay to rescue the people. One hundred fourteen Alutiiqs were taken to the Creole village of Afognak north of Kodiak on June 12, where they were housed in the schoolhouse, in vacant houses, and with residents. There they stayed until the beginning of July.

The reactions of the Afognak residents to the refugees from the mainland, as reported in the story of one Swedish/Creole family, are instructive:

> The strangers that were living in the schoolhouse and in the yard around Orloff's place were unlike other people they had known. Papa said they were from way across Shelikof Strait, from a place called Katmai. . . . Eunice and Enola, though curious, were afraid of them. . . .
>
> These men and women were dark-skinned with dark slit-eyes and black hair, straight and close-cropped. The women wore calico dresses and kerchiefs, which lessened somewhat their scary appearance to the girls. The men, however, wore dark hats, and coarse dark-colored suits with heavy knee-high *turbusii*, the skin boots typically worn by mainland natives. Both girls had seen some

children as they ran past the schoolyard, but they were not going to stop and ask them to play....

When rescue came, [Ivan] Orloff and his wife, Tania, let some of the people stay in their barn and *banya*. Others were sheltered at the schoolhouse. The revenue cutter left an officer in Afognak to oversee the distribution of rations of food and gear to the refugees....

Herman told his family that he had made arrangements for the Katmai men to carve a number of the crochet hooks [of ivory] and some miniature skin *bidarkas*, with carved men, to sell in the store. He thought the work would be a good occupation for the men, and, of course, he hoped to sell all the items they could produce. (Harvey 1991: 110–11)

This selection indicates the social and cultural gulf between Afognak Creoles and Alaska Peninsula Alutiiqs despite their common ancestry, religion, and language and their participation in the same economic system. The passage is also instructive in contrast to the very brief mention Alutiiq storytellers make of their time in Afognak. That month or so is passed over as an inconsequential interruption of the pilgrimage to Perryville, a time when the refugees temporarily placed their lives on hold.

Relocation

It was apparent to both cutter personnel and the inhabitants of the Katmai coast that their old homes were no longer habitable. The cutters made two trips to Douglas and Katmai so the residents could retrieve as many belongings as possible. Government officials began seeking a new village site for the refugees.

According to Revenue Cutter Service documents, Captain Reynolds, commander of the Bering Sea Fleet and the *Tahoma*, made the decision to move the people down the coast beyond Chignik. In a dispatch sent from the *Tahoma* on June 24, 1912, he wrote,

Recommend the 98 mainland natives now destitute and depending on Government aid be located immediately peninsula westward of Chignik, probably Stepovak [a bay southwest of Ivanof Bay]. Good summer fishing. Winter trapping and hunting. Should be moved by July 10th to insure winter supply fish ... soon self supporting.... Probable cost [of building material] one thousand dollars.... Agent acquainted with natives, possibly Bureau

Education, should be sent to compel fishing, building, etc., and handle rations. (USRCS 1867–1914)

The 1913 annual report of the USRCS talks of "the *Tahoma* [with Orthodox priest and interpreter Father Aleksandr Petelin and five Katmai/Douglas Natives] having left several days previously to select the site" (USRCS 1913: 93). Local villagers were apparently to choose the specific location for the new village within the area southwest of Chignik. Oral tradition agrees with this view, although not all residents were aware of the mechanisms through which the choice was to be made. George Kosbruk states, "We spent about two weeks there [Afognak] till the Coast Guard boarded us to proceed on our journey west. Where? Japan? We never knew where they were bringing us" (Kosbruk 1976: 18). Father Harry Kaiakokonok, on the other hand, recalls,

I don't know where they—where we were going, but the people had the Coast Guards give the people quite a long notice for them to make decisions which way they wanted to go. Southwestward or eastward from Kodiak. The people don't know which way to go, which way would be better for them for living; and a lot of people wanted to go further southeast; and some people wanted to go [to] the west. And one lady was so anxious, and she been telling people even when she's got no business, "We go to the west, west,—westward!" Oh! And then her husband, tempting the chief of Katmai, make people go westward and the lady, his wife, advise him to beg him to go westward. Okay, they decide. (1975a)

First Landing
The first place the people landed was at the head of Ivanof Bay. In its protected harbor, they set up tents and began to seine for fish, using a net given them by one of the canneries (USRCS 1913: 99). They started immediately to dry fish for the winter. However, local tradition has it that there were already two Norwegian trappers living at the bay. They told the people that it was not a good place for a village, for snowslides occurred, ice formed in the bay in the winter, and land animals were scarce. Kaiakokonok says,

Oh, the people get excited. "We not going to select this kind of place where we can't go in and out...." The people didn't know any better that they were further down south than where they used to be up here in Katmai and Douglas. Right away the people have a meeting, and then they go out and look for location for village. And they selected Perryville, here where we are today. And these two Norwegians, they ... fooled the marshal escorting the people.... They all believe it. (1975a)

George Kosbruk is more direct about the Perryvillers' attitude toward the Norwegian trappers: "That guy, the guy called bullshit. The winter time you got snow right down to the water." [Interviewer's question: "This is what the guy told you?"] "Yeah. And never. Never snow right down there" (1975a).

Home at Last

And so the village was moved two bays east to the present site of Perryville—though, as a postscript, a number of villagers soon built winter trapping *barabaras* at Ivanof Bay because land mammals were in fact much more abundant there than at Perryville. In 1965, six families moved permanently from Perryville to Ivanof Bay (Davis 1986: 8).

Alutiiq Narrative Genres

The Alutiiq versions of the Katmai story and the tales of events which are said to have taken place there before the eruption express a unique understanding of both the past and the present, a perspective which places the Novarupta eruption simultaneously at the center and beginning of modern history. In fact, the story of the eruption is so powerful that it has collapsed traditional narrative genres into a single story type.

The dangers of equating narrative genres across cultures are well known (see McClellan 1970a), but the English designations *myth* and *legend* are similar enough to traditional Alutiiq genres to warrant a closer look. Most definitions of myth contain the following elements: They are "prose narratives which, in the society in which they are told, are considered to be truthful accounts of what happened in the remote past" (Bascom 1984: 9). The stories generally "contain information about decisive, creative events in the beginning of time" which function as models and "can be characterized as *ontological*: they are incorporated and integrated into a coherent view of the world, and they describe very important aspects of life and the universe.... The *context* of myth is, in normal cases, *ritual*" [emphasis in the original] (Honko 1984: 50–51). Legends, on the other hand, are described as "prose narratives which, like myths, are regarded as true by the narrator and his audience, but they are set in a period considered less remote, when the world was much as it is today. Legends are more often secular than sacred, and their principal characters are human" (Bascom 1984: 9).

Because Alutiiq lore is largely undocumented, a brief discussion of narrative genres in the folklore of the neighboring Yupiit provides a framework for its examination. The Yup'ik stories which most closely resemble myth as defined here are *qulirat* (plural; singular form, *quliraq*). *Qulirat* include

> tales which are not ultimately attributable to any known storyteller, and which include stock characters, rather than named persons who are known to have existed.... Etiological stories, detailing origins of celestial and geographic features, human customs and ceremonies, and animal characteristics; accounts of the legendary exploits of culture heroes; and ancient tales of animals in their human forms and of human/animal transformations.... (Morrow 1994)

Morrow further notes that "*quliraq* narratives often begin with generalized locations ('there was a village by a river')" (1994). The Alutiiq word glossed as "myth" is *unigkuaq* (plural, *unigkuat*), a cognate of Siberian Yup'ik and Iñupiaq terms.

A second Yup'ik genre consists of *qanemcit*. These stories describe events which took place after the current world order was established. They "include anecdotes and historical accounts—for example, personal encounters with ghosts or other beings, accounts of famines or illness, and feats of great shamans or hunters whose names are generally known" (Dauenhauer and Dauenhauer 1984: 26). A word translated as "story" or "account," *quli'anguaq* (plural, *quli'anguat*) seems to be the analogous Alutiiq genre.[10]

The analogy between Yup'ik *qanemcit* and European legend is incomplete. For instance, two nonlegendary forms of *qanemcit* are the personal memorate and the radio/television broadcast. Further, supernatural elements are prominent in both *qulirat* and *qanemcit*. This fact mirrors the Yup'ik worldview, which does not separate phenomena into the discrete categories of the sacred and profane, the supernatural and the natural (Fienup-Riordan 1990: 78). In fact,

Morrow cautions that *qulirat* and *qanemcit* are not firmly bounded nor mutually exclusive categories. She describes the "basic, although not rigid distinction" as relative, for "stories are sometimes classified ambiguously" (Morrow 1994).

The Alutiiq pre-eruption stories I recorded were called by the tellers either *unigkuat*, *quli'anguat*, both, or neither. I found no firm agreement on their definitions or the distinctions between the two. In fact, they were described by some as synonymous. Alutiiq elders explained:

> "*Unigkuat* are the same as *quli'anguat*."
> "*Unigkuat* are bedtime stories; *quli'anguat* are stories told by some-
>   one who has come from somewhere else."
> "They're the same thing."
> "*Unigkuat* are fairy tales."
> "*Quli'anguat* are stories; *unigkuat* are fiction stories."

Jeff Leer (personal communication with the author, October 1992) reported like findings in other Alutiiq villages, where the distinction between *unigkuat* and *quli'anguat* is becoming blurred.

Alutiiq genres, like their Yup'ik counterparts, probably have never been strictly delineated. The disagreement over the respective meanings of the two terms results from several factors. On one level, it may represent an example of "the philosophical expression of multiple simultaneous reference [which] pervades Yup'ik society and encompasses phenomena . . . [and] a negative reinforcement of analysis and specification" (Morrow 1990: 152). Second, the apparent confusion indicates the uneasy fit between Alutiiq and English folklore genres. There is no single English word that adequately renders either Alutiiq term.

Third, informants' characterization of *unigkuat* as "fairy tales" or "fiction stories" is partly a reaction to derogatory comments by American teachers about the "superstitions" described in the stories. One man confessed to me, "A lot of people are ashamed of our stories." When I asked why, he explained that his generation had been punished whenever they spoke Alutiiq in school. This made them wary of mentioning anything related to their language, including the old stories, in front of white people.

I have concluded, though, that the confusion springs from something else, something more basic than these three factors: a collapsing of the two genres which represents a shift in Alutiiq conceptions of their lore and history. It appears that for contemporary Alutiiq storytellers, particularly those from Perryville, there is no longer a difference between the two types of stories. It is certainly true that the youth who do not speak Alutiiq know nothing of the genre distinction. Even elders who know the terms and heard examples of each when they were young tell "old" stories that are different in an important way from those they heard. On the one hand, their narratives are largely mythic in the primary role the supernatural plays and in their remote, unchanged, and paradisiacal setting. On the other hand, some contain nonmythical, *qanemciq*-like characters and plot elements and often describe conflict or action involving particular, named people who are asserted to have a direct link with the present.

At the same time, the types of stories considered *qulirat* among Yupiit are rarely told by peninsula Alutiiqs today. That genre, as formerly understood, seems to have all but dropped out of the local folk repertoire. I was told no Raven trickster or origin stories, nor did I meet anyone who remembered hearing any. I recorded only three transformation tales, two involving wronged wives who were transformed into (or from) bears and the third involving a race of killer whales who beat the people of Katmai in a gambling game. People remembered hearing other animal stories as children but could not recall them.[11] *A'ula'aq* stories about wild hairy beings who sometimes abduct people are also commonly told, but most of them are recent memorates.

The near disappearance of an entire genre of stories—which is said by local Alutiiqs to have occurred only in the last thirty years—is due in part to the deaths of all the Katmai survivors and in part to the discontinuities between life in Katmai and Perryville. The new community required new stories with new messages. Once people with links to the old way of life had died, their stories died with them. Today's elders grew up in what has always been considered a progressive and forward-looking community. The canneries began to employ Natives not long after the relocation, and people were soon completely entwined in a wage-earning economy. An American school opened in the early 1920s. Traditional locales for storytelling changed from the "community house" or *qasgiq* to the trapping cabin, from communal locations to individual homes.

Furthermore, for contemporary storytellers, life in Katmai exists only in stories. I spoke with no living Alutiiq who has visited the ancestral village site. Propelled by the descriptions of the elders who survived the eruption, Katmai has become a symbolic, mythical place.

The Katmai Story as Myth

Structure

The story of the eruption at Katmai is not precisely myth as conventionally understood by folklorists, although it is an origin story that mimics widespread mythic structure. Like myth, it serves as a major identifying symbol to contemporary Perryville Alutiiqs. An image of a volcano is painted on Perryville School's gymnasium wall, alongside a portrait of Father Harry Kaiakokonok and the school mascot, the eagle.

As an origin story, the tale contains a literary structure and symbolism common to both biblical and Yup'ik origin stories (see, for instance, stories of the flood and the theft and retrieval of light in Nelson [1899: 452, 461, 483]). Briefly stated, the story's structure is as follows:

  I. Original paradise
    A. Premonition of impending danger is felt
    B. Preparations are made
 II. Disaster which induces a liminal experience inside tomblike houses
    A. Divine help is received through prayer
    B. Three messengers embark across the water on a pilgrimage for human help
III. Flight of the people from the destroyed original paradise (Katmai, Douglas, and Kaflia Bay)
    A. Pilgrimage of the whole community begins
    B. People spend a month in exile in Afognak (an element rarely discussed in Alaska Peninsula narratives)
    C. Pilgrimage continues to a new location (Ivanof Bay), whence people are expelled again
 IV. Complete reintegration after settlement in Perryville; members of three communities merge to form a single new one.

The number of structural elements is unimportant; they can be rearranged to form three, four, five, or more main topics. The important point is the origin/mythlike movement from paradise through liminality to the modern era, suggestive of the birth and maturing of a people and their community. This movement mimics Van Gennep's (1960) tripartite structure for *rites de passage*, comprising separation, margin or *limen*, and reaggregation. Further, it mirrors Turner's extension of that structure to social activities aimed at strengthening solidarity or *communitas* (1974: 231–32). Turner explains that liminality, the ambiguous state between two normal states, is a particularly potent time for generating *communitas*. The experience is "frequently likened to death, to being in the womb, to invisibility, to darkness, to bisexuality, to the wilderness, and to an eclipse of the sun or moon" (1969: 95). This is an apt description of the time between the eruption and final settlement in Perryville, a time characterized by temporary passivity, literal nakedness within the sweltering houses, and an illusion of timelessness. Furthermore, through its physical and emotional hardships, the experience fostered a newfound sense of unity among the former residents of Katmai, Douglas, and Kaflia Bay and produced in them a sense of having seen something of the divine. It confirmed their role as a chosen people and their story as part of the divine one (see Turner 1969: 96; 1974: 238).

Symbols

Several locally important symbols are embedded in the Katmai story, including the characterization of the place as a paradise, the anonymity of the kayakers sent to Afognak (resulting in their representing the group as a whole rather than individual heroics), and the mushroom-shaped cloud rising out of the volcano as a symbol of the destruction of the old way of life. All signal that the story has metamorphosed into a symbol-rich, communal oral tradition. They further lend a mythlike character to it.

Another telling symbol is the emergence of the people from their buried houses after the eruption. This is reminiscent of Christ's rebirth from his tomb and the emergence of a shaman from his journey to another world, itself a sort of rebirth (see the Pugla'allria story to come; see also Fienup-Riordan 1990: 53). Similarly, their pilgrimage in search of a new home is comparable to the expulsion from Eden, of landfall after the great flood, of the Exodus out of Egypt. It reinforces the Perryvillers' sense of being a chosen people.

Parallels with Christian images are probably no accident: Father Harry Kaiakokonok, a lay reader until 1971 when he became an ordained priest, was intimately familiar with the Bible, as indeed are all Perryville elders. I often heard layfolk relate biblical teachings to everyday life, so the practice is a common one. Intentional references to shamanic rituals are also possible. Despite a century and a half of Christianity, talk persists today that at least one resident, dead less than thirty years, was a practicing shaman.

The Mythic Pre-eruption Era

Euro-American histories of Alaska customarily divide time into three periods: the precontact, which covers the archaeological era; the Russian period from 1741 to 1867; and the American period after 1867. Contemporary Perryville history also divides time into three eras, but the categories cover different years. Alutiiqs speak of the pre-eruption period (the years up to 1912), the Perryville years up to World War II, and the present. The division between the pre- and post-eruption eras is thought to have much greater magnitude than the one separating pre- and postwar Perryville.

People describe life in Katmai very differently from existence after the eruption. Humans had ready access to the supernatural, through which they learned proper behavior, which serves as a model today. People spoke Alutiiq, ate healthy Native foods almost exclusively, traveled in sealskin kayaks, and lived in warm, draftless *barabaras*. There was no drinking of alcohol, and people helped each other. They were hardy and healthy, able to work with an intensity unimagined by today's youth. There were community houses where people learned their Native dances and the proper rules for hunting and disposing of animals.

On the other hand, Perryville was a modern village from the beginning. Seventy-year-old women today insist that they never saw carved ivory or bone dolls but instead played with porcelain dolls and china tea sets. They recall their beribboned straw hats ordered from catalogues. They wore sno-packs rather than mukluks and played on swings rigged between the pilings of cannery docks. Men remember the Perryville baseball team, the Bears, which used to play Navy or Coast Guard teams on summer patrol along the Alaska Peninsula coast. In effect, the residents of Katmai, Douglas, and Kaflia Bay invented themselves anew when they became Perryvillers.[12]

The pre-eruption time is mythlike also in its portrayal as a single, seamless era in which life changed little from day to day, year to year. No distinction is made between precontact and postcontact time. This is illustrated by the fact that two major Russian and American influences figure prominently in the stories, Russian Orthodoxy and the fur trade which exploited the Alutiiqs. Storytellers do not see these elements as non-Alutiiq, nor as evidence of an essential shift in lifestyle or worldview from what they consider "traditional ways." They admit that Christianity and the fur trade came with the arrival of the Russians, but since they know nothing of the culture in existence before that time, these are part of the earliest stage in their known history.

The Russian Orthodoxy that permeates the pre-eruption stories is a syncretic mixture of Alutiiq shamanism and animism with Christianity. The fact that religion is important in the stories derives from both traditional *unigkuaq* structure and local interest. Most contemporary peninsula Alutiiqs are deeply religious.

The second imported element in pre-eruption stories, Alutiiq economic exploitation, is associated with the Russian fur trade, although in fact it continued for a generation during the American period as well. The economic system and its inequities are personified in the story about Macintine. He is portrayed as a greedy, stingy, bossy, dangerous, self-serving Russian.[13] He is an example of what has become a stock character in Alutiiq folklore, though this person is no longer necessarily a Russian (any white man will do), is often stupid as well as stingy, and in modern memorates is frequently bettered by the Alutiiqs among whom he travels.

Not only is there no expressed distinction between pre- and post-contact in the stories, but the Russian and American periods before 1912 are also collapsed and confused. The tale of the death of Macintine is again a case in point. Macintine was described to me before I began recording the story as the "king of Russian America." His tyranny and that of the fur trade in general are remembered as Russian phenomena, while in fact the events described in the story occurred in 1886, almost twenty years into the American period.

The merging of Russian and American times in Alutiiq conceptions of history is understandable, for life on the peninsula changed little as a result of the 1867 sale. The fur trade continued much as it had during Russian days, though now with American traders. Villages still interacted with company officials through a *tuyuq* or village chief, apparently chosen from among respected men, with a great deal of input from the itinerant priest (see AOM 1902: 432). The company continued to encourage worker dependence on its store, issuing credit to hunters which could only be repaid through future hunts (ACC correspondence: 8/7/1877; AOM 1899: 91). In several instances, Alaska Commercial Company officials were Russians who had chosen to stay in Alaska after the sale. Russian Orthodox priests maintained their yearly trips to the villages, speaking Russian and church Slavonic (and, in the case of Creole priests, Alutiiq as well). The absence of schools until the 1920s meant that the English language was neither promoted nor required in daily life.[14]

Pre-eruption Stories

Three recorded stories told by the current acknowledged story-teller in Perryville, septuagenarian Ignatius Kosbruk (son of George Kosbruk), illustrate the collapsing of genres and historical periods: "Piculi," about a hunter who tempted fate; "Pugla'allria," a "good" shaman who accepted Christianity at the end of his life; and "Mac-intine," the "Russian king" who was killed in retribution for his meanness to Kodiak Alutiiqs.

Ignatius Kosbruk learned most of the stories he knows at trapping camps or at night over tea from "the old man," Wasco Sanook. Was-co's widow, Martha, described the setting in which Kosbruk most likely learned the stories: Each night many of the boys in the village gathered at the Sanooks' house. Wasco Sanook would begin telling stories as the boys lounged on the floor and furniture. The storytelling continued well into the night, with Martha going to bed long before her husband relinquished his audience. Finally, he would announce that he had no more stories to tell, and the boys would go home. The Sanook house served as a sort of modern-day *qasgiq*, its main innovation being the fact that he was the only adult male instructor. Hence it was his own idiosyncratic view of Alutiiq folklore and history, rather than a consensus, which was passed on.

Ignatius Kosbruk told me the stories while I was a houseguest in his and his wife Frieda's home. I was an out-of-town visitor, a non-Native English speaker with very limited knowledge of the Alutiiq language. I generally sat across the kitchen table from Ignatius as he recorded his stories. I sipped tea while Frieda Kosbruk worked, listened, and occasionally commented from the cooking area.

Piculi[15]

Kosbruk identified the first story, "Piculi" (not the name of the man, but a descriptor meaning "great hunter"), as an *unigkuaq* (myth). The story is reproduced here in English translation, written with the assistance of Ignatius Kosbruk and Ralph Phillips. The comment to Jeff Leer at the beginning refers to Kosbruk's understanding that Leer, with whom he has worked in the past, will listen to the tape. Kosbruk switched to English when he felt it was especially important that I

Frieda and Ignatius Kosbruk, March 1992. Photo by Patricia Partnow.

understand what was going on. Portions originally told in English appear in italics.

"Piculi" as told by Ignatius Kosbruk[16]
March 30, 1992
Perryville, Alaska
English translation

There's another story, Jeff Leer. There used to live at Katmai an expert hunter. *I don't know his name.* He was a great hunter. *But I don't know his name. Anyway, this guy was a real good hunter and— great hunter. He used to hunt year round. Fill all his garages up for the winter, with whatever they had, I guess. I don't know how they were made, made out of grass or wood. He let his servants make him three big warehouses for winter. Dry up meat. All the meat he put away. So I think it must [have] been in the fall. Finally, he came back from his hunting.* When he came back, they were putting up fish; he saw them down at the river. The Alutiiqs were putting up fish. There used to be lots of fish in the past.

Then he said to his wife, "My new shoes. I've never used them." He put them on and went for a walk. He put on clean clothes and went to visit. He went to the village by way of the river.

While—the sun was shining; it was fine weather, and that man had on clean clothes; he went to the ones who were fishing at this river. While he was going along the road, he stepped on some fish—*you know*—they were exposed to the sun.

Then he splashed his shoes with the rotting fish. *Boy, then he cursed.* He cursed about the fish, even though it hadn't done any-thing to him. He cursed God. For no reason. "Why did you send fish here?" *Because it just dirty his shoes when he stepped [on] that fish, rotten fish. And he splash it on his new shoes. Boy, then he cursed God. He cursed God for no reason. And then He answer him from the air without nobody. Nobody around. And [He] answered. The word came out from the air. All the people that were along the creek listened to it. Every one of 'em. And listened to Him and stopped, and were—*

And then He said, God tells him Himself, "I sent this food, fish, down so the kids wouldn't go hungry. I sent it down due to the people that will go hungry, so they wouldn't go hungry."

And this guy, he answered Him right back and told Him, even if he doesn't eat any fish, *he will make it through the winter.*

And then God gave him the best of luck. All the game he wanted— came. And he dried all the meat he can, and put away three big warehouses, just full of dried meat. He went out, and God gave him all the luck he wanted. He didn't punish him. But at the end he was punished.

And then he—he filled all his warehouses full. When time to quit, then he quit. And then winter came. Winter came. Oh, I don't know how big those warehouses were!

Then it became fall; it was snowing and cold, and he quit hunting. These caches were full to the top.

Then he must have had a wife. He said to his wife—I don't know how many times—to open that first warehouse. He sent his wife *to open that first warehouse. She opened it as she was advised to from her husband. She opened it, but [there was] nothing but sod. All the meat: all dirt! And then he send her to the other one. Same thing: It was all sod. All that work he did. And then the third one, it was same thing: Nothing happened. No meat, all dirt. That's when God punish him.*

And then she ate in the table with him, tried to feed him, and couldn't. She feed him out of her own plate and put it in his mouth, and it turn into mud. And everything what he tried to put in his mouth, turned into mud. He died from starvation.

He hollered. Three times he answer Him. God told him that He sent the fish down so the children wouldn't go hungry; that's why He sent the fish to the earth.

Then that one answered Him, "Even if I don't eat fish, I will survive the winter." He died from starvation.

That's why they always tell us not to step on the fish when we're around the creek. Because it is just like bread—bread and butter. That's what they call it, how big the fish is. That's the meaning of it.

That's all.

The story melds a common Eskimo theme with a Christian message, illustrating how completely Alutiiq and Christian values have been combined. The motif of mockery or disrespect of a valuable food resource (Thompson 1975: motif nos. C94.3, C 934, Q288) is common among Alaska Native lore (see McClellan 1970b; Johnson 1975). It involves a person who is inconvenienced or upset by the resource and curses or mocks it. In this case, drying salmon, exposed too long to the sun, has rotted and splashed the man's new shoes. Later, retribution is exacted for this thoughtless and disrespectful act. In "Piculi," the man is punished by God Himself in a manner reminiscent of the European Midas punishment (Thompson 1975: motif no. D476.2), a motif not reported in other examples of North American folklore (see Thompson 1966: 362).

The story's messages are several: Treat the resource with respect, or it may be denied you (a common Eskimo theme); avoid the sins of pride and love of material objects (a Christian theme); be a sharing member of society (an Eskimo theme); and do not blaspheme God (a Christian commandment). Taken together, these messages represent solid contemporary Alutiiq values.

Pugla'allria

The second story is about Pugla'allria, a shaman who was said to have lived during the last days of Katmai.[17] Ignatius Kosbruk also termed this story an *unigkuaq*. He explained that Pugla'allria had actually lived; he had been the hunting partner of Simeon Takak, the last chief of Katmai and first chief of Perryville.

The following English translation of the Pugla'allria story was written with the assistance of Ignatius Kosbruk, Ralph Phillips, and Jeff Leer. The parts originally told in English are in italics.

"Pugla'allria," as told by Ignatius Kosbruk
March 24, 1992
Perryville, Alaska
English translation

I used to hear this story in the past from that old man; his name was Wasco Sanook. He used to tell me stories. He used to tell me stories there in the trapping grounds, when we used to be there, trapping. Then, I didn't understand what he told me. He was really talking about a shaman. Then, when I thoroughly understood it, he made me tell that story back to him.

From Naknek to Katmai, a maternal uncle went down there to two old people. They had only one son—one. Then that uncle made that son into a shaman—but the uncle didn't tell the nephew's two parents anything.

When he was about to go home, he took that boy out, the one he had made into a shaman, and he put him into a garbage pit. *It was about in the fall, in September, I guess, or October, whatever.* So he made him stay there the whole winter, through the entire winter, in the back of the pit. *We call it a garbage hole.* He was there the whole winter.

Then, when spring came, that uncle went down from Naknek to Katmai. Then he asked the two parents, "Where on earth is your son?" Then his mother got all excited, not having known where he was since the fall; she had lost him, her *boy*. Then that uncle told her to look for him out there in the garbage hole. *In the pit—the garbage pit.* His mother did as she was told; she went down to that pit. Then she saw him there in the pit, in the process of leisurely cleaning his teeth, taking fish eggs out from his teeth. She took him down to his father, to his dad.

Now that boy knew every last thing in the world. He knew what was on everyone's minds. He knew how people would live in the future. He was a person who knew things. Now that uncle was just beginning to make him a shaman.

From then on, being a shaman, he didn't hurt his fellow humans; he just helped his fellow humans.

He became a shaman. People in those villages didn't know what kind of person he was. That Pugla'allria, *he knows everything what was going on.* He only killed his uncle. He killed him because of the fact that he had made his parents cry. *The only person he killed; that was the only one.* When he was just leaving, when that uncle got ready to go home again, Pugla'allria tied a hair around his neck. That uncle didn't know it; *he didn't know he tied a hair around his neck. He didn't know. So he went back, back to Naknek, and that same year, one year after that, he went back. He went back to Naknek, and looked at him. He was almost cut by the hair what he put around his neck.* As a shaman, the only person he killed was his uncle. On the way, he helped people out.

Then again one time when people were hunting for sea otters in the sea, when they were way out in *qayaqs*, in three-man *baidarkas*, there were lots of them hunting sea otters. The wind came up, it blew really hard, and they had absolutely nowhere to go. Then that Pugla'allria, he called those who were hunting sea otters, *the ones that went out for sea otters. And all a sudden,* suddenly all the *qayaqs* went towards each other; they gathered without anyone doing anything. *Nobody touched them.*

They were out in the storm. They didn't know. And they all touch them, and they didn't know what happened. They all go through that one path—right up to Qa'irwik *gathered in one place and made a path for them to go up to—back to Katmai.*

There was no human agent—*nobody touch them, and they didn't know what happened. They all go through that one path—right up to* Qa'irwik [Katmai], *right where they live. And when they landed, Father,* Apawak [the Russian priest told him not to do that anymore].

Then he, that shaman, lived among the people. He was kind and nice to the people. He only helped those people. He used that magic.

Now, once, unexpectedly, this couple's child got a fish bone stuck in his throat—in the village—a bone got stuck in his throat. His parents asked shamans to come help. That Pugla'allria watched all those shamans from somewhere or other *in their home. They couldn't do nothing to him. And Pugla'allria was watching them from his home—and wondering what kind of kallagalek are they.*

At last, finally they think of him. They call Pugla'allria *down. And he went out. And when he entered the house, he told them,* "What are you shamans good for anyway? You just torture people in their minds; you're just killing people instead of helping. Is this child suffering here? You can't seem to help him." *So he just take the child and put him on his lap. I don't know what he did. And he take the bone out and show it to them kallagaleks, every one of them.* "Was this hard?" *He take the bone out and show it to them—every one of 'em.* Then he told them to look, that "a person who pays attention to himself can be a shaman. He helps people, doesn't do anything bad to them." *And they said some of 'em were real criminal in that group. He seen them, their mind.*

And then after that, then the shaman lived there helping people.

This chief there, *the one I told you about, the chief, he never hire nobody, only* Pugla'allria *for partner. He say he never carry no gun. And fall of the year, when they watch for bears at night, he let the bear come right close to them, up to them right there. He had no gun. That's something amazing. He never let the bear see him.*

Then he used his shamanism as a means of helping people out. He helped people out with his shamanism.

Then he lived and just helped people.

Then once he started to ponder, "Am I doing the right thing?" Then, then when he started to think about it, he started to think he wanted to quit it, what he was doing, being a shaman. Then he started to become sick. He was sick then. Then one time, once, all of a sudden his shaman helpers came back to him. They broke his joints. *Arms and legs were broken up without nobody touching 'em. And he hollered,* "Whoa! I wouldn't come with you guys!" *And his arms and legs started to break up without nobody touching them.*

And he hollered, "I wouldn't come with you guys, because I think that we are doing something that is wrong." He screamed that it wasn't right. *"It's not right. It's all devil's work."* And it got worse and worse and worse. *His legs start to break without nobody touching them.* Then it got worse and worse. *His arms and legs start to break without nobody touching them.* Then he screamed, saying he will not go with his spirit helpers; they're not doing right. He said he would follow only the true God.

Then the poor thing died. He just vomited blood until Good Friday. I heard this, that the poor creature died on Good Friday, vomiting blood.

That's the end, it's all done.

Pugla'allria experienced a conventional initiation into shaman-hood—his maternal uncle put him into a pit used to ferment fish heads and left him there for a year. At the end of that time, Pugla'all-ria emerged a clairvoyant, healer, and controller of weather. The story recounts a number of his exploits but makes a point of noting that each was for the good of the people, and that Pugla'allria, unlike other shamans of his day, did not use his powers for his own benefit or to harm people (with one exception, justified on the grounds that the murdered man had "made his parents cry"). Despite Pugla'allria's stellar career and good motives, when he was on his deathbed, he re-alized that shamanism was essentially evil and that his spirit helpers were agents of the devil. He threw them off, dying in excruciating pain. As with Yup'ik shamans, the locus of his spiritual power was in his joints, which burst open when he expelled his helpers. He died on Good Friday, but not before he was able to accept the true God and Christ.

The story of Pugla'allria, like that of the *piculi*, is a statement of contemporary Alutiiq values, particularly as they apply to religion and worldview. This story demonstrates that shamanism was not entirely bad; when it conformed to the Christian exhortation to help others, it was beneficial to the people.[18]

At the same time, shamanism is shown to have been powerful, re-gardless of the motives of its practitioners. There is no question that Pugla'allria has powerful abilities. Interestingly, the less beneficent shamans are portrayed as less successful in doing good deeds, but they have no trouble performing feats for their own benefit. The story thus shows that Christianity did not dissolve the beliefs that existed in precontact days. Instead, through a syncretic mixture, it incorpo-rated and overpowered them. Although people claim to know little about shamanism nowadays, the bone-breaking episode at the end of the story indicates that portions of the previous belief system are remembered. It is likely that the Alaska Peninsula Alutiiqs, like the Yupiit about whom we have more information, broke the bones of a shaman when he died to ensure that he would not come back to life (Elsie Mather, personal communication with the author, June 1992; Fienup-Riordan 1990: 54).

This story indicates that both Alutiiq and Russian supernatural systems were powerful, but Christianity, through its emphasis on good works, was preferable. Even today the powers and methods of the two religious systems are seen to be analogous. I was told of innumerable incidents when holy water, a cross, a prayer, church bells, or consecrated ground saved people or structures from natural disaster in precisely the same way that Pugla'allria was able to calm the waters for the sea-otter hunters.

A central theme in Kosbruk's telling of the Pugla'allria story thus concerns the victory of Christianity over shamanism.[19] For Kosbruk, the story symbolizes not just one shaman's conversion but the conversion of all Katmai Alutiiqs. The shaman's death on Good Friday is particularly significant. It invites comparisons between Pugla'allria's life and that of Christ, reinforcing each as a model for future generations. Good Friday itself is shown to be spiritually powerful, an active force in Pugla'allria's conversion.[20]

Taken together, "Pugla'allria" and "Piculi" reveal much variation in what Ignatius Kosbruk termed *unigkuat*. "Piculi" might have been a typical *unigkuaq* except for its Christian elements, but "Pugla'allria," as an account of a named and fairly recent person's deeds, would probably have been called a *quli'anguaq*, following traditional genre distinctions.

Macintine

The story about the death of Macintine illustrates Alutiiq attitudes about the fur trade, provides a striking symbol of ethnic distinctiveness, exemplifies the merging of historical periods in pre-eruption stories, and illustrates the way that ancient motifs have been reworked with modern situations and characters. The story is an account of the November 1, 1886, murder of the Alaska Commercial Company's Kodiak trader, Benjamin G. McIntyre.

Ignatius Kosbruk told me that the story "belonged" to the Kodiak Alutiiqs, for Katmai hunters and trappers did not deal with McIntyre but with the trader at Katmai who sent the furs to Kodiak. Kosbruk did not identify the tale by genre.

The English translation of this Alutiiq story was written with the assistance of Ignatius Kosbruk and Ralph Phillips. Again, portions originally told in English are italicized.

"Macintine," as told by Ignatius Kosbruk
March 24, 1992
Perryville, Alaska
English translation

I used to hear this one, too; it belongs to Kodiak Alutiiqs especially. Macintine was the king here in Alaska. He tortured Alutiiqs, the ones that went sea-otter hunting. He gave them for their sea-otter catch only *one pound of tea.* He made them go out hunting, the Kodiak Alutiiqs, out to sea. He made fun of them. A little flour, a little sugar was all he gave them.

Now one time they made a plan from the Lower 48, from Seattle, before we bought Alaska. That boss owned *the whole Alaska.*

Well, they made a plan from down there: Someone would kill him. Their minds were made up, all the Alaskan Alutiiqs.

Then the assassin from Seattle came from down there; the government from the Lower 48 sent him to Kodiak.

Kodiak was really full of gunpowder. So [he went] to the place under the bluffs, where he [practiced] shooting.

Then that assassin got to Kodiak. He walked among the people, and they didn't see him. *He was invisible. He was some kind of man, I guess.* People touched him, not knowing it.

Then *that first day when he got into Kodiak, Macintine himself, he went to him and ask him, "Macintine, would you let me buy a cow today for lunch?" Macintine saying, "No, you got to pay a lot of money for a cow." Says, "You know it."*[21]

Then that one said to Macintine, *"Today is your last day you will have supper in your table." Or tomorrow, whenever is a better time for him to be dead.*

Lots of those other people in the village were scared of him; they thought Macintine would kill all of them. They didn't think he'd be able to kill Macintine.

The next day the assassin [was there], just as they were sitting at a big table just about to eat. That Macintine was *right on the end of the table; he was sitting with his, with his treasurer or whatever he was, second to him, he was sitting down eating. Getting ready to eat.*

And then he sneak up to the window and aimed at him. He was clear. With the shot. And his partner was nearby him, and he aim at him and shot him right there—stone dead. And his partner, he must have talked a little bit Native language. He hollered, "Kina maani caligta [What's happening here]!?!" *He was crawling around all over on the floor.* "What's happening here!?!"

And then after that, soon as he killed him, he went over and blow that ship up, so nobody would know. He blowed it up. And then he wandered around. And about three days after that, they heard it from Seattle. And they were gonna come up and bomb the Kodiak Island, but Kodiak didn't put its flag up. That's the only—[if] the flag would have come up, they would have blowed Kodiak up, but the people knew that they were gonna do a dirty trick like that. They didn't put their flag up for three days. The third day they went out.

That was the end of it.

Like the Katmai story, "Macintine" has been remembered and recorded differently by various parties.[22] The first of four printed versions was published in an 1887 travelogue by Heywood W. Seton-Karr, who had been a member of the *New York Times* expedition to Alaska during the summer of 1886. Seton-Karr was dining with McIntyre when the manager was shot in the back of the head. The second is an unpublished account written by Ivan Petroff, who had been responsible for the 1880 United States census of Alaska. Petroff was deputy customs agent at Kodiak in 1886 (Pierce 1968: 7), and was also a witness to McIntyre's death. His observations were incorporated into a chatty narrative intended for publication in a magazine under the nom de plume, Boris Lanin (Petroff n.d.); a copy of this version is in the Bancroft Library archives. The third account is based on a family oral tradition recalled by Wesley Frederick (Fred) Roscoe (1992), who was an infant when the murder occurred. In his memoir, *From Humboldt to Kodiak*, he recounts the story as he remembers hearing it from his father, Wesley Ernest Roscoe, Kodiak's recently arrived Baptist missionary and schoolteacher. This memoir also includes the fourth version, a letter written by the same W. E. Roscoe shortly after the murder. The elder Roscoe was a witness to McIntyre's death when he entered the room immediately after the shooting, which he did not witness. His letter was published in the December 9, 1886, edition of *The Weekly Humboldt Times*.

Seton-Karr's account follows as a contrast to Ignatius's oral tradition. He corroborates the fire in the murderer's sloop mentioned by

Ignatius, although he explains that the attempt to blow up the boat was unsuccessful.

"Murdered at Table," by Heywood Seton-Karr
Reprinted from *Shores and Alps of Alaska* (pp 231–232)
St. Paul, Kodiak Island, Alaska,
November 3, 1886

The night before last I was the eye-witness to a shocking murder—none other than that of the general agent, whose corpse is on board. We start at noon for California, nearly two thousand miles distant.

We were seated at supper at six o'clock in the evening—McIntyre at the head of the table, and Woche, a storekeeper, at the foot. Ivan Petroff was by my side. The meal was nearly over, and McIntyre had half-turned to get up from his chair, when a terrible explosion suddenly occurred, filling the room with smoke and covering the table with fragments of plates and glasses.

McIntyre never moved, for he was killed stone-dead in a moment. Woche fell under the table, and then rushed out streaming with blood in torrents, for he was shot through the lower part of the head. The double glass window was smashed to atoms, for a cowardly fellow had fired through it, from just outside, with a spreading charge of slugs, presumably aiming at McIntyre, who received the main part of it in his back. Meantime the murderer who had thus shot into a group of unarmed and unsuspecting persons had time to escape.

I succeeded in stopping the bleeding from Woche's wounds, everyone appearing paralysed!

The suspected man, Peter Anderson, a Cossack of the Don, cannot be found. He had, we found, attempted to fire his sloop, lying at anchor near the wharf; and had refused employment at cod-fishing, in order, as he said, to be present at the departure of the schooner. He had also been seen loitering with a gun behind the house. He owed money to McIntyre, who had twice fitted him out for sea-otter hunting, but both times he was unsuccessful.

We have been scouring the woods with rifles, but the natives are frightened to death. Not a light can be seen in any house after dark for fear of its being shot into by this madman, who is still at large if he has not committed suicide. Nor can any of them be got to stir out at night, or to keep watch like sentries over the sloop, in case he should return, unless a white man is with them.

There is little chance that Ignatius Kosbruk's story is the result of his or his mentor having read an account of the murder. Newspaper articles are easily ruled out, for the only newspaper in existence in Alaska in 1886 was the *Alaskan* in Sitka, which was not published for half of November and all of December in 1886 due to the foreman's illness.

Both Seton-Karr's book and W. E. Roscoe's newspaper letter may have been available in Alaska after 1887, but until the 1920s, they would have been inaccessible to Alaska Peninsula Alutiiqs because they are in English. Neither of the other two authors could have been a source for Ignatius Kosbruk: Petroff's account was never published, and Fred Roscoe's only appeared in 1992.

It is more likely that Kosbruk learned the story indirectly from a locally renowned "Russian" (Creole) named Spiridon Stepanoff. He had been born in the tiny village of Eagle Harbor on Kodiak Island in 1883, and at the age of twelve had moved to Mitrofania on the Alaska Peninsula with his family. A renowned storyteller, he spent the rest of his life in the Mitrofania and Chignik areas, with occasional trips to Unalaska, Unga, and Port Moller to work in the canneries. I was given a copy of an audiotape Stepanoff had recorded in 1969, in which he recounted the tale of Macintine.[23] This tape provides a fascinating bridge between the eyewitness narratives by McIntyre's friends and Kosbruk's oral tradition.

Assuming that Spiridon Stepanoff was the source for Kosbruk's story, the narrative has undergone an interesting transformation through the years. Like the Katmai story, it has become part of the Alutiiq self-definition, converted from a diverting anecdote about the murder of a particular individual to a narrative about the destruction of a symbolic social persona. Whereas Stepanoff maintains narrative distance from the characters and action of the story, Kosbruk identifies closely with the Alutiiq hunters and the assassin in turn.

Stepanoff maintains distance in two ways. First, he reminds his audience that the murderer was a Russian (not an Alutiiq or Creole) from "outside" (i.e., from the Lower Forty-Eight). Second, the man was a lazy good-for-nothing: "He wouldn't do nothing!" Spiridon implies that it was only natural that Macintine denied him his request for part of the slaughtered cow: "So this fella he come up too. 'Won't you give me a little piece for my supper?' Macintine says, 'Ah! You! You're not my man. You're not a working man. You don't do nothing! You don't get nothing from me! You get home!' " (Stepanoff 1969).

Stepanoff also recognizes that Macintine suffered from moral weakness: At the beginning of his narrative, he implies that Macintine may have been partly responsible for the death of an Orthodox bishop he resented because this prelate would not allow the Alutiiqs to hunt on Russian Orthodox holidays.[24] Furthermore, Macintine had sold the Russian stranger defective gunpowder at the beginning of Stepanoff's narrative. It was apparently partly in retaliation that Macintine was killed.

More importantly, Stepanoff frames his narrative about the "Kodiak king" in terms of the fur trade that exploited generations of Alutiiqs, including his father. Stepanoff begins the story only after explaining that during the nineteenth century, Mitrofania was the site of a major sea-otter hunt. The teacher making the tape comments, "Yeah, used to make a lot of money?" and Stepanoff answers, "Yeah, not *people*! *People* for nothing! But they say company made a lot of money. They could get two thousand dollars for the skin; they pay sixty dollars."

Stepanoff's perspective is most like that of neither the assassin nor the fur buyers in the story, but rather the Alutiiq onlookers. Seton-Karr, Petroff, and Roscoe make much of the fact that the local Natives and Creoles were afraid to chase the murderer and so did nothing to apprehend him. Stepanoff depicts the locals not as fearful but as clever opportunists who were able to benefit from a drama that did not directly affect them by feeding unhelpful information to the American "bosses" for money:

> And there was [unclear] right on the post, "Anybody seen somebody walking strange places, and you get $10...." Lots of people made the money for nothing. Once in a while they'd say, "There he is, up there! See the man up on the hill!" One of the bosses would go, go find him; they find nothing. Never find him, all over the Kodiak, and they're climbing mountains, look for that man. Never find him. Never find him. (Stepanoff 1969)

Ignatius Kosbruk, on the other hand, has recast the story in a form reminiscent of traditional Eskimo tales about the redistribution of wealth (see Lantis 1953: 164; Norton 1986: 79–88). In depicting the Russian Macintine as greedy, selfish, and despotic, he portrays a man who is in direct conflict with the Alutiiq values of sharing and downplaying good fortune or superior ability. Macintine is similar to the rich men in many *qulirat*, but as an outsider to the culture, he does not understand that according to Alutiiq mores, he must willingly give away some of his goods. Instead, he demands a large payment for them. There seems to be no way to correct the imbalance brought on by his greed and arrogance other than murder.

Kosbruk is also alone in transforming Macintine's assassin to a folk hero whose story "shaped the past into narrative that made inevitable changes more bearable" (Ives 1988: 3). Kosbruk shows the way the assassin avenged the economic exploitation that the Alutiiqs had experienced throughout the nineteenth century. Like another folk hero, George Magoon (chronicled by Edward Ives), Macintine's killer is an outlaw hero, a type "which arise[s] in a time and locale of economic and social crisis and become[s] symbolic champion of one segment of this highly particularized society" (Meyer 1980: 116). Outlaw heroes, Ives reminds us, need not be approved of by the storyteller or audience. Rather, they allow a sensitive subject to be aired without anyone having to take an explicitly illegal stand (Ives 1988: 295–96). Further, the fact that Macintine's murderer is an outsider and a man of considerable spiritual power allows for a measure of distance between his actions and the storyteller's values. In this case, it is obvious to Kosbruk's audience that he approves of the assassination, but it does not follow that he would support a person he knew doing such a thing.

For Ignatius Kosbruk, then, this is the story of the Alutiiqs' victory over the Russians, and by extension over all white men, through the agency of a stranger sent to save them. Its parallels with the story of Christ as savior are marked. In addition, the story shows the power of the traditional (i.e., shamanic) religion, which enabled the assassin to escape detection both before and after the murder. The tale recounts a turning point in Alutiiq history, a time when the people were victorious over the white man because they possessed a spiritually and morally superior culture.

As would be expected, the written versions of the death of McIntyre display different attitudes about Natives, Creoles, Russians, and Americans. For instance, all printed documents (and Spiridon Stepanoff's oral testimony as well) declare that the murderer, Peter Anderson, was a Russian.[25] This fact accounts for some assumption about his character by the American raconteurs, for relationships between the recently arrived Americans and the Russians who had remained in Alaska after its sale were strained at best. Baptist missionaries like Ernest and Ida Roscoe resented the Russian Orthodox priests, who hampered their attempts to establish a mission and orphanage on Kodiak. In 1887, Ida Roscoe wrote,

> The old priest … is very much displeased with the American school. He told some of the men that as soon as the children learn to read English they would leave the Greek church, so he does all he can to make them go to the Russian school which they started two days after E. commenced his. They even went so far as to send a man around to gather the children up in the morning, when they first commenced, but I think we will come out best in the end. (1992: 10)

Several years later another missionary, C. C. Currant, echoed the anxiety about the priests: "The Greek priest here is doing what he can to oppose. Pray God that he may not harm us" (Roscoe 1992: 124). Following his 1899 survey of the fishing industry in southcentral and southwestern Alaska, Capt. Charles P. Elliott expressed similar sentiments: "The Indians [sic] under the domination of the Russian church, and the personality of the priest in charge determines to a considerable extent the condition of the Indians. The priest at Kadiak [sic] preaches sedition against the United States, his influence being distinctly for evil" (Elliott 1900: 741).

The Orthodox priests' point of view is reflected in an 1898 article in the *American Orthodox Messenger* entitled, "Short Church Historical Description of the Kodiak Parish": "Only this year on Woody Island the Baptists, weaving a nest for impertinently taking Orthodox children, are building a prayer house, and, it seems, not so much for vagrants without pastors of the heterodox, as much as for the seduction and luring of Orthodox Aleuts" (266). The strained atmosphere in Kodiak between Americans and Russians at the time of McIntyre's murder may have been a factor in the murder itself and undoubtedly influenced the way it was perceived and reported.

The younger Roscoe adds a new twist to this tale of interethnic conflict. Writing fifty years after the murder occurred, he depicts negative attitudes not toward Russians (who were no longer a threat to the Protestants in Alaska) but rather toward Natives. In Roscoe's account, Peter Anderson was no longer a Russian. Instead, he was a dissolute white man living among the Alutiiqs. He "was a shiftless, irresponsible sort of person. He lived with his squaw by the Aleut village outside the town of Kodiak" (1992: 6). Anderson had sunk to what Roscoe implies was the Natives' uncivilized level and was immoral as well. Roscoe has restructured the story to demonstrate the rift not between Russians and Americans but between whites and Natives.

The character of the victim likewise differs in the various accounts. In contrast to the oral traditions recounted by Ignatius Kosbruk and Spiridon Stepanoff, all written versions show McIntyre to have been a reasonable, responsible manager who fulfilled his duties well. Seton-Karr and Petroff, the two eyewitnesses, agree that McIntyre was competent. Petroff depicts him as so valuable that his vacation was delayed to deal with company matters no one else could handle. He is also shown as exceedingly generous; he assists Anderson one (Roscoe), two (Seton-Karr), or three times (Petroff) before finally refusing to outfit him again for trapping.

As already discussed, the Alutiiq Macintine story ignores the distinction between the precontact, Russian, and American periods and, except for its chronological setting and the identity of the victim, sounds very like a traditional Yup'ik *quliraq*. First, there is the suggestion that the assassin had strong spiritual powers connected with ancient Alutiiq beliefs which, like Pugla'allria, he used for the good of the people. Second, this is a story about the restoration of social balance and order that had been upset by the despotic deeds of a rich man. And third, the task was accomplished, as in many *qulirat*, by an unnamed hero whose own social position was marginal (see Lantis 1953: 114, 158). Instead of an orphan whose only known ancestor is a spiritually powerful grandmother, we have an itinerant hero with no known home but, similarly, a great deal of spiritual power. The story of Macintine serves as a model for proper behavior, for it distinguishes between the righteous and unrighteous, the Alutiiq hunters and the Russian traders.

Conclusion

The stories reproduced here exhibit characteristics of both myths and legends, *qulirat* and *qanemcit*, *unigkuat* and *quli'anguat*. Further, they describe a world in which Eskimo, Russian, and American elements meld smoothly to project a pre-eruption Alutiiq worldview and delineate the image that today's Perryvillers have of that time. The diverse cultural strands that historians and anthropologists delight in discovering and separating are inextricably woven together in the stories—and presumably in the minds of Perryvillers as well.

These stories are also part of Alutiiq history. Combined with the story of the Novarupta eruption, they illustrate that the essential separation between mythical time and modern time occurred not with Raven's machinations or the first glimmerings of human society, as among the Yupiit, but when the catastrophic eruption of a mountain on the Alaska Peninsula buried all that was old. People were left to reconstruct their lives and reinvent their culture.

This point is illustrated in several ways. First, the preeruption period is characterized as a paradise. It is also seen to be substantially different from modern times. It was a time when God spoke directly to people, when a shaman-in-the-making spent an entire year in a pit before emerging in his full spiritual strength, when only a spiritually powerful stranger was capable of vanquishing the evils of the "Russian" economic system. Second, the structure and content of the eruption story mimic origin myths, and third, with the death of all the survivors of the disaster, this story has become the primary origin narrative within the villagers' communal oral tradition.

Finally, Katmai has become an imaginary place for today's Alutiiqs, none of whom has seen it. Although pre-eruption stories are set in a named location (as are Yup'ik *qanemcit* and, presumably, Alutiiq *quli'anguat*), the people actually have no visual referent for that place. Katmai has become a symbolic setting similar to the generalized locales in Yup'ik *qulirat*.

The fact that Alaska Peninsula Alutiiqs can no longer distinguish between *unigkuat* and *quli'anguat* is thus not merely a product of translation difficulties but also derives from the conception of history embedded in the stories. All "old" stories are seen as essentially alike, parts of the same genre, having taken place during a homogeneous epoch. People see only one major discontinuity in Alutiiq folklore, a rupture that coincides with the major historical break between the pre- and post-Katmai eras. Events that occurred before the eruption and move to Perryville are stories. Those that happened afterward are history.

Notes

1.   This account appears to be the source for most of the information contained in a book written by a teacher who lived in Perryville for five years during the 1960s (Johnson and Johnson 1977).

2.   Vansina (1985) suggests that specific predictable changes occur as eye-witness report turns to oral tradition. There is disagreement among oral historians and folklorists about the timing and causes of some of those changes, but most agree that variations in form and content conform to a general pattern.

3.   In the Alutiiq language, the plural term is Alutiit, while the dual is Alutiik. In this article, I follow common Alaska Peninsula usage: When speaking English, the people call themselves either "Aleuts" or "Alutiiqs."

4.   The term "Russian Aleut" describes people who recognize both Russian and Alutiiq forebears. Indeed, the vast majority of today's Alutiiqs can claim such ancestry, but those who call themselves Russian Aleuts believe they were and were regarded by others as distinct from the Alutiiqs they lived with. They grew up in homes where Russian rather than, or in addition to, Alutiiq was spoken. Their parents were literate, usually church readers. Many Russian Aleuts on the Alaska Peninsula trace their ancestry to Kodiak or Mitrofania, which was founded in 1880 by Creoles from Kodiak Island (Tanner 1888: 36).

5.   This locale is no longer called Cold Bay, which is now the name of a village and bay located 250 miles to the southwest near the tip of the Alaska Peninsula. The bay which contained the 1910 Alutiiq settlement of Cold Bay is now called Puale Bay.

6.   Also spelled "Wrangell" and called "Port Wrangell" or "Wrangell Bay," this locale should not be confused with the town of the same name in southeastern Alaska.

7.   The name "Savonoski" is a corruption of the Russian term *severnovskie*, which was originally a designation for a group of people (*severnovskie* being the plural form of the adjective "northern") who lived in several settlements in the region around what are now Naknek, Grosvenor, and Brooks lakes in the interior of the Alaska Peninsula, northwest of Katmai. The name Savonoski was eventually applied by the local people to a particular village near the mouth of Iliuk arm of Lake Naknek. There is also a New Savonoski on the Naknek River, established after the Novarupta eruption and inhabited by the people from the original Savonoski but recently abandoned.

        The ethnicity of the Severnovskie people is uncertain. Russian Orthodox church records report their self-ascription as Aleut (the English version of the term Alutiiq [Dumond 1986: 5]), although Spurr notes that "even between two such closely adjacent settlements as Savonoski and Katmai there is a marked difference in the speech" (Spurr 1990: 93).

8.   In 1911, sea otter hunting was prohibited altogether by law and international treaty.

9.   Although Wasco and Vanka are nicknames for Wasillie, or Vasilii, and Ivan respectively, neither man is ever referred to by his formal name.

10.   The postbase *-nguaq* (plural, *-nguat*) used with nouns means "little, small."

11.   One animal story recalled was an Aesop's fable from the woman's childhood schoolbook.

12.   For extended discussions of this and related phenomena, see Wagner (1975) and Hobsbawm and Ranger (1983).

13.   I did not hear Alutiiqs generalize about the overall effect of Russian contact. Instead, I most often heard them discuss particular Russian imports, such as religion or the fur trade. Most Alutiiqs characterize Russian Orthodoxy as beneficial and the Russian fur trade as detrimental to their culture.

14.   Even the Americans who carried on commerce in the area understood the importance of the Russian language. Father Harry Kaiakokonok explains,

> [Foster, the owner of the Kaflia Bay saltery] speak a little Russian too! All those people that lives in Kodiak speak little Russian. That the language Kodiak used to use—even the Kodiak natives hardly speak their dialect, mostly in Russian. That's why this Foster guy speak a little Russian, too, so the people can understand whenever they inquire for something. (1975b)

Alfred B. Shanz, who gathered information on the Nushagak district for the 1890 census, similarly reports,

> The fact that the territory is now owned by the United States cuts no figure and many of the native members of the church are not even aware of that fact. The natives of the north peninsula villages divide mankind into two classes, Russians and non-Russians, and to all of the latter class they apply the generic term Americanski, no matter whether the individual specimen be a German, a Scandinavian, a Finlander, or a Kanaka. One unable to speak any Russian whatever is looked upon as pitifully ignorant and is treated with contempt. (1893: 96)

15.   I have titled the narratives for easy reference, but Kosbruk did not name the stories. Rather, he would say, "Have I told you that one about the *piculi*?" or "Did I tell you that one about Macintine?"

16.   The narratives that follow are arranged in paragraph form pending a more detailed analysis of pauses (see Tedlock 1983). Each paragraph begins with a lexical marker indicating the beginning of a new thought or episode. Ignatius Kosbruk's most common marker is *"nu-taan tawaken,"* meaning roughly, "now then ..." or "and then ..." or "and after that. ..."

17. Ignatius Kosbruk used the term *kallagalek,* which he glossed as "shaman," to describe Pugla'allria. French scholar Alphonse Pinart, who traveled in Alaska in 1871 and 1872, referred to two types of Alutiiq spiritual practitioners: the *"kahlalik"* (which Leer transliterates as *kallagalek*) or shaman, and the *"kachak,* un homme supposé avoir des relations avec les [sic] *hlam-choua* [person or power of the universe] et connaître l'avenir; il était en même temps le dépositaire des traditions et de la foi religieuses de ces populations; ils étaient ... tres-révérés et placés bien au-dessus du *kahlalik"* (Pinart 1873: 677).

18. Not all Alaska Peninsula Alutiiqs agree with this characterization of shamanism. Several people became uncomfortable when I introduced the topic, disclaiming any knowledge of *kallagaleks.* They stated that the practice was the devil's work. The region's current priest, Father Maxim Isaac, does not share this view. He is a Yup'ik who has great respect for the healing ability of the shamans of the past. He recounted to me his father's recovery from an accident, reportedly made with the invaluable assistance of the local shaman. Father Max's attitude toward shamanism may have facilitated the discussions of the topic that I was privileged to hear.

19. "Pugla'allria" contains many interesting motifs, most of which are beyond the scope of this paper. For instance, shamanistic contests are common themes in Eskimo lore (Lantis 1953: 156). In addition, the maternal uncle's role is significant as an indication of precontact social structure. Davydov notes that in the early nineteenth century among the Koniag Alutiiqs, heredity passed from uncle to nephew, precisely as it did among the Tlingits (1977: 190). Ignatius Kosbruk's story lends support to the idea that the Katmai Alutiiq social system was similar. Further, Golder reports the motif of the cruel uncle in Kodiak folklore (1903: 90–95), and Boas compares the motif with similar Northwest Coast stories (1919: 796–817, 951–52). Lantis sees the motif as an indication of close cultural contact between Koniag and Tlingit cultures (Lantis 1938: 128, 154).

20. Jeff Leer (personal communication with the author, April 1993) reports that a common folk belief among Russian Orthodox faithful is that a person who dies on Good Friday automatically goes to Heaven. See also Fienup-Riordan (1988) for the story of the death of a Yup'ik Christian, also during Holy Week.

21. I did not understand this detail about the cow until I heard a 1969 recording made by Spiridon Stepanoff, in which he explained that Macintine and his crew were slaughtering a cow for their dinner when the assassin asked for a share.

22. See Partnow (1993) for a detailed discussion of the differences among the Katmai story versions.

23. See Partnow (1993) for a transcript of Stepanoff's Macintine story.

24. The bishop in question is undoubtedly Bishop Nestor, who died in 1882

during McIntyre's tenure at Kodiak while on a visit to the west coast of Alaska. Almost a century later, the *American Orthodox Messenger* described his death as follows:

> In 1882 he was in the far north, at Mikhailovsky Redoubt [St. Michael]. On the return trip to San Francisco, Bishop Nestor unexpectedly disappeared. Apparently he was washed completely overboard off the little steamship on which he was traveling. After some time, Aleut fishermen from Mikhailovsky Redoubt found Bishop Nestor's cassocked body. Over him circled a seagull. The body was taken to Unalaska for burial. (AOM 1972: 113)

To my knowledge, there was no suspicion of foul play at the time of Bishop Nestor's death. Spiridon's motif of discord between the economic activity of hunting and the religious observance of holidays also appears in Fred Roscoe's memoirs (1992: 50–51).

25. Anderson is not, of course, a Russian name. Vladimir Stafeev, an agent stationed at the Alaska Commercial Company's post at Tyonek, received word of the murder and wrote in his diary that Anderson was a "Russian Finn" (Diary: April 18, 1887). Roscoe posits that the man's name was Andresoff in Russian (1992: 6).

References

Alaska Commercial Company (ACC). Correspondence of the Kodiak Post 1868–1891. University of Alaska.

Alaskan Russian Church (ARC). Russian Orthodox Greek Catholic Church in America Archives. Geographical File 1733–1938. Kodiak Island and Area 1815–1933. Reel 180. University of Alaska Anchorage Archives.

Anchorage Archives. Microfilm. *American Orthodox Messenger* (AOM). See *Pravoslavnyi Amerikanskii Vestnik'*.

Bascom, William. 1984. "The Forms of Folklore: Prose Narratives." In *Sacred Narrative: Readings in the Theory of Myth*, edited by Alan Dundes, 5–29. Berkeley: University of California Press.

Boas, Franz. 1919. *Tsimshian Mythology*. Bureau of American Ethnology Annual Report 34. Washington, D.C.: Bureau of American Ethnology.

Chichenoff, Katherine. 1975. Interview by Nancy Freeman. Tape recording. Kodiak Alaska. Oral History Archives, Elmer E. Rasmuson Library, University of Alaska Fairbanks.

Dauenhauer, Nora Marks, and Richard Dauenhauer. 1984. "Alaska Native Oral Tradition." In *1984 Festival of American Folklife*, edited by Thomas Vennum, 25–27. Washington, D.C.: Smithsonian Institution and National Park Service.

Davis, Nancy Yaw. 1986. *A Sociocultural Description of Small Communities in the Kodiak-Shumagin Region*. Minerals Management Service Technical Report, no. 121. Washington, D.C.: U.S. Department of Interior.

Davydov, Gavriil I. 1977. *Two Voyages to Russian America, 1802–1807*. Translated by Colin Bearne. Kingston, Ont., Canada: Limestone Press.

deLaguna, Frederica. 1972. *Under Mount Saint Elias: The History and Culture of the Yakutat Tlingit*. Washington, D.C.: Smithsonian Institution.

Dumond, Don E. 1986. *Demographic Effects of European Expansion: A Nineteenth-Century Native Population on the Alaska Peninsula*. Anthropological Papers, no. 35. Eugene: University of Oregon Press.

Ellenak, Larry, and Katie Ellenak. 1976. Interview by Carolyn Elder. Tape recording. Ouzinkie, 12 November. Oral History Archives, Elmer E. Rasmuson Library, University of Alaska Fairbanks.

Elliott, Capt. Charles P. 1900. "Salmon Fishing Grounds and Canneries." In *Compilation of Narratives of Explorations in Alaska*. Washington, D.C.: U.S. Government Printing Office.

Erskine, Wilson Fiske. 1962. *Katmai: A True Narrative*. London and New York: Abelard-Schuman.

Fienup-Riordan, Ann. 1988. "The Martyrdom of Brother Hooker: Conflict and Conversion on the Kuskokwim." *Alaska History* 3(1): 1–26.

———. 1990. *Eskimo Essays: Yupik Lives and How We See Them*. New Brunswick, NJ: Rutgers University Press.

Golder, Frank A. 1903. "Tales from Kodiak Island." Parts 1 and 2. *Journal of American Folklore* 16(1): 16–31; (2): 85–103.

Goodwin, Sister. 1986. "Piksinñaq." In *Alaska Native Writers, Storytellers and Orators*, edited by Nora Dauenhauer, Richard Dauenhauer, and Gary Holthaus, 168. Anchorage: University of Alaska Press.

Harvey, Lola. 1991. *Derevnia's Daughters: Saga of an Alaskan Village*. Manhattan, Kans.: Sunflower University Press.

Hobsbawm, Eric, and Terence Ranger, eds. 1983. *The Invention of Tradition*. Cambridge: Cambridge University Press.

Honko, Lauri. 1984. "The Problem of Defining Myth." In *Sacred Narrative: Readings in the Theory of Myth*, edited by Alan Dundes, 41–52. Berkeley: University of California Press.

Hussey, John A. 1971. *Embattled Katmai: A History of Katmai National Monument*. Springfield, Va.: National Technical Information Service, U. S. Dept. of Commerce.

Ives, Edward D. 1988. *George Magoon and the Down East Game War*. Urbana: University of Illinois Press.

Jessee, Tom. 1961. Letter to Dr. L. S. Cressman, Head of the Department of Anthropology, University of Oregon, 12 June.

Johnson, Andrew P. 1975. *Kiks.ádi Dog Salmon Legend*. Anchorage: Alaska Native Education Board.

Johnson, Fremont, and Harriet Johnson. 1977. *Da-Ne-Hi: Come in to Alaska and Men of Katmai*. Arkansas Pass, Tex.: Biography Press.

Kaiakokonok, Harry O. 1956. Untitled story said to have been printed in *Island Breezes* (newsletter). Sitka: Public Health Service. Mimeograph.

———. 1975a. Interview by Michael J. Tollefson. Tape recording. King Salmon, 29 April. Katmai National Monument, King Salmon, Alaska.

———. 1975b. Interview by Michael J. Tollefson and Harvey Shields. Tape recording. Perryville, 22 October. Katmai National Monument, King Salmon, Alaska.

Kosbruk, George. 1975a. Interview by Michael J. Tollefson and Harvey Shields. Tape recording. Perryville, 21 October. Katmai National Monument, King Salmon, Alaska.

———. 1975b. Interview by Michael J. Tollefson and Harvey Shields. Tape recording. Perryville, 22 October. Katmai National Monument, King Salmon, Alaska.

———. 1976. "We Were Very Lucky." In *Elwani* (Kodiak Aleutian Regional High School) I(1): 16–19.

———. n.d. Tape recording of performance at the Elder's Conference, Dillingham, in the 1970s. English translation by Jeff Leer. Alaska Native Language Center, University of Alaska Fairbanks.

Lantis, Margaret. 1938. "The Mythology of Kodiak Island, Alaska." *Journal of American Folklore* 51(200): 123–72.

———. 1953. "Nunivak Eskimo Personality As Revealed in the Mythology." *Anthropological Papers of the University of Alaska* 2(1): 109–74.

Martin, George C. 1913. "The Recent Eruption of Katmai Volcano in Alaska." *National Geographic* 24(2): 131–80.

McClellan, Catharine. 1970a. "Indian Stories about the First Whites in Northwestern North America." In *Ethnohistory of Southwestern Alaska and the Southern Yukon*, edited by Margaret Lantis, 103–33. Lexington: University Press of Kentucky.

———. 1970b. *The Girl Who Married the Bear*. Publications in Ethnology, no. 2. Ottawa: National Museum of Man.

Meyer, Richard. 1980. "The Outlaw: A Distinctive American Folktype." *Journal of the Folklore Institute* 17(May–December): 94–124.

Morrow, Phyllis. 1994. "Oral Literature of the Alaskan Arctic." In *Dictionary of Native North American Literature*, edited by Andrew Wiget, 19–32. New York: Garland Publishing.

———. 1990. "Symbolic Actions, Indirect Expressions: Limits to Interpretations of Yupik Society." *Etudes/Inuit/Studies* 14(1–2): 141–58.

Nelson, Edward William. 1899. *The Eskimo about Bering Strait*. Eighteenth Annual Report of the Bureau of American Ethnology to the Secretary of the Smithsonian Institution. Washington, D.C.: Bureau of American Ethnology.

Norton, Laura. 1986. "The Boy Who Found the Lost." In *Alaska Native Writers, Storytellers and Orators*, edited by Nora Dauenhauer, Richard Dauenhauer, and Gary Holthaus, 79–88. Anchorage: University of Alaska Press.

Partnow, Patricia H. 1993. "Alutiiq Ethnicity." Ph.D. diss. Department of Anthropology, University of Alaska Fairbanks.

Petroff, Ivan [Boris Lanin, pseud.]. n.d. "Presentiments: An Alaskan Reminiscence." Manuscript C-B 989, Folder 2. Bancroft Library, University of California, Berkeley.

Pierce, Richard A. 1968. "New Light on Ivan Petroff, Historian of Alaska." *Pacific Northwest Quarterly* 59(1): 1–10.

Pinart, Alphonse. 1873. "Eskimaux et Koloches: Idées Religieuses et Traditions des Kaniagmioutes." *Revue d'Anthropologie* (Paris) 2: 673–80.

Pravoslavnyi Amerikanskii Vestnik' (*American Orthodox Messenger*) [AOM]. Available at the University of Alaska Anchorage Archives. 1898. "Short Church Historical Description of the Kodiak Parish." Translated by P. H. Partnow. 2: 265–66, 508–10.

———. 1899. "Report on Kodiak Parish." Translated by P. H. Partnow. 3: 91, 160.

———. 1902. "Report of the Voyage of Vasilii Martysh, Taken in 1901." Translated by P. H. Partnow. 6: 431–33.

———. 1904. Excerpts from "Travel Report of Vasilii Martysh on a Trip Taken in 1902." Translated by P. H. Partnow. 8: 13–15, 32–34.

———. 1911. "Oldtimers of Alaska," by Father A. Kedrovskiy. Translated by P. H. Partnow. 15: 273–74, 323–24.

———. 1912. Excerpts "from a Report by Priest A. Kedrovskiy." Translated by P. H. Partnow. 16: 77.

———. 1972. "Bishop Nestor." Translated by P. H. Partnow. 68: 111–13.

Roscoe, Fred. 1992. *From Humboldt to Kodiak.* Fairbanks: University of Alaska Press.

Seton-Karr, Heywood. 1887. *Shores and Alps of Alaska.* Chicago: A. C. McClurg.

Shanz, Alfred B. 1893. "Chapter VI: The Fourth of Nushagak District." In *Report on Population and Resources of Alaska at the Eleventh Census*, edited by Robert Perceval Porter, 91–98. Washington, D.C.: U.S. Government Printing Office.

Spurr, Josiah Edward. 1990. *A Reconnaissance in Southwestern Alaska in 1898.* Washington, D.C.: U.S. Government Printing Office.

Stafeev, Vladimir. Diary. Translated by Marina Ramsay and Lydia T. Black, edited by Richard A. Pierce. Personal files of Richard A. Pierce.

Stepanoff, Spiridon. 1969. Interview by Don Kinsey. Tape recording. Chignik Lake. Personal files of Patricia Partnow.

Tanner, Z. L. 1888. Vol. 8 of *Bulletin of the United States Fish Commission.* Washington, D.C.: U. S. Government Printing Office.

Tedlock, Dennis. 1983. *The Spoken Word and the Work of Interpretation.* Philadelphia: University of Pennsylvania Press.

Thompson, Stith. [1929]1966. *Tales of the North American Indians.* Reprint, Bloomington: Indiana University Press.

———. [1955] 1975. *Motif-Index of Folk Literature.* Reprint, Bloomington: Indiana University Press.

Turner, Victor. 1969. *The Ritual Process*. Ithaca: Cornell University Press.

———. 1974. *Dramas, Fields and Metaphors: Symbolic Action in Human Society*. Ithaca: Cornell University Press.

U.S. Bureau of the Census. 1900. Census of Alaska. Roll 1832. National Archives, Anchorage, Alaska.

———. 1910. Census of Alaska. Roll 1750. National Archives, Anchorage, Alaska.

U.S. Revenue Cutter Service (USRCS). 1913. *Annual Report of the Revenue Cutter Service*. Washington, D.C.: U.S. Government Printing Office.

———. Alaska File 1867–1914. RG 26. Records of the United States Coast Guard. Microfilm M641, roll 16. National Archives. Anchorage, Alaska.

Van Gennep, Arnold. [1908] 1960. *The Rites of Passage*. Translated by M. B. Visedom and G. L. Caffee. Reprint, with an introduction by Solon T. Kimball, Chicago: University of Chicago Press.

Vansina, Jan. 1985. *Oral Tradition as History*. Madison: University of Wisconsin Press.

Wagner, Roy. 1975. *The Invention of Culture*. Chicago: University of Chicago Press.

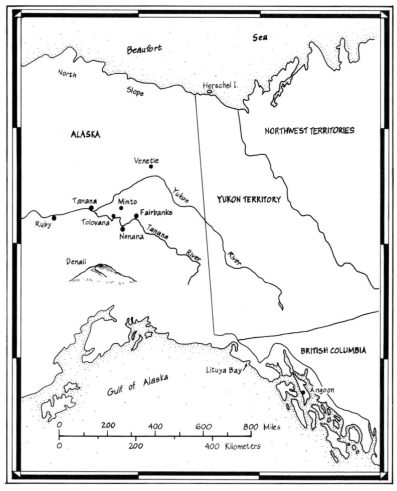

Alaska, Yukon Territory, and the Northwest Territories, showing locations mentioned in the text. Map by Robert Drozda.

Lessons from Alaska Natives about Oral Tradition and Recordings

William Schneider

In this essay, William Schneider focuses on the record of remembrance that is bequeathed to future generations. As an oral historian and archivist, Schneider is sensitive to the differences between remembering in context and "freeze-drying" memories on tape.

Although we know that neither writing nor recording necessarily inhibits oral transmission (we habitually retell the plots of movies and novels, remember urban legends, and write stories that reflect our society's most cherished folktales), we have good reasons for wanting to keep a diversity of traditions alive. To do so, however, we need to know and appreciate the contexts which have nourished them.

Unlike Partnow, Schneider does not deal with reshaping memories for the present, but he does take an active stance toward remembering. His examples reveal that what people find memorable, and want others to recall, are things which continue to have relevance and importance. For example, the resilience and defiance of indigenous individuals (and, by extension, their cultures) in the face of Western domination are a pervasive overt and covert theme that transects the oral traditions of otherwise-varied Northern peoples. Similarly, Schneider notes that the same story "can be grounded and thrive in two or more folk groups" that have little contact with each other, especially if an appealing universal theme, such as self-sacrifice, makes it memorable.

Schneider portrays the oral historian's work as a way of deciding what to remember in the absence of the conditions which triggered remembrance. That is, recording, by its very existence, marks a telling as worthy to preserve but removes it from the teller who decided why it was worth remembering at that particular time and place. Recorded materials are simply unintelligible without contextual dimensions.

While he does not mention it in this essay, Schneider is turning toward computer technology to create a wider context for understanding recordings. With a "jukebox" program, audio and visual elements can be combined; collectors can incorporate maps, photographs, biographical data, and other descriptive material into the narrative. While it does not fully hydrate them, this approach at least moisturizes these freeze-dried recordings.

Schneider's essay is an important reminder that recording traditions is a form of remembering, not simply a documenting of things remembered. Although recordings may appear complete and faithful to their source, they are actually as problematic as writing.

Years ago, Alan Dundes (1964) pointed out that stories contain at least three elements: text—what the story is about; texture—the way the story is told; and context—the circumstances surrounding the telling. These three elements are not always obvious and clear-cut, but the categories point to the fact that storytelling and comprehending its meaning depend upon an appreciation of what is said, the way it is expressed, and the particular setting that prompted the telling. These considerations have become basic to our understanding of *oral literature* and the *verbal arts*, terms which are often used interchangeably but carry slightly different emphases (Finnegan 1992: 9–11). *Oral literature* connotes structured presentation, recognizable genres, and the speaking styles of people who share a common body of knowledge and ways of conveying it to others. *Verbal arts* reflects the creative and skillful use of language to communicate meaning within a group that expects, appreciates, and recognizes individual variation in storytelling. Taken together, the terms point to the hallmarks of oral tradition. It is creative and personal, but it is also structured and experienced by a group of people who share a basic understanding of the way stories are told and how to comprehend their meaning.

This tension between structure, creativity, and meaning is easily lost in oral recordings, which are made at one point in time and passed on to an audience of people who don't know the speaker and his or her culture. This dilemma challenges us to ask: What have we captured on tape and what eludes us on the machine but is integral to the telling?

These are some of the challenges that I faced when I wrote the oral biographies of Moses Cruikshank and Waldo Bodfish, Sr. In my work with Moses Cruikshank, an Athabaskan elder, I was concerned that after I transformed his stories through tape and transcript, I would create something very different from my experiences listening to him tell stories over the years and foreign to those who know him. I wanted to preserve as much as possible of the way he speaks and the settings where he shares his stories. In order to do this, I had to go beyond the text, back to Moses' choice of words, the way he strings certain stories together, and the settings where he tells them. I had to go beyond the words and rely on the ways I know him.

The second volume in the oral biography series is Waldo Bodfish, Sr.'s book, *Kusiq: An Eskimo Life History from the Arctic Coast of Alaska*. Preparing it, I continued to ask how I could convey the meaning which lies in the stories but is clear only to those who know the man. I found that I had to describe to readers how my relationship with Bodfish affected the types of stories he told me and the way he told them. I came to see myself not as a neutral conduit but as a strong influence on the content, style, and context of his storytelling.

In this essay, I intend to illustrate these and other dynamics of storytelling through a patchwork of examples from Native oral traditions. I focus on stories from Native cultures because here in Alaska and the Yukon, many Natives still rely on oral tradition as their primary source of knowledge, so who better to show us how it functions. Then I contrast oral tradition with what actually gets recorded to point out that the oral record captures only a small part of what is actually shared. I conclude that oral recordings provide a comparatively rich portrait of the way people express meaning to others (Dundes's text and texture), but that too many of them fail to adequately document the circumstances surrounding the telling and the relationship between tellers and listeners: the context.

The best way I know to begin this investigation is by sharing a very personal experience with Chief Peter John of Minto, the traditional chief of the Tanana Chiefs Region in Interior Alaska. Peter John has been interviewed many times, and a wealth of his stories exist on tape and in manuscripts. The last couple of times, we have met primarily because I wanted to ask him important questions about how to live. A few months ago, I asked him to speak about family responsibility and help me think through ways to lead that part of my life. As I recall, that's the way I presented the question to him.

He responded with the story of a starvation time he and his family had experienced. Without food and in winter during a cold stretch, Peter John went out hunting. He found fresh moose sign and started to follow it, but then he turned away, weak from hunger. He thought about his family and returned to the tracks. After many miles and using his last three shells, he finally killed three moose.

The image of Peter John turning back to the moose tracks is now a very powerful picture in my mind, and I often think about his personal strength and the depth of his love for his family. That's the way I remember the story. But I know from conversations with Dave Krupa, who has been working with Peter John for several years, that he also tells this story to illustrate his faith in God and his strong belief that we must trust God completely to provide for us. When I heard the story, I wasn't open to that message. What I focused on was Peter John's personal fortitude. I now know that if I really want to understand what he means, I can't dismiss his faith in God. My fuller understanding resulted from discussions with Dave Krupa and a subsequent visit with Peter John.

I believe Peter John responded to my original question about the way to live in the best way he could, by telling me his experience. He probably also knew that my understanding of his story would increase as I got to know him better and heard more of his stories. Sometimes he will stop and ask if we understand, and then he'll laugh at our cautious response; he is patient and knows how difficult communication is and that it requires many more tellings. Oral tradition is built upon repeated tellings in different contexts and the depth of understanding that emerges as we listen each time and open ourselves to different themes. Knowing Peter John means knowing what he means without having to ask for explanation. Oral tradition demands that we know storytellers to really understand what they are saying, and that takes years!

I am beginning to realize that it is a disservice to Peter John if I retell this story without mentioning the depth and power of his faith, even though for me the most powerful message is still that family members must work as hard as they can for each other, and that takes strength. Peter John would probably respond that his strength comes from faith in God.

Without knowing Peter John, what prompted the story, his intentions, and my understanding at the time, you are left with only a small part of the meaning. This illustrates the types of challenges we face if we want to understand oral tradition and use oral sources. We must go beyond the text as much as possible to approach a complete meaning. To do this, we must know a great deal about speakers and learn how and why they tell stories. Only recently have we begun to realize that the text is not enough, that the type of sharing experienced in oral tradition cannot be mechanically preserved on tape. We can record Peter John's laugh, but to understand what it means, we have to take the time to get to know him and see how he uses it. We need to consciously ask ourselves how and why stories were told to us and then document that information for other people who want to use the recording. We must produce what Renato Rosaldo calls an "analytical narrative" (1980: 90). Our starting point and frame of reference must be oral tradition itself.

Oral Tradition

By *oral tradition*, I mean all accounts which are deemed important enough to pass on in the collective memory. Barre Toelken puts it very clearly: "Folklore is made up of informal expressions passed around long enough to have become recurrent in form and content, but changeable in performance" (1979: 32). Unlike Vansina (1985: 12–13), I don't discount recent personal narratives (stories based on individual or group experience), as long as they are known and shared by others and are acknowledged by a folk group as worthy to be passed on. I don't require a certain number of people to constitute a folk group, nor do I have strong feelings about how long a story needs to be told before it can be considered part of the oral tradition. Following Toelken, I think a key feature of the folk group is "the extent to which its own dynamics continue to inform and educate its members and stabilize the group" (1979: 51).

So I'm more concerned about the reason stories continue to be told than how long they have to be told to be part of the oral tradition. Do they, for example, explain characteristics of animals and the social and natural world, or do they teach lessons of proper behavior, or are there other reasons for telling them? My sense is that the stories that continue to speak to people's experiences and needs will last the longest. I can illustrate this point by an example from southeast Alaska.

For the people of Angoon, the United States Navy's shelling of their village in 1882 is still a very vital part of their oral tradition. The Navy shelled Angoon because the Tlingit of that village were holding members of the Northwest Trading Company hostage to force the company to make payment for the death of a shaman killed in a commercial whaling accident. By all reckoning, the Navy's show of force was totally inappropriate, and the atrocity has never been forgotten. The anthropologist Frederica deLaguna collected an account in 1950 from Homeless Raven. In telling the story, Homeless Raven inserted several other grievances into the account, including his comments on current fish and game laws, the building of a local fertilizer plant, and mandatory service in the military, all to demonstrate the way the government still mistreats and misunderstands Angoon people (de-Laguna 1960: 170–71). Ten or so years ago, I was indexing U.S. Forest Service tapes and came across some made in Angoon. I recall how surprised I was to find many of them contained the bombardment story. I now know that the story survives in the oral tradition not only because the original action was so atrocious but because people continue to see a pattern of grievances that matches the events of 1882.

There are other examples of the way stories highlight clashes between Native and white ways during the early years of contact. Often they celebrate individuals who defy the outsider's authority and use their own power to prevail. One of the stories that Inuvialuit elders tell when asked about Herschel Island features Kublualuk, a powerful shaman. I have had the chance to hear two accounts about Kublualuk, and I am impressed by the way he seems to symbolize the tension between old shamanistic practices and Canadian national law and order. Several accounts of Kublualuk have recently been published (Nagy 1994: 30–32; also Nagy 1991a, 1991b). At least two stories from the newest volume tell about the shaman and the way he freed himself from jail. The story goes that he was locked up by the Royal Canadian Mounted Police (RCMP) at Herschel Island; one version states that he had been drinking with the "sailors" (commercial whalers) and had gotten drunk and out of control. Despite the policemen's efforts, they couldn't contain him in jail; he kept escaping. The police finally gave up trying to restrain him and made him a special constable.

In both accounts, the shaman's power is matched against the police; he proves more powerful, and the authorities back down. These stories are testimony to the way people remember Native power in the early days of contact with the RCMP. I think the story survives because the theme of Native strength and legitimacy amidst the Westerners' display of might remains important, memorable, and worth passing on to future generations. This doesn't mean that the tellers condone all the actions of Kublualuk or even that they prefer shamanism to Canadian national law and Western religion, but it does demonstrate how much they still respect his power, which was exercised at a time when there was extreme pressure to conform to Western ways.

In a similar way, I am reminded of Shahnyaati', a powerful trading chief from the Yukon Flats. Unlike many of his followers, he exerted a great deal of control over other people, food, and material wealth. He was respected for his ability and willingness to provide for others and is remembered as merciless toward those who crossed him. He lived during the latter half of the nineteenth century, at a time when the Hudson's Bay Company and the American traders were operating in the interior of Alaska, and he established himself as a broker between the Indians he supported and the fur-trading companies. His success in this role depended upon the support he got from the traders and his fellow Athabaskans.

I have heard several people talk about Shahnyaati'; often they tell about the way they are related to him. Some go on to relate his exploits. My most complete accounts have come from Sophie Paul, who was eager to tell me about him because she wanted her grandchildren and future generations to know about this man (see Schneider 1976: 315–27 for the details of Paul's stories about Shahnyaati' and her close kinship ties with him).

In all the accounts, Shahnyaati' takes responsibility for feeding and supporting a large number of people, a major accomplishment at a time when people sometimes starved to death. This message has particular meaning for today's elders, who recall difficult times in their own lives when they didn't have enough to eat. Because Shahnyaati' was a provider, the Yukon Flats Gwich'in supported him. They hunted and trapped, and he did the trading. People wanted to be around him. Old Birch Creek Jimmy told me, "Shahnyaati's sons weren't going far for wives" (Schneider 1976: 208). Shahnyaati' himself had many wives, a sign that he was able to provide. When he wanted to make war, his band stood by him. Even beyond his own people, neighboring groups and their leaders backed him in war.

Today people don't condone all that Shahnyaati' did, but I think they excuse many things. His actions, even his most violent ones such as killings, are explained and excused because he looked after people. I recall Sophie Paul saying that when the minister told Shahnyaati' to give up all his wives and only keep one, he said he'd take his first two, but he still gave food to the others (Schneider 1976: 326).

Unlike the Angoon bombardment stories, where the reasons they persist are perfectly clear to group members and outsiders alike, in the cases of Kublualuk and Shahnyaati', we are on shakier ground. I think people continue to tell stories about these two men because they so successfully defied the newcomers. The stories are an antithesis to the usual accounts, which highlight suppression of Native ways. And I think because of this positive image, people deem the stories worth passing on to future generations. (See Partnow's essay for "Macintine" and other clever Alutiiq tales that exemplify this genre.)

Is it going too far to call these men culture heros? Will they fade from the oral tradition when the elders are gone who remember what life was like when they lived or heard about these "great" men from a close relative? Or is their message of lasting value to the group? I don't know the answers to these questions, for, unlike the Angoon bombardment, the reasons for telling these stories remain unstated. I can only say that they are important enough to people that they continue to be told, and my sense is that is the case because they are success stories at a particularly critical time in the group's history, when its members were negotiating power relationships and verifying their values to each other and the dominant culture. While I know that the Angoon story is told to people outside the group and the Kublualuk story was played on the radio, my sense is that Shahnyaati' is mentioned to outsiders as a great chief, but stories about him are rarely told to them and may even be largely confined to his relatives.

While stories survive because they have meaning for the folk group and serve a purpose, we must go beyond a functional analysis to understand the way oral tradition works. Dundes and other folklorists (see Toelken and Scott 1981) remind us that meaning extends beyond the text to the contexts or settings where the stories are recalled and told. In Athabaskan tradition among the Koyukon, winter is the time for *kk'adonts'idnee* stories. The tellers are reputed to shorten the long winter when they tell these epic stories at night (Attla 1983: 1–2, 1990: viii). Yup'ik storyknifing is a specialized type of storytelling for young girls in summer, when they can draw in the mud. They learn the stories from older girls and from their mothers (Ager 1974; Oswalt 1964). In southeast Alaska, some Tlingit, Haida, and Tsimshian stories are owned by clans which control when and who can use them. They resist certain types of tape recording and distribution because clan members would lose control of the way the tapes are used.

In each of these cases, the meaning of the story goes deeper than the text to the people who are present and the setting where the story is told. We are reminded that the stories are intended for those people at that time. The folk group's identity is reinforced not only by the story and the people there when it is told but also by the cultural rules that govern how and when it may be retold.

Audience also plays a vital part in all storytelling. For instance, in

Iñupiaq culture, an old man will turn to other men of his generation and ask for their confirmation. They may respond with something like, "Yes, that's the way I remember it." Older Athabaskan women may tell their stories to a young girl, periodically addressing her, "Granddaughter . . . ." Belle Herbert's book, *Shandaa: In My Lifetime*, is an example of this form of address (Herbert 1982). When Athabaskan elder Poldine Carlo was hired to record stories for the Alaska Library Association's Songs and Legends program, she was told not to interact much with the narrators: "Don't say a word; don't say anything." She tried to follow the instructions until one old man, puzzled by her social distance, asked her why she wasn't responding to his stories: "Grandchild, how come you're not saying anything? You're supposed to say every now and then, 'Aha!' " (Women's Oral History Panel, 1992: tape no. H-93-06-02).

These storytellers remind us that we learn oral tradition from individuals in personal and particular social contexts and our knowledge of a story includes our recall of the text along with the conditions of the telling. In our retelling, we convey a sense of this social context and the people who have told us the story. Past tellers and the circumstances in which we heard the stories are our human connection with the event; they are a part of what we know about what went on.

I remember the first time I heard about John Fredson, a young Athabaskan boy who was along with Hudson Stuck on the historic climb of Denali (Mt. McKinley) (Stuck 1914). There are many interesting stories about Fredson, covering his early years at the mission, his travels with his father, his formal education, and his experiences starting a school at Venetie (Mishler 1982). But stories of the climb are particularly noteworthy because they are told by two quite distinct groups of people: Native elders, who have little interest in mountain climbing, and mountain climbers, who, as a group, have no particular interest in Native history and culture.

On the climb, Fredson's job was to stay at the base camp and look after things while the others went up the mountain. He is remembered because he carefully saved all the sugar so that when the others got down, they would have something sweet for their tea, an act which is recognized by both groups as very important and indicative of his good character. I first heard this story from a group of Athabaskan elders gathered around a table at the Fairbanks Native Association. I later read it in Clara Mackenzie's book, *Wolf Smeller* (1985: 48–49, 55–56), and it is also reported by Stuck in his account of the climb (1914: 129). Recently I was surprised to learn from a friend

Johnny Fred who kept the base-camp and fed the dogs and would not touch the sugar.

Photo and caption from Hudson Stuck, *Ascent of Denali (Mt. McKinley): A Narrative of the First Complete Ascent of the Highest Peak in North America* (New York: Charles Scribner's Sons, 1914), between pp. 128 and 129.

that climbers also tell the story. Now when I think about this account, I also think about the two quite different settings in which it is told and the people who tell it.

The book reference pales in comparison to personal retellings because they come from distinct folk groups which happen to share the same lore. Mountain climbers learn the story from other mountain climbers and perhaps from reading Hudson Stuck's classic, *The Ascent of Denali*. I suspect that Natives learn it from other Natives and also from the written accounts by Mackenzie and Craig Mishler's biography of Fredson in McGary's book. I doubt that mountain climbers know other stories about Fredson, and Native stories about mountain climbers are equally rare. For both groups, the storytellers and their social contexts are the critical link for any retelling. And for me, when I recall this story, the image of each group with all their apparent differences, including the settings where they may tell the story, have to be part of the human connection which weaves through my retellings.

In oral tradition, the relationship between teller and audience guides the retelling. This relationship is implicit in all renditions and grounds the story in human reality. The grounding can be formal, as in the cultures of southeast Alaska, where clan affiliation and kinship determine rights to know and tell, or highly personal, as with my story from Chief Peter John. A story can also be grounded and thrive in two or more folk groups, as in the Fredson case.

So far in this essay, I have concentrated on textual and contextual issues. Now I turn to textural elements to investigate how we can derive meaning from the way people express themselves. Patty Bowen, a schoolteacher for many years in Tanana, has been indexing old recordings from that village. Because of her familiarity with the elders and her sensitivity to the way they use words, she has been able to identify and highlight their special expressions. For instance, "gather up" refers to the coming together of many people at a particular place, often used to describe the historic spring gatherings at the mouth of the Tanana River, where groups from hundreds of miles away came each year when the ice cleared. This was a time for trading, celebrating, and sharing news from distant groups. Another expression, "before the big wind comes," refers to the strong winds that blow in the fall near Tanana and make travel difficult (see Edwin and Luke, tape no. H78–184).

These expressions are common knowledge to the people in Tanana, and to these listeners they convey a verbal image of an activity or seasonal phenomena. "Gather up" may be less familiar to younger people, since the spring gathering hasn't taken place recently. Both expressions will undoubtedly change over time, and new ones will emerge. However, our understanding of elders like Lee Edwin and Teddy Luke is dependent on identification and explanation of the old expressions. In this project, the oral record has preserved the use but not the meaning. Only with the help of people like Patty Bowen, who are active participants in the folk group and know the oral tradition, can we hope to explain to future generations the ways elders express themselves, their choice of words, and the meaning behind them.

The best way to describe oral tradition is to say that it is dependent on people; it can grow and change, or it can be forgotten. The control rests completely with the folk group, which decides consciously or unconsciously what will be preserved and how.

Oral Sources

When oral traditions are recorded, the recordings take on their own life, independent of the interaction between tellers and audience, the setting, and the original reasons a story was told. They function as a created record that is widely accessible and outside the control of the narrator and his or her folk group. As we have seen, this creates interpretation problems because meaning is intricately tied to our knowledge of the speaker, the context of the particular telling, and the narrator's choice of words. If these are missing, then we can't hope to understand the full meaning.

When recordings are made of interviews, testimonies, hearings, and speeches, individuals are asked or choose to share their personal knowledge which may or may not be unique. This creates an added challenge to distinguish what is personal from what is part of oral tradition.

The Alaska Native Review Commission hearings are an illustration. Native people were asked to share their opinions and experiences on issues raised by the Alaska Native Claims Settlement Act. When Alfred Starr spoke, he addressed other Natives with information that he thought they might not know: "Thank you. First, I want to talk about a long time ago when there were not white people here. There are some Natives here that I want to talk to, too, you know" (Schneider 1990: H-2). Starr's testimony contains some familiar themes: the difficulty for leaders to get time and money to travel so they could meet and plan for land claims and their rejection of cash as the sole basis of settlement. He also provides some personal history and opinions such as his efforts, starting in 1951, to get people in Nenana to talk about land claims and his feeling that the original Tanana Chiefs' delegates who met in 1915 really didn't reject reservations outright but were concerned that they be big enough to accommodate hunting and trapping. We're left with an intriguing and nagging question—is Alfred Starr correct that the Indians would have accepted reservations if they were large enough, or is this his personal conclusion, based upon his experiences with reservations in other parts of the country?

Unlike oral tradition, which is grounded in personal participation in a folk group that tells the story over and over again, oral sources such as Starr's testimony become part of the record at one point in time and are accessible from then on to everyone, some who know Alfred Starr and the circumstances surrounding the story but many more who don't. As time goes by, fewer and fewer people will know Alfred Starr and be able to reconstruct the context of his story, whether they are members of his folk group or "outside experts." It becomes increasingly important to document these aspects before they are lost, while people still live who knew Alfred Starr.

The 1915 Tanana Chiefs' Conference alluded to by Starr is a good example of the difficulty of reconstructing context and meaning years later. Judge Wickersham convened that meeting of the chiefs, and a transcriber faithfully recorded the comments of each participant. The transcript is an official part of Wickersham's archival collection and is available at the Alaska State Library. Excerpts from the transcript were unearthed and popularized by journalist Stanton Patty at the time of Native land claims (1971). Both documents are important because they tell us what the chiefs said and the responses of Wickersham; Guy Madara, the Episcopal priest; and Thomas Riggs, head of the railroad commission. We learn about plans for the development of the Tanana Valley, the coming of the railroad, and the options that Wickersham thought existed to protect the Natives from exploitation. We also learn that the Indian leaders refused to accept solutions that would limit their ability to hunt, trap, and fish over many miles of country, seemingly a rejection of reservations.

For many years, I have quoted from this document and listened to elders talk about the meeting. Most often they pay tribute to the particular chiefs and refer to the gathering as the first public interaction with government people on land issues. As I began to look more closely at the impact of whites on Indians in the Tanana Valley, I wanted to reconstruct more of the circumstances surrounding the meeting: basic questions like how Wickersham knew who the chiefs were and what issues they were concerned about before the meeting, questions not really addressed in the transcript. I went to Wickersham's diary and was rewarded with a few entries which I will paraphrase here:

May 19, 1915—Wickersham, after visiting with Chief Charley at Tolovana, reports that the Indians are protesting against white men coming into their hunting grounds.

May 21, 1915—Wickersham reports meeting with Chief Alexander and talking about game laws, reservations, and schools.

May 23, 1915—Chief Alexander gives Wickersham the names of chiefs on the Tanana River.

Do these really tell us what prompted Wickersham to convene the meeting? How do we weigh his experiences with the chiefs out in the country and his dealings with the railroad commission and the church? If only he had given us more information on the transcript of the meeting!

Much of the oral record is like the Tanana Chiefs' Conference transcript: meticulous detail on who said what but little information about the circumstances surrounding the meeting. It is as if there's a photo of people, and someone takes scissors and neatly cuts out the figures and discards the rest in the trash. We're glad to see the people, but we'd really like to know the setting. Going through Wickersham's diary is a bit like hunting through the trash to find discarded photograph clippings so we can reconstruct the background. Perhaps most research is like working with the Starr interview and the Wickersham transcript; we end up searching for more information from multiple sources so we can fit pieces together in a way that accurately describes the narrator and the setting in which the event took place. We keep trying to go back and reconstruct meaning, and we sometimes end up kicking ourselves when we wait too long and miss the opportunity to talk directly with people who could tell us.

Historians often use the term *oral history* to refer to both the record produced and the activity of making recordings. Up until now, I have chosen not to use the word "history" because it implies interpretation of the source(s), which isn't possible unless we know the context of the recording and have access to other material which we can employ in an analysis, the type of thing I did with Wickersham. Rosaldo says, "Doing oral history involves telling stories about stories people tell about themselves" (1980: 89). This definition implies interpretation and a conscious choice of when to retell a story and what should be emphasized. Unfortunately, oral recordings don't always contain sufficient contextual clues for anyone but the most familiar to understand and retell in an historically and culturally appropriate way.

Narrators and their folk groups certainly interpret stories and have ideas about history, but their analysis doesn't necessarily end up on a recording of limited length, which is made at one point in time. For narrators and their audiences, meaning is embedded in their knowledge of each other and based on hearing similar stories over many years. These are the dynamics that we recognize as important to oral tradition, so unless we participate in the tradition or find ways to get the folk groups' reactions to our interpretation, we are operating at a loss. Some oral records provide interpretation, but most of the time we just don't know how the group interprets something until we ask, or as in the following example, they have an opportunity to correct our misinterpretation.

This past semester I had the pleasure of working with Phil Albert, an Athabaskan from Ruby, Alaska, and a graduate student in our Northern Studies program. He's researching the history of his village, and we got talking about the St. Patrick's Day celebrations they had in the old days. Back then there were quite a few white gold miners in the Ruby area, and they liked to celebrate. John Honea, in his oral biography (Yukon-Koyukuk School District 1979), talks about the dances, good food, dog races, and boxing. I was left with the impression that it was a good time. When Phil Albert spoke about it, he said it was like a spring carnival with dances that featured great fiddle players, Native and white. I was surprised, then, to hear him say that there were separate dance halls, one for Natives and one for whites. This led me to conclude that the Natives felt offended by the prejudice and apparent injustice.

Phil's reaction was quite different. He said they thought it was silly, that they laughed at the fact there were separate dance halls. I had confused the way I would feel with the way they actually felt. Until I speak with more people in Ruby, I'm not in a position to talk about their reactions to this, but Phil Albert's comments confirm the importance of dialogue in interpretation, particularly when we are dealing with an area as personal as feelings. Only then can we hope to represent the range of sentiments and provide accurate interpretation (see Tedlock 1979 and Mary Odden's essay in this book).

As we've seen, the best way to understand oral sources is to experience the stories with the folk group and have the chance to hear them many times so we can observe the range of sentiments, but in the case of real old stories, that's not possible. Sometimes we just have the recording; the subject matter has faded in significance for the folk group. With oral recordings made years ago, our only recourse may be to compare other versions of the story to see how it has changed and what elements have persisted. In this way, and exercising great caution, we can begin to account for the way people have used the narrative to verify what is important to them over time (Portelli 1991).

There are, however, many pitfalls to this approach. For instance, Tlingit stories of Lituya Bay tell about the first contacts with Euro-Americans. Some accounts say that when the ship arrived, the Tlingit thought at first it might be their creator Yehlh appearing in the form of Raven. Fearful of his power, they sent an old man out to see if it was indeed Yehlh. Some versions are not clear as to who the whites are, and then there are several that link the ship's appearance with the first Russian contact; the details concerning first impressions remain the same, except in some cases we learn that the Russians were attracted to the area because they had picked up bundles of fur which had floated from Tlingit canoes wrecked in the treacherous bay. (See Dauenhauer and Dauenhauer 1987: 293–309, 432–42; deLaguna 1972: 258–59; Emmons 1911: 294–98; Gunther 1972: 141–42.)

It is generally assumed that the story about Lituya Bay originally described the Tlingit reaction to the arrival of the French explorer LaPerouse in 1786. Given the lengthy Russian presence in this area and the fact that the Russians arrived in 1788, just two years after LaPerouse, it is understandable that Russian fur traders could, in some versions of the story, replace what was for the Tlingit an obscure Frenchman. Since the Russians were after sea-otter pelts, it is also logical that the Tlingit would identify furs as the commodity that lured Russians to the bay. However, the situation is a bit more complicated because the story was first recorded by Lieutenant Emmons in 1886, and it is unclear from his version whether the Tlingit were talking about the Frenchman LaPerouse, or whether Emmons made that assumption because LaPerouse was the first European to visit the Tlingit there.

Now it may be that various versions of this story each reflect what really happened, that some people are referring to the French and some to the Russians, and some just to the first whites, hence the differences. Another possibility is that the stories have merged in oral tradition and the oral record, and certain themes or motifs have been reinforced. I say this because so many of the story's elements remain the same from version to version: the idea of the newcomers as creator Yehlh in the form of Raven, the Natives' way of viewing the ship through skunk cabbage leaves, and the experiences of the person sent out to the ship to investigate.

I don't know if we'll ever be able to determine whether the stories are separate or have intermingled, but that question is secondary to what the comparative oral record can tell us about Tlingit perceptions of the first whites, their ships, and the food that was offered them. These are elements which persist no matter what the story specifies about the newcomers' nationality. If these elements are products of intermingling then this may very well point to their continued importance over the years. Without the oral record, it would be difficult, perhaps impossible, to gather comparative evidence for the way Tlingit ancestors perceived the new arrivals and to document the range of perceptions and various versions of the story. The record is now over a hundred years old, starting with Emmons's documentation of the oral tradition in 1886, which was another hundred years after LaPerouse came to Lituya Bay. (See also Partnow's essay, which addresses blending in oral tradition.)

So far we have been looking at the oral record as a source for text analysis. The comparative record of oral recordings is also important when we study texture, the way stories are told. Sometimes we remember the way a person speaks, and then we are led back to recordings to see if this is a pattern or an anomaly. My colleague Dan O'Neill is fond of recalling Moses Cruikshank's description of Gunga Din, a sled dog he used when he was mushing dogs for the ministers: "powerful dog, wide chest, flopped eared, old worker from way back, that one" (1986: 33). Whether you know anything about sled dogs or not, Moses Cruikshank's description, stacked with adjectives, conjures up the image of a super dog that would always pull his load and then some. This verbal image sticks with us as Moses Cruikshank goes on to tell about Gunga Din's exploits. It sets the stage for the way he wants us to consider this dog.

Many of Moses Cruikshank's stories are like this, rich in descriptions and images that either prepare us to hear the story or sum up the feelings he wants to leave with us, what he considers important. This is particularly true of his characterizations of people. Phrases like "real old-time Alaskan," "one of the best miners," and

202   *William Schneider*

"old-time Native way" set the tone and convey a strong sense of his judgment. The carefully crafted descriptions create a strong image of Moses Cruikshank and his personal code: what he considers right and wrong, good and bad, strong and weak. They leave little doubt about how he wants us to interpret his stories.

In both the Tanana project described earlier and Moses Cruikshank's stories, the oral record is an invitation for future generations to experience the way storytellers create meaning by their choice of words, the expressions they use, and the ways they construct their stories. The big winds still come to Tanana each fall, and people may still refer to them in the same way, but when we hear Teddy Luke use the expression, it provides a sense of time and connection with the elders of his generation that is preserved only in the words of a few of his living contemporaries, in our memories of these people, and in the oral record. Unless we pass on both our understanding of the oral tradition and the oral record, future generations will have few clues to the richness of our experience.

I want to conclude by reemphasizing the necessary connection between oral tradition, characterized by a folk group that knows the stories and the tellers over time, and the oral record, what will someday be, for most of us, our closest tie to today's elders, their stories, and their particular ways of conveying meaning. The oral tradition which we experience with elders today contains our most important clues on the way to know, interpret, and evaluate the oral record that we commit to audiotape. To experience oral tradition is first and foremost to meet and know elders, to learn how to listen, and to come to know what they mean over many tellings. This knowledge is key to any evaluation of the oral record. Our biggest problem is not too few tape recordings but not enough documentation of how and why elders shared their knowledge at a particular time, in a particular way, and what we think they meant in each telling. Answers to these questions are the basis for sound interpretation and comparison of recordings now and in the future. For too long we have collected and interpreted just the text and lost track of these other expressions of meaning.

References

Ager, Lynn Price. 1974. "Storyknifing: An Alaskan Eskimo Girls' Game." *Journal of the Folklore Institute* 11(3): 189–98.

Attla, Catherine. 1983. *Sitsiy Yugh Noholnik Ts'in', As My Grandfather Told It: Traditional Stories from the Koyukuk*. Translated by Eliza Jones and Melissa Axelrod. Fairbanks: Yukon-Koyukuk School District and Alaska Native Language Center.

———. 1990. *K'etaalkkaanee, The One Who Paddled among the People and Animals, The Story of an Ancient Traveler*. Translated by Eliza Jones. Fairbanks: Yukon-Koyukuk School District and Alaska Native Language Center.

Bodfish, Waldo, Sr. 1991. *Kusiq: An Eskimo Life History from the Arctic Coast of Alaska*. Fairbanks: University of Alaska Press.

Cruikshank, Moses. 1986. *The Life I've Been Living*. Fairbanks: University of Alaska Press.

Dauenhauer, Nora Marks, and Richard Dauenhauer, eds. 1987. *Haa Shuka', Our Ancestors: Tlingit Oral Narratives*. Vol. I of *Classics of Tlingit Oral Literature*. Seattle: University of Washington Press.

deLaguna, Frederica. 1960. *The Story of a Tlingit Community: A Problem in the Relationship between Archeological, Ethnological, and Historical Methods*. Bureau of American Ethnology Bulletin, no. 172. Washington, D.C.: U.S. Government Printing Office.

———. 1972. *Under Mount Saint Elias: The History and Culture of the Yakutat Tlingit*. Washington, D.C.: Smithsonian Institution.

Dundes, Alan. 1964. "Texture, Text, and Context." *Southern Folklore Quarterly* 28: 251–65.

Edwin, Lee, and Teddy Luke. n.d. "Songs and Legends." Alaska Library Association Oral History Project, tape no. H-78-184. Elmer E. Rasmuson Library Archives, University of Alaska Fairbanks.

Emmons, G. T. 1911. "Native Account of the Meeting between LaPerouse and the Tlingit." *American Anthropologist* 1: 294–98.

Finnegan, Ruth. 1992. *Oral Traditions and the Verbal Arts: A Guide to Research Practices*. London: Routledge.

Gunther, Erma. 1972. *Indian Life on the Northwest Coast of North America As Seen by the Early Explorers and Fur Traders during the Last Decades of the Eighteenth Century*. Chicago: University of Chicago Press.

Herbert, Belle. 1982. *Shandaa: In My Lifetime*. Edited by Bill Pfisterer and Jane McGary with the assistance of Alice Moses, and translated by Katherine Peter. Fairbanks: Alaska Native Language Center, University of Alaska Fairbanks.

Mackenzie, Clara Childs. 1985. *Wolf Smeller (Zhoh Gwatsan): A Biography of John Fredson, Native Alaskan*. Anchorage: Alaska Pacific University Press.

Mishler, Craig. 1982. "John Fredson: A Biographical Sketch." In *John Fredson: Edward Sapir Haa Googwandak. Stories Told by John Fredson to Edward Sapir*, edited and translated by Jane McGary 11–20. Fairbanks: Alaska Native Language Center, University of Alaska Fairbanks.

Nagy, Murielle. 1991a. *Qikiqtaruk (Herschel Island) Cultural Study: Final Report*. Presented by the Inuvialuit Social Development Program. Heritage Branch, Government of the Yukon.

Nagy, Murielle. 1991b. *Qikiqtaruk (Herschel Island) Cultural Study: Interviews 1–20*. Presented by the Inuvialuit Social Development Program. Heritage Branch, Government of the Yukon.

———. 1994. *Yukon North Slope Inuvualuit Oral History*. Occasional Papers in Yukon History, no. 1, Heritage Branch, Government of the Yukon.

"Native Women's Oral History Panel." 1992. Oral History Program, tape no. H-93-06-02. Elmer E. Rasmuson Library Archives, University of Alaska Fairbanks.

Oswalt, Wendell H. 1964. "Traditional Storyknife Tales of Yuk Girls." *Proceedings of the American Philosophical Society* 108(4): 310–36.

Patty, Stanton. 1971. "A Conference with the Tanana Chiefs." *The Alaska Journal* 1(2): 168–70.

Portelli, Alessandro. 1991. *The Death of Luigi Trastulli and Other Stories: Form and Meaning in Oral History*. Albany: State University of New York Press.

Rosaldo, Renato. 1980. "Doing Oral History." *Social Analysis* 4 (September): 89–99.

Schneider, William. 1976. "Beaver, Alaska: The Story of a Multi-Ethnic Community." Ph.D. diss., Bryn Mawr College, Bryn Mawr, Penn.

———. 1990. "Elders' Voices Echo Links to Land." *Fairbanks Daily News-Miner*, 11 February 1990, Heartland, H-2.

Stuck, Hudson. 1914. *The Ascent of Denali (Mt. McKinley): A Narrative of the First Complete Ascent of the Highest Peak in North America*. New York: Charles Scribner's Sons.

Tedlock, Dennis. 1979. "The Analogical Tradition and the Emergence of a Dialogical Anthropology." *Journal of Anthropological Research* 35(4): 387–400.

Toelken, Barre. 1979. *The Dynamics of Folklore*. Boston: Houghton Mifflin.

Toelken, Barre, and Tacheeni Scott. 1981. "Poetic Retranslation and the 'Pretty Languages' of Yellowman." In *Traditional Literatures of the American Indian: Texts and Interpretations*, edited by Karl Kroeber, 65–116. Lincoln: University of Nebraska Press.

Vansina, Jan. 1985. *Oral Tradition As History*. Madison: University of Wisconsin Press.

Wickersham, James. Journal. Wickersham Collection. Alaska State Library, Juneau.

Yukon-Koyukuk School District. 1979. *John Honea: A Biography*. Blaine, Wash.: Hancock House Publishers.

The Weight of Tradition and the Writer's Work

Mary Odden

In the introduction to this book, we noted that stories, to be recognized as important cross-culturally, must move beyond the interestingly exotic or inaccessibly esoteric. Throughout these essays, even where they focus on oral traditions from some academic distance, the writers hint at numerous ways that we all take stories home with us at the end of the day, identifying their values in terms of our lives. Peter John has given William Schneider moral strength in his family life; Robin Barker and her son have looked to see if the crane's eyes really are blue; and the places Robert Drozda documented have clearly become part of his "sense of being."

It is Mary Odden, however, who most clearly articulates for all of us the interweaving of the intellectual with the deeply personal. Her intimate and poetic writing expresses the pain and ineffable beauty of traditions lost and found. In this essay, Odden moves from an abandoned homestead, a place her father wanted her to know in some urgently inaccessible way, to a contemplation of issues raised by the preceding articles. The search to create personal meaning from both familiar and elusively distant oral traditions is simultaneously a search for the intangible connections that can bond people together across cultures and generations.

This is, perhaps, what beckons us all to listen, write, and remember oral traditions.

Nearly the last thing my father said to me, certainly the last thing I remember, was "You know what I mean, Mim." Mim was a nickname he had for me, a special name between the two of us, reserved for the times when we would sit in the back door of the family grocery store and watch the eastern Oregon thunderstorms roll across the sky, or when I had just won a ribbon on my horse—something extraordinary like that. My mom never called me Mim, and Dad wouldn't have used

Mim in the third person, as in "Mim did this or that." Mim was only for me from my dad, for my ears and my heart to hear.

When Dad said, "You know what I mean, Mim," he wasn't talking about anything in particular. His eyes could be bluer than any ocean, and his eyes were about all that was left of the father I knew as he lay there, so I couldn't say that I didn't know what he meant, especially if it was anything in particular that he wanted me to understand. I just held onto his hand and nodded and let pass between us whatever it is that can pass, without words. I didn't ask him to explain, and after I left that room, I never saw him alive again.

My dad always wanted me to understand what he knew, in the way that he had lived and understood it. One time my sister-in-law took a picture of the old homestead out in the middle of Flag Prairie, broken-down grey buildings in the middle of a sagebrush flat where the pioneers used to flag antelope. In the distance, you could see the juniper-covered hills that wrapped around the prairie. My dad asked me if I would paint it for him. He had the photograph, but it wasn't enough. He wanted the isolation, the trying to live there, the heat and the hidden water, the stories. He wanted the flat, cold, plastic film to pass through a human heart—mine—and come out again, complete with all the dimensions he knew and felt about that homestead. And he thought I could do that for him, that somehow there was a complete Bill Looney—my father—inside me like a truth about the world that I could paint or write or say for him. I never did paint that picture. It was beyond my skill, even if I had been a very good painter.

In 1977, I was twenty-two years old and working out of Galena, Alaska, as a forest-fire dispatcher for the Bureau of Land Management. I spent several weeks on the Seward Peninsula fighting a fire that had covered hundreds of thousands of acres. During that time, I lived and worked with a crew of young firefighters from Noorvik, an inexperienced village crew put together in a hurry, the fourth or fifth group taken out of the village in that incredibly busy year of lightning fires. The first two crews taken out of Noorvik would have been the experienced firefighters, led by older bosses who were also village leaders. But the Noorvik crew on our sector of the fire was comprised of people in their late teens and early twenties, kids just out of high school who had taken the two-day training class but most of whom had never been on a fire before.

I was a newcomer to Alaska, and I had never been around many Native people. Bannock and Shoshone people were nearly invisible in eastern Oregon when I grew up. When Indians were pointed out to me, at laundromat or bus station, I was disappointed that they looked ordinary, even a little more beaten-down than ordinary, and nothing like the grand Plains Indians in the books I had read hungrily all through my childhood, nothing like what I had imagined myself to be when my best friend and I tied feathers in our horses' manes and tore around the ditch banks on her dad's sheep ranch.

In the proximity of fire line and camp, my first impression was how alike we were, all of us still kids, laughing as we ran our hands around the black edges of the fire feeling for the heat left in it, walking all day through the tussocks next to Imuruk Lake, then huddling together in little groups, waiting for the helicopter to shuttle us back to camp. The crew members would be jostling each other and teasing about boyfriends and girlfriends. Sometimes we waited to be picked up for hours, since there was only one helicopter and there were many crews scattered around the perimeter of the fire. It was more than twenty miles back to the base camp, across burned tundra that in some places was already growing green again. Sometimes the young men and women from Noorvik spoke Inupiaq, and then I felt some of our difference. I felt both excluded to hear words I didn't understand and privileged to be in the country where they were spoken. Most of the time the Noorvik crew spoke Inupiaq mixed with English, and I could gather the gist of the teasing or the story, though I missed most of the references and the cues for laughter. We were all young and earning money and camping out together, so there was a lot of laughing and little to be sad about. But one day I heard one young man tell another, "You're not an Eskimo. You don't even know your traditional culture." The accuser pronounced "traditional culture" as one might say "multiplication tables," words from a vocabulary both formal and remote, as if "traditional culture" were a thing to be achieved and then recited, something you could get a ribbon for mastering. The person accused of not knowing his traditional culture was quiet and seemed ashamed. How could he not be an Eskimo, I wondered?

I heard this note of shame many times in the next few years, in the several summers I worked along the Kobuk River. One time a young friend from Kobuk told me that I knew her country better than she did, though she had lived there all her life. I could rattle off place names from my big wall map in the dispatch office, mispronunciations of names misspelled by United States Geological

Survey orthographers from the 1950s. I could even connect a few of these generally disembodied names with the textured landscape I had flown over, walked on, fished in. This strange litany seemed to Ahka to be a more "legitimate" kind of knowledge than all of her experiences growing up in a place where much of an earlier Eskimo life was still practiced—fishing, hunting, berry picking, celebrating, grieving.

Because of Ahka's statement, and occasional comments I heard from people in Kobuk and Shungnak, I began to see that between the oldest residents who spoke Inupiaq exclusively and the people in their twenties who spoke almost none, there seemed to exist a boundary, a paroxysm of memory begun in earlier generations from the onus of being an Eskimo at all and speaking that "primitive" language—both forbidden and discarded in favor of the "melting pot." The division was deepened by the elevation of this "traditional culture," by the time of my friend's coming of age in the 1970s, as something to be admired and longed for, though lost. Perhaps it was especially admired because it was regarded as lost. Some of the young people felt as though they were failing at a responsibility they had inherited as Eskimos, although the obligation to achieve a certain past is an impossible one to fulfill, as impossible as the longing I will always feel to know what my father meant, to see what he saw in the broken buildings at Flag Prairie, the desire I will always feel to express his vision in art or words.

When I think about traditional knowledge as something I have to enter, like another room, or absorb, like a foreign liquid, I have already locked myself away from seeing it as something that can ever belong to me or be a part of me. As writers writing about folklore and oral tradition, whether we are dealing with our own traditions or those of another group, we tend to objectify and probe and analyze tradition as if it were a lump of slimy stuff on the dissecting table, as if this were the way to "know" it. How much of our difficulty in learning about ourselves or others is a product of this stance?

Elsie Mather tells us in this book that part of young people's problem in entering Yup'ik tradition, in taking it into themselves and making it their own, is that they have lost an older generation's "art of learning." Instead of learning in built-up layers of experience, watching and listening and accepting that some things are "not explainable in mere words," she says contemporary students of Yup'ik culture are in a hurry to gather up knowledge. They want to "get it in a nutshell" and make instant sense of it, as if the knowledge of aging elders could be "collected" in a bushel basket together, or lifetimes could be gathered up and saved for winter.

The word *knowledge* means different things depending on who you are. A few summers ago, I was transcribing and indexing tapes of interviews with Koyukon Athabaskan elder Susie Williams of Hughes. I was fascinated with the way Susie was so careful to specify that any stories she told were from a particular time and place: "those people, that time." It seemed to me she was refusing to create any false generalizations about her culture, or that enough of her original language carried over into English to circumvent the creation of universals which English accomplishes so easily with its copula "is."

Anthropologist Wendy Arundale and Koyukon culture and language specialist Eliza Jones were interviewing Susie about place names and historical sites along the Koyukuk River. At one point they asked her about a particular place, and she said she didn't know it. "But we know you camped here," said Eliza. "Yes," Susie agreed, "but I don't know the stories that belong to that place." Susie was teaching them, and me the listener, and now you the reader of this essay, that she meant something different than her interviewers by the word "know," even though Eliza is a Koyukon and an insider to most of the information Susie offered in the interviews.

Susie's usage signified a process deeper than mere recognition or recitation of a name. It is something slower and more respectful to acknowledge that stories belong to places and are a part of their certain place and time. Even as we as listeners and writers borrow them into ourselves, taking and retelling any story we can "catch," as Yup'ik tradition seems to give us permission to do, I am asking myself about that translated word *catch*. A cat catches a mouse and tears it apart or plays with it until it is dead. This could work as a fitting analogy for analysis, but Phyllis Morrow tells us that Yupiit tend to leave their stories open, without explaining or analyzing. Perhaps "catch" represents a concept more like the "knowing" of places in Susie Williams's interview—respect and long acquaintance.

It is an underlying theme of many of the articles in this book that there are no shortcuts to knowledge about a folk group, yet this medium of written words is a shortcut, as are the taped voices in the archive—words cut away from the life that gave rise to them. The danger inherent in taking these shortcuts seems analogous to the danger of any listening between cultures: that I will wrongly understand and that in talking and especially in writing about what I have wrongly understood, I will silence a voice that belongs to a person of another culture, as a starling is able to displace the indigenous bluebird whose nest is so like but not identical to its own. William Schneider expresses this concern when he writes that he understood the Peter John story about killing the moose as a measure of the strength of his concern for his family—later discovering that Peter's telling probably also meant to convey his deep faith in God as provider. We have a responsibility to storytellers to know what they "mean," but written words, even taped voices, rob us of most of the context and dynamism of the telling situation and provide only an extremely limited acquaintance with the teller.

Still, I know that some voices become a part of my own fabric, written and taped voices layering into the memories of real experiences along rivers and in kitchens and gardens. I have been privileged to hear Susie Williams speak, though I have never seen her face. I have been in Hughes, and I can imagine her there and at the mission at Allakaket when she was young, the latter a place I can know only through the faded film of pictures and what I read from books, those books that Elsie Mather aptly calls "necessary monsters." The most respect I can show to Susie, as an eavesdropper on her conversations with Wendy and Eliza, as a writer still hungry to tie feathers on my horse, is to allow the particularity of time and place to remain in what I write about her, a particularity that her eloquent "village English" insists upon. I want to find a way of writing that allows a reader to "hear" Susie's words. I also want to be visible, to let a reader see my enthusiasm for wall tents and Blazo boxes and Coleman lanterns that allows some understanding of Susie's stories, as well as the fact that I do not know Susie and that I only hear her through headphones, sitting in front of my computer.

My summer's work in 1992 was to write down Susie's stories for Wendy and Eliza (Williams 1988), and since then the stories have often found their way into my thoughts. Sometimes I find myself "thinking with" a story I did not understand as I wrote it down. Sometimes Susie reminds me that she is also a woman of my mother's generation, when I remember hearing her talk about her family's first radio or making clothing from flour sacks (and trying to scrub out the inked letters). In a way, Susie's words have selected me and not the other way around.

Other people's words carry certain obligations. As a writer, I want to give my reader something of both Susie and why her words are important to me. Sometimes this means imparting a sense of a story's "otherness," its inscrutability, its deferral of interpretation. It might mean leaving in the text the part of the transcript that "bumps" or is uncomfortable, leaving in the snatch of singing which is a seeming non sequitur. It might mean wondering, self-consciously and in the writing, about how a word like "know" or "catch" is negotiable between speaker/writer and listener/reader and how the negotiation is complicated by translation from another language.

As a writer of nonfiction about the north and its people, I want to dispel the "disguise of certainty" of objective writing, just as many anthropological writers are struggling to do. Objective writing has tended to angle civilization above the heads of cultures, a perspective that is a "particular epistemological stance of Western civilization," according to Michel Foucault (as paraphrased in Phyllis Morrow's essay). How can I reduce the steepness of this angle as I regard the culture and the individual life process of a person who is my "subject"? How can I offer enough context so that my readers can find their own importance in this person I find so important, yet defer interpretation of a subject's words so that a story does not turn into "why the beaver slaps its tail on the water"? How can I make my participation (my interpretive frame) visible and yet remain respectful and maintain a sense of the "other's" ownership?

Julie Cruikshank begins her introduction to *Life Lived Like a Story: Life Stories of Three Yukon Elders* with the following words: "One of the liveliest areas of discussion in contemporary anthropology centers on how to convey authentically, in words, the experience of one culture to members of another" (1990: 1). If this is impossible, the struggle to achieve it can be lovely.

The Angle of Power

A coldness blows between writer and subject in the very word *subject*. It rouses an issue of political and social power. Oral historian Alessandro Portelli suggests that "the very need for anthropological research in western societies implies the recognition and observation of otherness in subjects who are not on the same social and political plane with the observer" (1991: x). In this view, the very act of observation is a position of power, typified by the fact that the observer has a mobility in and out of the situation that is generally not shared by the object of study. The student of culture has typically been an outsider, notebook and camera and tape recorder at the ready. This is the model of learning that anthropology has presented.

In the 1968 film, *Yanomamo: A Multi-Disciplinary Study*, an anthropologist bends down to a woman in a hammock. The woman is holding a baby, and the scientist bends over them to write "B101" on the woman's arm. Some twenty-five years later, I find this very hard to watch (and so would most contemporary anthropologists), even though the film has prepared viewers for the numbering of subjects by telling us that the study is being conducted "in a culture where there are strong prohibitions against using people's names." This statement is one of the most interesting in the entire film. There must be a context for using people's names if people have them. So the prohibition must be against using people's names in a certain way. What is naming in that society, and how is it antithetical to labeling or numbering? In the anthropologist's frame of reference, like my own, numbers and names are nearly interchangeable. If I want to discuss my taxes or my phone bill, I am more likely to get results by telling the official at the other end of the line one of my numbers—social security or telephone—than my name. So if the Yanomamo people have prohibited the use of names in the way anthropologists want to use them, there is something for me to learn about the Yanomamo, those anthropologists, and myself. Why am I so offended by a scientist marking a number on a human being as if that human being were a bottle of urine?

In much objective writing—third person, present tense—there is a clear sense of looking down, from scientist to subject, from civilization to culture. I have been thinking about maps lately: how maps are made from a certain elevation and include selected features; how they turn elevations and spatial distances into all there is, devoid of spiritual dimensions, devoid of stories, devoid of the way one route can be immeasurably harder to travel than another blue line of the same length. I have been thinking that I am the center of my particular map of the universe. That map notes only the places and routes I know, not by population or distance from each other but by their importance to me, my memory of them. Is Susie Williams the center of her own map of the places she knows, in her way of knowing? Or does her sense of particular places and times and people as owners of stories "decenter" her in this abstraction I have made by flattening and mapping Susie's worldview? And as Eliza lays the inch-to-the-mile chart down in front of Susie—something I cannot see; I only hear the voices and the large map crinkling and hissing across laps—what translation is being made between Susie's memory of the time it took to go from one camp to another and the cross-hatched green-and-white paper in front of her?

Some people can't pass their private pilot's examinations just because they can't learn to read a map. This may be because they will not trust that the map is a metaphor for topography, or because what is on the map does not look like what they see out of the airplane window, those passing, changing shapes. It is a kind of algebra, to let an unchanging symbol stand for a changing thing, even to let your life rely upon it.

The mapping of culture, like that of topography, is a flattening of what is round and multidimensional, held in many different forms and memories, into a common representation that stands for the whole. It is useful if I understand it as an interpretation, dangerous if I begin to see it as the thing itself. In Robert Drozda's words in his essay: "The authenticity of the land is detached from the landscape and conveyed to paper, where it can be further divided and legally manipulated." When the cemetery sites or berry-picking places or hunting areas of a certain group of people are set down on paper, with a list of who's buried here and who goes there, then according to a Western cultural convention, it seems possible to make rules about privilege and ownership, compartmentalizing significance as if we can regiment the activities and concepts the map represents.

We, as in the Western civilization "we," are the heirs of Aristotle's ideas about the universal nature of human minds and also his metaphysics, which says we have to stop the world and remove ourselves from it in order to look at it.[1] This is a dangerous combination of theories. Once we have removed ourselves in order to be scientific, it is then possible to draw conclusions about categories and forms and assume commonalties of concepts as if we were not part of the process, to proceed with our production of one-dimensional maps.

The conversion of information to map or words is interpretation in which the interpreter is invisible. Maybe what is most shocking to me about B101 is that I actually see the anthropologist writing on the woman's arm.

English and "Still Time"

I remember as a young person reading about my ancestors and others in James H. Hawley's *Idaho: The Gem of the Mountains* (1920). The country described was the Boise Valley, Silver City, and Jordan Valley, Oregon, the very country I was living in, but in the book it was peopled with family accounts from the early 1900s. Some described my own great-grandparents' farms and ranches. The present tense in those accounts, coupled with their great distance from my life, heightened my sense of nostalgia, of loss. I read about the heads of stock, the amount of acreage put under irrigation, and the names of children born in that immediacy of long ago. The writing was meant for a contemporary 1920s reader who would recognize many of the names and nod his head at that progressive, modern West. The Shoshone and Bannock and French explorers were already ghosts and the Idaho of the 1960s and 1970s undreamed of. My then-present landscape and experiences became footnotes to that powerful, still time—the real Idaho, lost forever. This was the place and time my father was born into, and I think the little rock houses and the broken grey homesteads all led him back to longing for that childhood place.

If the angle of political power in some anthropological writing is downward because of the impulse to classify and objectify, another byproduct of objectification angles the point of view upward to a subject on an impossibly static pedestal, nearly platonic and outside time. Romantic absorption with the object of study can also devalue the cultural position of the examiner and *create* a nostalgic reality for the moment or person or culture being described—the noble savage, the Gold Rush.

My father's longing for those places of memory and invention and the books and pictures my family kept of those times helped to draw me into my own intellectual life. There is a hunger for many lives that draws us past ourselves. But the dead are dangerous—this is our life, not theirs. The present-tense description of a moment in time is a snapshot from a moving train. The objectification it creates and its accompanying power to generate nostalgia and longing proceed from the use of language, not experience.

The very structure of English and other Indo-European languages puts a stop to the world. English is noun-rich, whereas Alaska Native languages are verb-rich, so that translation into English flattens the complexity of narrative and other verbal art. Also the English verb *to be* has the double function of copula, joining subjects and predicates, or standing alone as in God *is*, meaning *exists* (Benesch and Krejci 1992: 77). We can say, "Society is changing." But we can also say, "Society *is*," creating the very thing we will then look for evidence of. Employing this one handy feature of our language, we can fill up the world in less than seven days ourselves!

First Person

I am particularly interested in what happens when an anthropological writer or anyone else writing "about" something shifts to the
first person. It seems very like getting out of the pew and going up
to the front of the church, not to turn around and sing or preach,
but to kneel in front of the altar, separately and visibly committed
to whatever subject we are all focusing on. I don't think it is stretch-
ing the metaphor beyond the breaking point to say that whatever we
turn our attention to is on a kind of altar, selected from the chaos of
events and ideas in our lives. The author, visible or not, is the initial
supplicant in the proliferation of meanings between author/teller
and reader/listener. While all subject-pointed writing continues to
employ third-person stances, and we all benefit from the rich objective writing of anthropological observers before us, it is fascinating
and useful when ethnographic accounts offer a first-person view of
contemporary observers in the midst of their own observations.

When Jean Briggs's *Never in Anger* was published in 1970, its first
person viewpoint was regarded as unusual.[2] *Never in Anger* is a field
study of a small group of Eskimo people living north of Hudson's
Bay. In this section from her introduction, listen to Briggs's concern
with the issues of movement versus the anthropological present tense
in which she feels she is expected to write:

> The book is a still life also in the sense that Utku life, like that of
> other Eskimo groups, is changing. Some of the practices and at-
> titudes described here already at this writing belong to the past;
> and there is no telling how long the Utku will remain in Chantrey
> Inlet. But having made it clear that the book describes a particular
> moment in time, for simplicity's sake I shall avail myself of anthro-
> pological privilege and refer to that moment in the present tense.
> (1970: 7)

This paragraph is ironically noteworthy because Briggs only employs this expected present tense for a few introductory pages, and
the remainder of the text, three hundred pages or so, is written predominantly in first person, past tense, which highlights motion and
intimacy in a particularity of experience absent in more general,
objectifying texts.

The following passage from Briggs describes a permissiveness
and affection toward small children: "I, like her family, delighted

in luring her onto my lap, in feeling her warm, wriggly little body in my arms, and in snuffing her small dark head. I delighted in society's permission, more accurately, in its injunction, to respond to all Saarak's commands" (1970: 117). Briggs's account is a scene, a narrative of a particular place and time. The presence of anthropologist as participant is inescapable in Jean Briggs's way of writing, as is the momentary nature of experience. Briggs's form is corporeal, seated in the picture. The position of the observer is inside the observer's consciousness, so the narrative is first person. One of the central issues of the Briggs book becomes the learning experience and changing attitudes of Briggs herself, visibly germane to her observations of the Eskimo group.

I believe that the first-person, past-tense storytelling mode comes close to acknowledging the lever-pushing, ventriloquizing author function and frame while still allowing the careful "those people, that time" of the Susie Williams accounts. It seems to me to be respectful of the particular ownerships of time and place. By itself, or interspersed with other types of presentations, it allows insider or outsider readers and students of culture to break into, even to argue with, observations made by a flesh-and-blood person. Could it be that past characterizations of what Eskimos "are" and what their culture "is" have pointed a still life which is difficult for young Eskimo people to crawl out of, to claim their lives as "Eskimo" lives? Can books, those necessary monsters, become less monstrously distant and static and allow young people to enter into a dialogue with their pages?

I've been back to Jordan Valley, Oregon, where my father was born many times. I've felt the rough, pink cinder stones of the house he was born in. When I was in my late teens, I had a job on a lookout near Jordan Valley, and I had friends living in the rock house, which had long ago passed from my family's ownership to that of my friends, the Skinners. One night I sat in the swinging chair on the front porch until the stars came out, wondering whose life I was living. Both sides of my family had their roots in this part of the country, a mining district since the mid-1800s, and here I was, drawn to the scene of all their encounters, only the mine shafts were abandoned, and the people in the stories were all gone. I wondered how my life could ever be as important as that of the little girl who had grown up in the big white house next to me and given birth to her children in the rock house behind me. I had no sense of my fresh memories joining my grandmother's and my father's words about this place, just a sense of loss that I hadn't listened enough. Like my father, I felt the loss of stories I hadn't heard, names of places I hadn't learned. Stories and even the places they belonged to were washing off the map, robbing me of the real. It was always a "they" when I thought about my family, never an "us" in all our continuing, changing, differing connections with the country. As I grow older, I see myself sitting at the foot of family stories, still listening, and I can forgive myself for only hearing what I can hear.

In her essay, Julie Cruikshank writes of herself in relation to her subject. She describes ethnography as conversations between "anthropologists and our hosts," dialogues that "open the possibility that we may learn something about the *process* of communication [emphasis added]." Dialogue and conversation are diction from level ground, a respectful discourse between equal parties, but when Cruikshank goes to first person to narrate the story of her involvement with Angela Sidney, she often refers to their relationship as that of student and teacher. Cruikshank gradually incorporates Sidney's way of relating traditional narratives into her present life experiences: "Even though she is no longer able to participate actively in our dialogues, they continue whenever her words surface unexpectedly while I am puzzling about some problem, just as she undoubtedly hoped they would." Cruikshank views ethnography as dialogue, but when she enters her own picture, it is also as a younger person approaching an elder with questions, not just about the past but about the way to conduct her present life.

William Schneider says the best way he knows to illustrate his point about how important it is to know tellers' circumstances is "by sharing a very personal experience with Chief Peter John of Minto." He tells us that he met with Peter John primarily to "ask him important questions about the way to live ... to speak about family responsibility and help me think through ways to lead that part of my life." Even if the reader is more interested in Peter John's life than William Schneider's, I think it is important to know Schneider's stance and attitude at the telling, how he also came to Peter John as a younger person to an elder, asking about how to live.

Communication takes place between living persons in a certain situation. Phyllis Morrow told me a story about her early fieldwork, how she found it impossible to write up her field notes because she couldn't adopt a stance without a sense of writing *to* someone. Assigning a static "meaning" to her experiences proved impossible because she recognized that it would put a stop to the conversation and learning process. She refers to something like this when she writes about collaboration in her essay: "Personal meanings proliferate through tellers and listeners." In the field situation, she finally ended up sending long letters to friends, finding it necessary to use the first person because it encompassed her own involvement in the fieldwork and also invited responses from her correspondents.

Robert Drozda's third-person description of the interethnic difficulties between Yup'ik informants and historical-place and cemetery-site examiners is interesting and informative in itself, yet he finds it important to switch to first person later in his article identify himself as an investigator moved by his experiences from "ignorance and naïveté" to a position of thankfulness to "the patient (and impatient) teachers and lessons that have helped me along the way." He closes his essay with a letter from Marie Meade, a Yup'ik woman involved in the examinations, written to a Bureau of Indian Affairs manager of the project. Drozda tells us that this letter "adds a dimension which extends across cultures and contrasts to the starkness of mere physical description. Perhaps such experiences and values truly capture the deeper meaning that the preservation of Native historical places possesses."

Drozda seems to be saying that third-person description can give us the "what" of ethnography or situation, but we depend on something more personal to give us the "why." In Meade's words: "I especially will not forget the thrill and joy of my uncle Nickolai Berlin when we took him to his birthplace. It was wonderful to watch as he spoke of his first years of life on that land." It is the sense of Meade listening to her uncle that makes me eager to hear him speak of those first years. For me, too, it would be important to carry a sense of niece listening to uncle into a session with the tape or transcript from that occasion. Interestingly, when Drozda gives us a glimpse of himself, his stance, like that of Cruikshank and Schneider, is that of an increasingly respectful student.

When some first person is included in ethnographic or any subject-oriented accounts, we can't squirm away from the issue of motivation. Alaskan oral traditions (and especially languages) may be like endangered species, to be protected in their living habitat for the sake of the cultural diversity of the world, but first-person accounts also allow me to see real people valuing knowledge in personal ways, wanting to "get some of the old wisdom." An author who lets me see him or her come to a tradition or a teller for old wisdom gives me a perspective from which I can both respect and respond to what the writing describes. That perspective helps move knowledge from something I should want to learn, like the multiplication tables, onto the intangible ground from which I draw my life.

Holding On, Passing On

Part of my definition of a human is maker of meaning. As a writer, a pursuer of a particularly virulent form of meaning making, I must acknowledge the power that language has to create and recreate the world—not just *a* language, but language in motion—a dynamic and powerful link between tradition and performer/writer, between performer/writer and audience/reader. To spread the author function around to whoever interprets and incorporates stories seems reasonable to me, without reducing the authorship of storytellers. Words stop with each of us for a while, long enough for us to invent our worlds with them.

Language is not the observer, not the observed, but a third, created world between the two. This is due not only to the difference between speakers but to the separate, active nature of language itself. Language does not weigh anything—it has no tangible surface to be measured—yet it exerts a force which makes things happen. It carries and creates our concepts, consciously and unconsciously, as we use it. As folklorist Charles Briggs writes, "Language is not a passive instrument for describing a world that is independently constituted. Through its performative force, language can affect action, whether it is the baptism of a baby or the delivery of a command" (1988: 8).

The power of words, their force and our need to respect them, is everywhere throughout this volume. Robert Drozda tells us, "The power of the word, gaze, and thoughts can make things happen in Yup'ik." Phyllis Morrow talks about why Yup'ik stories are not named and describes a Yup'ik sensitivity to both the creative and limiting power of words.

Patricia Partnow's article portrays a group of people inventing themselves anew, changing themselves as they modify the stories about the time before and after the Novarupta eruption. Partnow comes to Perryville asking for "old stories and history" and finds an active shifting of myth and history around a tangible boundary between past and present. Rarely are we privileged to consider such persuasive evidence that present circumstances change tradition and that language confirms it. Yet to a degree that varies by cultural convention, genre, and individual style, storytellers treat words from and knowledge about the past with a careful regard. Partnow lets us see Father Harry appending the words "must have been" to events he relates but did not himself witness.

It seems like a paradox that respect for ownership of words and the witness of people from another place and time are present in oral tradition alongside acknowledgments (and other evidence) that words also belong to the present. Even in Tlingit society, where ownership of stories is prized and fought over and fidelity to the exact repetition of words and expressions is a high virtue in traditional narratives, one of Tlingit-Tagish storyteller Angela Sidney's chief motivations for wanting to relate the K̲aax̲'achgóok story at the opening of Yukon College is to give her audience a story they can "think with."

Thinking with stories is not the same as knowing what they mean. In the introduction to *The Death of Luigi Trastulli and Other Stories*, Alessandro Portelli writes that he "stumbled inadvertently" into the Trastulli stories and realized he did not know what they meant. Not knowing, he returned again and again to the people who told them, gradually recognizing the way his own stance and research methods were affecting his "understanding of the other" and the stories (1991: 43). The deferral of knowing what the stories meant was more rewarding for Portelli than immediately understanding them would have been, because it caused him to question and redefine his own identity and gave him a longer time to live with them and learn. Not knowing exactly what my own father "meant," or what he thought I knew, is a memory that lives inside me, and I return to it again and again.

Can I, as a writer, pass on the discrepancy, the ambiguity, the thing that I don't know? Can I give the reader something to think with, instead of explaining why the crane has blue eyes? The discrepancy between the "fact" level of truth and the obscurity of meaning in a story needs to be preserved long enough for me to live with them, and this seems to require a certain openness on my part. I want to wonder over various tellings of stories and allow the differences to teach me, instead of nearly unconsciously consolidating and homogenizing. I'd like to be more hunted by stories than a hunter.

My mother told me so many conflicting proverbs that I finally found it necessary to peel truth off the saying and stick it on the situation, good training for a folklore lover. She not only shared the "Don't hide your light under a bushel" that Phyllis Morrow cites as a marker for a Western cultural tendency toward individualism, but she would also say, "There's nothing new under the sun." She said, "Look before you leap," but I liked it better when she said, "Faint heart ne'er won fair maid." I liked that long before I knew what it meant, because of the archaic sound of "ne'er," because of the balanced alliteration of "faint heart" and "fair maid," and most of all because of the mood she was in when she said it.

I haven't completely given up on that twenty-year-old's question about what family history and stories mean to me, what parts of them are my own life, as if they were dressers and china cupboards to be passed on in unchanging lumps. But I am beginning to see that the concentric circles of words and scenes and whole stories wash over me again and again during the different times I need them. As a writer, I can learn to respect both stories and tellers and the dangerous written word that fixes them in a misleading stasis. I can try to hold the writing open to the reader, like a letter from a certain place and time.

Notes

1.   "As writing, so also is speech not the same for all races of men. But the mental affectations themselves, of which these words are primarily signs, are the same for the whole of mankind ..." (Cooke and Tredennick 1962: 15). And as a basis for our Western science: If "there is to be a science of *knowledge* of anything, there must exist apart from the sensible things some other natures which are permanent, for there can be no science of things which are in a state of flux" (Apostle 1966: 218).

2.   Dennis Tedlock, who early on drew attention to many of the participant/observer dilemmas and championed dialogic and poetic representations, expressed caution about first-person monologues of anthropological experiences, which he deemed "confessional," while also admitting that such accounts keep "contact between individuals and between cultures" *visible* at the presentation stage (1979: 390).

References

Apostle, Hippocrates G., trans. 1966. *Aristotle's Metaphysics*. Bloomington: Indiana University Press.

Benesch, Walter, and Rudolph Krejci. 1992. "Three Legged Chicken's Travel Guide to Logical Space." Department of Philosophy and Humanities, University of Alaska Fairbanks. Unpublished manuscript.

Briggs, Charles. 1988. *Competence in Performance: The Creativity of Tradition in Mexicano Verbal Art*. Philadelphia: University of Pennsylvania Press.

Briggs, Jean L. 1970. *Never in Anger: Portrait of an Eskimo Family*. Cambridge: Harvard University Press.

Cooke, Harold P., and Hugh Tredennick, trans. 1962. *Aristotle: The Categories; On Interpretation; Prior Analytics*. Cambridge: Harvard University Press.

Cruikshank, Julie. 1990. In collaboration with Angela Sidney, Kitty Smith, and Annie Ned. *Life Lived Like a Story: Life Stories of Three Yukon Elders*. Lincoln: University of Nebraska Press.

Dauenhauer, Nora Marks, and Richard Dauenhauer, eds. 1987. *Haa Shuka', Our Ancestors: Tlingit Oral Narratives*. Vol. 1 of *Classics of Tlingit Oral Literature*. Seattle: University of Washington Press.

Hawley, James. 1920. *Idaho: Gem of the Mountains*. Chicago: S. J. Clarke Publishing Co.

Morrow, Phyllis. 1994. "Oral Literature of the Alaskan Arctic." In *Dictionary of Native American Literature*, edited by Andrew Wiget, 19–32. New York: Garland Publishing.

Portelli, Alessandro. 1991. *The Death of Luigi Trastulli and Other Stories: Form and Meaning in Oral History*. Albany: State University of New York Press.

Tedlock, Dennis. 1979. "The Analogical Tradition and the Emergence of a Dialogical Anthropology." *Journal of Anthropological Research* 35(4): 387–400.

Williams, Susie. 1988. Oral history audiotapes. Doyon Historical Project. Eliza Jones and Wendy Arundale, interviewers. Oral History Project, tape no. H-88–57. Elmer Rasmuson Library Archives, University of Alaska Fairbanks.

Epilogue

We offer this book with both humility and a sense of accomplishment. We feel a bit like a young girl who has completed her first basket or a boy who has killed his first game. Like them, we are pleased; we see our work as a significant start, and we are indebted to the traditions of our forebears as well as offering an original and unique contribution to that tradition. We sense that if we really want to understand oral tradition and contribute meaningfully to the dialogue which is well under way elsewhere, we must expand our audience, and we must broaden our investigations as well. There is much to learn about the way people in the North and elsewhere communicate meaning through the stories they tell and the ways they tell them. This book, then, our rite of passage, is an offering by northern scholars to the lively conversations about language and cultural expression now going on.

There is an urgency to this work, for while we expect oral traditions to evolve and change, we also know that the stories that are told now represent an important moment in time, a moment that deserves all the skills and perceptions we can muster. For this reason, we look both to our fieldwork and to scholarship in other parts of the world. In adding to the discussion, we wish to ensure that northern scholarship proceeds with both the benefits of "outside" knowledge and a sensitivity to the special conditions and local voices which teach us how to listen and learn.

The special conditions of the North are also those which should be urgently instructive to students of oral tradition elsewhere. In Alaska and Canada, the political climate is one in which the voices of indigenous peoples are becoming increasingly insistent as they struggle to maintain (or obtain) control of their land. As power relations between indigenous and nonindigenous residents shift, we have become increasingly sensitized to the subtlety and serious consequences of our work together. These are also worldwide political trends, but they are perhaps farther advanced in the North than elsewhere or at least more consistently in the forefront of our lives. In these essays, we have tried to offer others the benefits of a trail that has been at least partially broken in.

The trailbreaking ultimately involves trying to understand verbal exchanges that trigger and shape meaning in both our minds and the minds of narrators and audiences. In *Symbolising Boundaries*, anthropologist Anthony P. Cohen comments that "it is in the nature of the symbolic to be imprecise.... If we could pin down the meanings of symbols, then the symbols would have become redundant, because we would have moved from the symbolic to the technical" (1986: 3). Elsewhere, he elaborates that "much of what symbols 'mean' or express may be beyond or behind consciousness ... either because these meanings are so inchoate as to be inexpressible, or because their value depends on their being left unstated" (1987: 12). Because oral traditions are largely symbolic, we face the same dilemma as any other interpreter of such forms: when we want to talk about meaning, we are put in the particularly challenging position of trying to interpret that which is itself interpretive.

Another way to say this is that if we have trouble objectifying the oral tradition, it is because its very slipperyness is what makes it meaningful, or to be more precise, its imprecision is what allows people to make meaning with it. Our difficulty, then, is a logical consequence of its nature: the oral tradition is negotiated, performative, and interpretive. It cannot be captured. Yet we seem to have to continually relearn this. There is always the urge to "preserve" "it." The problem is that both the notion and the object of preservation are problematic.

They are problematic because oral tradition is less about tellers and texts than about relationships. Unfortunately, this truth is obscured by the words that we use for oral traditions (*verbal arts, oral literatures*), which tend to focus on either the performers or that which is performed. That makes it more difficult for us to remain mindful of the fundamental relational qualities that underlie both. In fact, it is people's relationships with each other and their experiences that prompt all telling, remembering, and hearing. Because oral traditions live when they are told, preserving texts on paper or in other static forms does nothing to maintain the relationships through which the cultural processes we term traditions are enacted. Because oral traditions are only told when they live, as the relationships among the people that tell and hear them change, so do the symbolic forms with which they make meaning. The conservatism of traditional *forms* notwithstanding, oral traditions are only meaningful when they connect people, places, and events in changing relationships. There are no meanings without meaning makers. So preserving the forms is like preserving fleshless bones. What we can reconstruct or infer from their structure at best lacks warmth and subtlety and at worst gives us a false sense of accomplishment.

That said, what gets "boxed" in our writings, the objects of preservation, have to be more than text, more than context, even more than performance. All of these suggest that an instance of narrative is something already accomplished. Narrative becomes past tense, an object of reflection. We have to find ways to convey a sense that narrative is, rather, always accomplishing. And we, as a sometime audience of narrative, are always learning, rather than learned.

One lesson that comes through clearly in this book is that it is easier to maintain a sense of humility, of not knowing (which more faithfully respects the inchoate nature of the symbolic), when we remain close to the communities that make a practice of relating through these narratives. When we as academics are drawn into relationships and are recognized as listeners who want to retell, people tend to keep us honest and on the run. To the extent that we cannot preserve and interpret but really only participate and retell, we can perhaps convey something of the relational qualities of oral tradition.

Can we do this in good faith? Can we write without appropriating and objectifying? Can we say something worth saying without making ourselves less or more than our sources? Writing itself can never be relational and interpretive in the same way as oral traditions. Yet it can be powerful. If we try, we can do more than merely capture the words. We can at least make readers aware of the environment that creates, nurtures, and sustains oral tradition. Each of these essays has made this attempt; collectively, they suggest that there are many ways to broach understanding. In the late twentieth century, both the oral traditions and the animals of the North remain largely unfettered. When we encounter them on this trail, it must be with humility and respect. We must not try to take them into intellectual captivity, or like nineteenth-century zookeepers, we will have preserved only their pale and distorted reflections. We need them to return.

References

Cohen, Anthony P. 1986. *Symbolising Boundaries: Identity and Diversity in British Cultures*. Manchester, England: Manchester University Press.

Cohen, Anthony P. 1987. *Whalsay: Symbol, Segment, and Boundary in a Shetland Island Community*. Manchester, England: Manchester University Press.

Appendix: Polar Bear Story

Two Tellings by Belle Deacon

"Polar Bear"

There was a village, they say, on the coast.[1]
It was a big village.
And a husband and wife lived in the middle of this village.
At the downriver end of the village, a poor, dear grandmother and
    her granddaughter lived.
From time to time, the old woman would go up to the village.
She would go to find out what was happening in the village, and
    then she would go back home.
As for this young hunter,
a very powerful woman was married to him.
She was tough and very strong.
Whenever he looked around outside,
she would suddenly attack him and beat him up.
"You looked outside at other women.
Why are you looking at the women walking around?" she said to
    him.

Then he paddled up to shore.
He didn't even look about, but he was really getting tired of her.
So at last he thought,
"It would be better if she left me alone.
Why, if I so much as look out at women, she always fights with
    me,"
he said, thinking.
He went back down into his *kashim*.
He towed seals to shore.
In his big boat, he went hunting on the sea.
I don't know where he paddled, but he hunted seals and towed
    them back.
Then this woman, his wife, would go down to the end of the village

and give food to that poor, dear old woman all the time.
With that food, she raised her granddaughter.
They lived there a long time.
Everyone liked them and spoke kindly of them.
As for him, he had a good reputation.
He never looked around, because she was jealous.
So, then, things were all right.

Then one time he paddled back out [to sea].
He was gone a whole day, and
in the evening, far out on the ocean,
they looked for him, and far out on the ocean there was a kind of
    black spot.
It was him, paddling back in.
He paddled back to shore.
All the people came out to the bank and looked at him.
The women, too.
He towed a great many sealskins to shore.
They were impressed when they saw them.
"He gets so many!" they thought.
At that, that wife of his got angry again!
I-i-y!
She started fighting with her husband right there on shore.
Meanwhile, all the people up there said,
"Why does she do that, that one?
She ought to just leave him alone.
She's just jealous, doing that again to the one she lives with," they
    said.

So then he went to his *kashim*.
In there she gave him a black eye.
She punched him in the face.
And then when she brought food in to him, he didn't eat.
He was very, very angry.
That was that.
He thought to himself,
"I should paddle away,
somewhere far across the water to where my bones will lie.
It's better that I should paddle away, for I'm really tired of her.
Well, for a long time now,
even though I don't speak with women,

she has been beating me with no reason," he thought.

She brought food to him, but he didn't eat.

"Well, eat," she said, but he didn't; he just looked down all the
time.

Meanwhile, down at the end of the village,

the poor, dear orphan girl was growing up.

She reached puberty, and

her dear grandmother raised her.

She didn't let her go out.

She went out only early in the morning.

"Don't look from shore out to sea.

Just keep looking down at your feet and come back in," she told
her.

"That is how we [behave] whenever we menstruate," she told her.

So she did just that.

Early one morning the young hunter got up.

There on the beach was his big boat, with his big paddle in it.

He went down to it there.

He launched it in the water.

He started to load it.

He stuffed it full with all his blankets and all the furs from his
cache.

As it was just starting to get light, he paddled away from shore.

Meanwhile, in the village, everyone lay sleeping.

The one who was menstruating went out.

She looked out on the ocean and saw a black spot on the horizon,
so she quickly averted her eyes.

But then she did not tell her grandmother.

Then out onto the ocean, outward

he moved, on water so calm it seemed frozen.

Then he paddled out to sea all day,

until at last the sun started to set in the west.

At last, being hungry, he ate some food,

and after that he rested, and then he started paddling again.

He paddled all night.

All night it was as calm as if it were frozen.

The next day he paddled all day again.

For two days and one night he paddled.

Once again, it started to get dark.

Poor thing, he paddled this way for two more nights and two days.

Then on the third day, at last, far across the water, he saw
signs of shore appearing.
"I-i-y," he thought, "How tired I am!
Thanks! Land is visible," he thought.
He kept paddling quickly until
very soon there he was, paddling right up to the shore.
Meanwhile, all around him seals and whales were swimming
    about.
He didn't look at them or pay any attention to them;
he just kept paddling; what else could he do?
He paddled to shore and landed on a nice beach.
He paddled on upstream [on a river there].
And just then, there, back from the shore, there was a slough.
He paddled to its mouth.
He stood still there.
After a while, he thought to himself,
"I ought to paddle up [the slough]; it seems good up there.
Up there I'll look for a suitable spot for my bones to lie," he thought.
So he just started paddling up [the slough].
He hadn't paddled very far
when he saw a house standing back from the river.
And a cache was standing up there, too.
"E-e-ey," he thought.
"I wonder who lives there?
I hope it's a man's place," he thought.
"I hope it's not a woman's place," he thought.
He paddled to shore, and up on the bank,
a big woman came slowly out of the house.
He looked at her.
I-i-y, she spoke to him in the other [Eskimo] language.
Then he said to her,
"I'm trying to go to where there are men.
I am doing this to find a place for my bones to lie.
I don't want a place where there are no people," he said.
"Don't say that; come up here and rest.
Why ever are you saying that?
Come, spend the night," she said to him.
So he walked up [the bank].
A big fish camp was there.
I-i-y, all around outside a lot of sealskins
were hanging up; nothing was lacking.

King salmon and plenty of everything was there.
It was after spring breakup.
Then she cooked and she fed him,
and he went to the bench across the room.
She handed the dish toward him over the fire.
"Come, have a little something to eat.
Then you can go to bed, you seem tired," she said to him.
"That's true—
While I paddled for three nights and three days,
fortunately it was calm for me."
"Come on," she said to him.
"Go to bed, go on," she told him.
She went to bed on one side [of the fire] and he on the other.

Meanwhile, during all this time, across the water—in his absence
      across there—
his wife, i-i-y, got furious.
She went out in the village, wrecking things.
"Where is my husband? You hid my husband!" she was saying
      angrily.
She rushed down to the end of the village, and she knocked down
      the cache there.
"Why, we didn't hide him. What are you doing anyway?" they
      said, but it was no use.
She rushed down to the end of the village, and
she went to that old woman, that poor, dear old woman.
"Now my husband is missing.
Now they've hidden my husband," she said.
"Now I'll kill you all unless you tell me something.
Now he will never [be able to] stay away from me," she said.

"What are you saying anyway? Why they didn't hide that one.
Here is a corner girl, in puberty seclusion.[2]
Well, she stayed there several nights.
Having gone out, although I told her not to look out to sea,
even so, she glanced out to sea," [the old woman] said.
E-e-y,
"She looked out, and she saw someone paddling out to sea,"
she told her.
"Aha ... well, I've wanted to know this.
I've been wrecking the village;

I should have spoken to you first," she told her.
"Tomorrow I'll just get a canoe, and I'll go in the canoe.
Then I'll paddle after him," she said.
"And as for this corner girl,
I'll take her along in the canoe, too."

"Oh, no," said the poor, dear old woman.
"You really mustn't do that.
Why, one who is having her period doesn't go in a canoe."

"Well, I'll just take her in it anyway, that one," she told her
       [laughing meanly].
Then she loaded the canoe, and
putting that corner girl in the canoe in front of her,
she paddled out to sea.
How could they stop her?
"I'll kill you guys," she told them.
Terrified, they just put [the corner girl] into the canoe.
All the way across [the sea], then, it seemed calm to them.
Far across, she paddled over to shore.
I don't know how long she spent in doing this.
She was so angry that she paddled along very fast.
She paddled to the beach and on up [to the shore].
There was a slough.

And as for the others [the husband and his new wife], this is
what was happening with them:
"Well, okay," [the new wife] said.
"Your wife, your wife has gotten smart.
Your wife has paddled after you.
You mustn't go outside now.
You go here under the blanket,
while I go to meet her alone."

"What will we do with one another?
I already married her, but I married you, too.
I already took her [as my wife] so I better not [hide];
I've already stayed with her a long while.
I still love her very much,
in spite of her always fighting with me,
but finally I got tired of it, and I came here," he said.

Here, it seems, that woman [the new wife] made a noise [making
    medicine],
while she [the other wife] paddled there.
"She's paddling along near here.
That's why I'm saying this," she said.
"Wait! Don't go outside," she told him.
Meanwhile, she ran back in.
"She's paddled into the slough, and
her boat is coming out there," she told him.
Mmm.
"A big boat is starting to appear," she told him.
"Get underneath this mat here,
for I don't know what we'll do to each other,
but if she attacks me first, I'll fight her," she said.

Then, down in the water, a boat was approaching shore, while
someone said "Yey . . . ," from out on the water.
"Adey, you have stolen my husband from me.
Can you keep living when you've stolen my husband from me?"
    she asked.

Meanwhile, [the new wife] stood up on the bank.
She began to descend toward the shore, walking along very slowly.
"Yey," [the first wife] said, and suddenly she charged up the bank
    at her.
Charging up the bank at her, she grabbed her, and they started
    fighting.
Meanwhile, down below, that corner girl
hid down in the canoe, while
out by the shore,
the ground started to shake.
The place was shaking and shaking, and
there was not another sound except the shaking.
After a long time it quieted down, and
[the new wife] came back inside,
The woman of this place.
"It's all right now," she said to him.
"Well, she did it to me first.
Don't feel sorry or be sad.
Whatever I did, she did to me first;
she wronged me.

Don't be sorrowful," she told him.
"Come on now, get up from under that blanket," she told him.
"Go back outside," she told him.
Yey, outside everything was destroyed!
His wife was out there,
and she was in pieces; she had torn her to pieces.
She had torn her up.
He went back inside and started crying,
Saying, "My wife," he started crying.
But she went back to him.
"Don't cry anymore," she told him.
"For a long time she has mistreated you.
I will be your wife.
I am a woman, too," she told him.
Thereupon he stopped crying.
Her hands and her fingers were nothing but blood.
For she had torn her entirely apart.
Having gathered all the pieces together and having piled them up,
they took the things down there in the boat,
and they piled them onto it, taking everything, and then they set
    it on fire.

And all of a sudden, as they were unloading the canoe,
there was a woman sitting in it, that young girl.
"Have pity . . . ," she said to [the new wife].
"Have pity . . . ," she said.
"Have pity . . . on this poor little orphan," she said to her.
She was crouching down there in terror.
So the woman picked her up and brought her up the bank.
"Don't worry about it;
you can stay up there and we'll adopt you," she told her.
Meanwhile, she put all those things into the fire.
The big paddle and the big boat were also out there.

They started living there.
The young man worked and started to do well.
He started hunting for her a lot.
He started hauling caribou back from the uplands.
He brought back a lot of caribou.
One day he woke up and his voice was gone.
"What's wrong with you?" she said.

"I just remembered my village; that's why I'm this way.
This girl she brought with her
was being raised by a poor person back over there.
Maybe her grandmother wants her," he told her.
"Hey we're living here quite well;
why are you saying that, anyway?" she said to him.

"We ought to go across there to get the news," he told her.
So they loaded the boat; there was a big paddle in it.
"Let's use the paddle that I paddled over here with;
let's use that one," he said to her.
"Oh, no . . . ," she told him.
"We will be safe only if I use my paddle."
"Your paddle is too big," he told her.
So they got into the canoe and left.
When they got out onto open water, a storm overtook them.
I-y, it got so cold;
the waves were as big as mountains and
the boat pitched and tossed.
With the fourth wave he paddled through,
the paddle shattered.
They capsized.
Up on the waves, the child came to the surface, that little girl.
Half of her was woman and half of her was fish.
And her hair streamed ahead of her, floating on the surface of the
        water.
Out in the ocean, she came up to the surface:
"Grandchild! Grandchild!" she said.
At the same time, that man and his wife came to the surface.
One of them, the wife, suddenly had become a big, white bear, a
        polar bear.
Her husband also surfaced as a polar bear.
All right then, it is finished.

"Polar Bear"
    Once upon a time, there was a big village on the coast. There's a
big village in there. In the middle there was this man and his wife.
They live with them. This woman, she wouldn't even let her husband
look at another woman. As soon as he turned little bit towards other
woman, she get so jealous and then she start. She just beating him

up all the time. And he had to look at his feet. Never look around nowhere because he's scared of her, because she's too powerful.

There was an old lady and her grandchild was below in the village, and every time that married man goes out to sea, he hunt for seal. Whale and seal and he kill lots, and he tow them. And then people comes and help him out. On the beach. And they skin it, all those women. They skin it. So they give them lots of whale meat and things like that. And they give this old lady some all the time 'cause she was good, that old lady and that little girl.

But this little girl was start[ing] to grow up. She never came up to the village. [The jealous woman took food] down to them and give them some meat and things to eat. These other womans, they're good to her, but they cannot look at her husband because she's too jealous of him. So they have big *kashim* where they give a party. She cook lots of meat, and she pass it all around to the older people and everything. And that way she has lots of friends, but her husband got no friends because she'd be too jealous of him. So at last he started thinking to himself, "Maybe I might go away."

One day he went out again, out to sea, and he killed lots and he came back, and all the womans came to the banks and look[ed] at him. "My!" they say. "What a good hunter. He sure brings in lots of things every day." And she heard that. She got really mad, and she just beat up her husband, right in front of everybody. "You fellas admire my husband. You're not going to have him," she say to them. So he, he went into the *kashim*. She brought some food to him, but he wouldn't accept it from her. [She sit] by him, and he wouldn't eat. He just feel so bad because his face and everything was just swollen up. She was hitting him so bad and just beating him for nothing. He decided, "Maybe I'll go away from her. I'm getting tired of this woman. I'm going to go someplace where my bone[s] will be. Where I'll die, and nobody [would] even know where I'll die. I'm going to find a good place where I'm going to be laying [down], and that way I wouldn't live. I don't want to live anymore," he was thinking to himself.

And this little girl, at the same time down there, she got pretty big. And she became a corner girl, you know. She had period. At those times they wouldn't look around [at anybody] till one year [later]. They're in the little place, and they let them stay, and there's nobody [would] see them, their faces or anything. So she wakes up early in the morning before the sunrise, and she goes out and look around.

She look at her feet, but this time she look way out to sea. And she see somebody going way out. She see black thing moving out. She keep looking and [it looked] just like a canoe or something. So she went in, but she never even told her grandmother about it.

Then [the jealous wife] woke up. Her husband was gone. Never come back. And she went to them, and she just bust their cache down. "You hide my husband, you hide him!" "No, we didn't do nothing. He's just not around here." She just beat up them people and just start to tear up the village, and pretty soon they tell her not to do that to them because it's just no use. "You know we're not powerful like you. We cannot take your husband away from you." And she went down to the old lady. She told the old lady and the little girl, "If you and your grandchild don't tell me anything, I'm going to kill you, both of you," she said to them. "No," [the old lady] said. "My grandchild, you know we never go up to the village. We don't know nothing." "Well, you must know something," she start[ed] to tell them. Then she grab this little girl: "You know anything?" (You know she's a corner girl. She's not supposed to look around.)

[The man paddled and paddled for three days, and he came to a slough. He paddled up the slough, and he saw a house. A big woman came out of the house and invited him in. Meanwhile, his wife started to paddle after him. She took that young girl, the corner girl, along with her.]

And at the same time, that one woman back there said, "Your wife is coming. You got to hide under the blanket, under our blanket. Because she [won't] leave me alone. She's going to fight with me because she is very mad already. I'm not mad, but I'm going to try my best to do what I can to her. Because I don't know, maybe she'll beat me up or I'll beat her up. But don't get sad." But he said, "That's my own wife. I love her. I love her very much. But I can't. I got tired. That's why I came this way, because I wanted to die someplace by myself alone," he said.

"Don't you ever think that way, because you're going to live with me," that woman told him. Soon she came in and said, "There's a boat coming out around the corner. Pretty soon she's going to land. We're going to start. I don't know what she's going to do to me. If she's not going to bother me, I'm not going to bother her."

So [the jealous wife] stop, and gee, she got awfully mad. She said, "You took my husband away from me. I'm going to just beat you up and tear you up," she [told her].

"Well, try it," she said, this woman. "I never fought before, but if you want it that way, we'll just start in anytime you feel like it," she said.

So she just came out, and they just started fighting. That place where they stayed, it was just shaking everything. The ground was just [going] bang, bang, and just no [other] noise, nothing. Pretty soon they were fighting quite a while, and all at once it just [became] calm. And [she] came in that place [and she] said, "I'm finish[ed]. I got ready for your wife. She started it. Now I tore her all up. I tore her into pieces." He say to her, he started crying, "You shouldn't do that to my wife. I love that woman."

"Well, we can't help it. [If] we never do that to her, she'd tear us both up," [she] say. "Well, we'll take the scraps up, and we'll put it in one place, and we'll burn her up with all that stuff she brought in that boat. We'll pile it up, and we'll put wood on it, and we'll put oil on it and burn it, burn her up." And so they did that. She wash her hand. Her hand was all full of blood and everything. Her clothes, she took off her clothes and she changed into new clothes. She was a beautiful woman, too. And they started to bring things up, and all at once they see this girl was sitting in amongst the things [in the boat]. She pack her up in her arms and brought her into the house. She tell her, "Don't feel bad, 'cause we're going to keep you good. You're going to be our little girl." But her husband say, "No," he say. "She's a corner girl and maybe her grandmother wanted her. Maybe we'll bring her back across, where she belongs to." "Well, I don't know," she say. "I don't feel like going, but if you feel that way, we'll go over."

I don't know how long they stayed there, and then they started to go across. She got big paddle, was just like big tree, was the paddle. Two big ones. "If I use this one, we'll be alive all the time. But if we take your paddle, the one you came with, we're not safe," she said. "No," he said. "We'll be safe. Leave your paddle in there; it's too big. That's too big to handle, that big paddle." So she said, "It's your will. It's not my will, but we'll do that. I'll take your word for it. And it's not safe," she said.

So they went out, they started to go out. It was calm weather. Way out they paddle all day and that night, and the next day this big wind came up. It was big wind, and the waves were so big it's just like hills. Maybe more than twelve feet high, the waves. And the fourth wave they start to go over, the paddle just bust. And that's the time that girl came up, you know. Half girl, half fish. And her hair, it's hang[ing] down on the water, you know, saying this: "*Choyalim'*,

choyalim'." From way long time ago. "It's going to be big flu [and] that's the [only] time they'll hear me on the coast." [When people had been starving, and there was going to be a big flu], they hear it. Some people hear it on the coast, this kind of half-fish, fish animal saying, "*Choyalim'*." They couldn't see it, but they hear it. Something say, "*Choyalim', choyalim',*" way off on the coast.

And these polar bear, man and wife, they became polar bear. That's why they're on the ice all the time on the coast. That's the story, Indian story. That's the end.

Notes

These tellings are reprinted with permission from the Alaska Native Language Center at the University of Alaska Fairbanks. They originally appeared in Belle Deacon, *Engithidong Xugixudhoy: Their Stories of Long Ago* (Fairbanks: Alaska Native Language Center and Iditarod Area School District, 1987). The texts as printed here have been copyedited to correct punctuation and typographical errors.

1. Belle thinks the story takes place in the Norton Sound area.
2. The term *corner girl* refers to a menstruating woman. It comes from the practice of sequestering these women in corners of houses.

About the Authors

Each of the contributors to this volume has sought out and found rewarding ways to pursue collaborative projects with Alaskan and Yukon Native peoples. In Alaska and the Yukon, trust develops slowly between people, and long-term personal relationships form only after the newcomer's words begin to return, contributions are recognized, and the inevitable mistakes and misunderstandings are exposed. The essays in this book demonstrate the value of community investment in each step of the research, whether it be analyzing stories, exploring historic sites, or writing an elder's life history. Many of us feel that these experiences have been as important to our personal and professional growth as our formal training.

The contributors to this book have also grown from working with each other as both professionals and friends. We come from a variety of professional and personal backgrounds and have worked with each other in various capacities. We don't fit into neat categories, nor are we easily labeled. In some cases our relationships have been those of "student" and "teacher." Here the labels obscure the rich backgrounds that these students have brought to the classroom. We include a school teacher, a Yup'ik language and culture specialist, a researcher of Alaska Native historical sites, a literary scholar specializing in Native American literature, a graduate student in English whose experiences in rural Alaska provide the heart and soul of her writing, and finally, four cultural anthropologists whose personal and professional experiences stretch widely across Alaska and the Yukon and who share strong interests in folklore scholarship.

Elsie Mather was born in Kwigillingok and raised in southwest Alaska. She holds a degree from the University of Alaska Fairbanks. For many years she has conducted language instruction and cultural research at Kuskokwim Community College. When she is not too busy cutting and smoking her family's winter supply of salmon, she willingly shares knowledge of her Yup'ik culture. She is often asked to speak at conferences, she has served as a translator at international meetings, and she has published several major works in and about the

Yup'ik language, most notably *Cauyarnariuq* (*It Is Time for Drumming*), the first full-length original work in an Alaska Native language.

Phyllis Morrow first went to the Kuskokwim region in 1974 as a Ph.D. student at Cornell University. She was looking for a field site and found a home. In 1979, she became director of the Yupik Eskimo Language Center at Kuskokwim College in Bethel. She held this position until 1981 when she began work for the Lower Kuskokwim School District, developing the Yup'ik language and culture program which is currently in use in high schools in southwestern Alaska. Since 1987, she has been on the faculty of the Anthropology Department at the University of Alaska Fairbanks. Her research on cross-cultural communication in the justice system and her work with Yup'ik oral traditions provide academic excuses to remain personally connected with people in the Kuskokwim Delta.

Julie Cruikshank received her advanced degrees in anthropology from the University of British Columbia. Her major work has been in the Yukon with elders, but she is no stranger to Alaska, where she has done research and conducted workshops. Her recent work, *Life Lived Like a Story*, has strongly influenced the direction of research in the North and is frequently praised as an example of the way to conduct long-term life-history research with elders sensitively. She is presently a professor of anthropology at the University of British Columbia in Vancouver where she lives during the school year, returning for a part of each summer to the Yukon. She is known for her amazing professional energy and her caring mentorship of students. This is probably due to the fact that she was mentored so well by Yukon elders.

Robin Barker has moved progressively farther north. She graduated with a teaching certificate and a bachelor of science in child study from Tufts University. After a couple of years of teaching in rural Vermont, she moved to Bethel, Alaska, in 1974 to do itinerant teacher education in the region's villages. Eventually, she worked in a variety of education programs for teachers and parents, who introduced her to Yup'ik culture. Robin and her husband Jim, a professional photographer, lived in Bethel for twelve years. Five of Jim's photographs are a handsome addition to this volume. For Robin and Jim, Maggie Lind's small red house by the river became a favorite visiting place where tea and storytelling followed a day of snowmobile travel or drift-netting for salmon. Up the slough from Maggie's, just past Elsie Mather's house, lived her friend Phyllis Morrow. When she wrote the essay for this book, Robin was a graduate student and instructor in the University of Alaska Fairbanks's School of Education. Her job took her to urban schools where she found the cross-cultural casting and catching of words to be just as compelling as her experiences in rural Alaska. Now she is education coordinator of the Tanana Chiefs Conference Headstart program.

Robert Drozda is an independent researcher and student of Alaska Native cultures. He has traveled and worked extensively in western Alaska from 1981 to the present. Much of this travel included visits to remote villages and surrounding areas as a federally employed field investigator of Native historical and cemetery sites. He has also made numerous personal trips to many of these same places, observing and listening to the residents and the land and learning through a form of participatory research he calls "hanging out." His training, for the most part, has been experiential, informal, and practical. He is currently working on a project documenting Cup'ig Eskimo place names and the cultural geography of Nunivak Island. When he's not traveling, he spends his time with his wife, little brother, their nine-or-so dogs, and his vegetable garden in Fairbanks.

James Ruppert enjoys a joint position in English and Alaska Native studies at the University of Alaska Fairbanks. He is past president of the Association for the Study of American Indian Literatures (ASAIL) and has published many articles on Native literature, both oral and written. His books include a description of the life and work of Native author D'Arcy McNickle and a volume forthcoming from the University of Oklahoma Press on contemporary Native American literature.

Patricia Partnow moved to Alaska in 1971, having lived in a variety of towns and suburbs as the child of a career Marine Corps officer. She arrived with a fresh master's degree in anthropology, which she put to work in museums and educational institutions (including a public school district), designing learning materials on Alaska Native cultures. She returned to graduate school at the University of Alaska Fairbanks in 1989 to study anthropology with dual emphases in folklore and ethnicity. Her dissertation research was conducted between 1990 and 1993 on the Alaska Peninsula. Her doctoral degree was awarded in 1993, and since then she has been doing anthropological contract work, writing a book on Alutiiq ethnohistory and directing a planning grant for the National Endowment for the Humanities Exemplary Award project.

William Schneider began his fieldwork in Beaver, Alaska, in 1972, where he met and worked with Turak Newman and Moses Cruikshank, two men who have strongly influenced his knowledge and appreciation of oral tradition in the North. Schneider's first professional employment was with the National Park Service, where he worked with Native regional corporations during the identification stage of the historical and cemetery-site selections for the Alaska Native Claims Settlement Act. He was then assigned to a major study of the National Petroleum Reserve on the North Slope, and this marked the beginning of his association with Waldo Bodfish, Sr., which eventually led to the oral biography, *Kusiq: An Eskimo Life History from the Arctic Coast of Alaska*. Since 1981, Schneider has directed the Oral History Program at the Elmer E. Rasmuson Library, University of Alaska Fairbanks, where he and his colleagues are pioneering Project Jukebox, which uses computers to access oral recordings and related texts, maps, and photographs.

Mary Odden writes essays on northern and rural subjects. She has served on the editorial board of *Northwest Folklore* and recently created a correspondence course which is an introduction to folklore and oral history. Her essays have appeared in such wildly diverse publications as *Northwest Folklore*, *The Alaska Trapper*, and *The Georgia Review*. Mary lives with husband Jim and daughter Kari, migrating seasonally between summer work in McGrath, Alaska, and her winter home in Nelchina, Alaska.